BEGINNING DIRECTX® 10 GAME PROGRAMMING

WENDY JONES

THOMSON
━━━━━━ ✳ ━━━━━━ ™
COURSE TECHNOLOGY

Professional ■ Technical ■ Reference

Important: Thomson Course Technology PTR cannot provide software support. Please contact the appropriate software manufacturer's technical support line or Web site for assistance.

Thomson Course Technology PTR and the author have attempted throughout this book to distinguish proprietary trademarks from descriptive terms by following the capitalization style used by the manufacturer.

Information contained in this book has been obtained by Thomson Course Technology PTR from sources believed to be reliable. However, because of the possibility of human or mechanical error by our sources, Thomson Course Technology PTR, or others, the Publisher does not guarantee the accuracy, adequacy, or completeness of any information and is not responsible for any errors or omissions or the results obtained from use of such information. Readers should be particularly aware of the fact that the Internet is an ever-changing entity. Some facts may have changed since this book went to press.

Educational facilities, companies, and organizations interested in multiple copies or licensing of this book should contact the Publisher for quantity discount information. Training manuals, CD-ROMs, and portions of this book are also available individually or can be tailored for specific needs.

ISBN-10: 1-59863-361-9
ISBN-13: 978-1-59863-361-0
Library of Congress Catalog Card Number: 2006909688
Printed in the United States of America
08 09 10 11 12 TW 10 9 8 7 6 5 4 3 2 1

Publisher and General Manager, Thomson Course Technology PTR:
Stacy L. Hiquet

Associate Director of Marketing:
Sarah O'Donnell

Manager of Editorial Services:
Heather Talbot

Marketing Manager:
Jordan Casey

Senior Acquisitions Editor:
Emi Smith

Marketing Assistant:
Adena Flitt

Project Editor:
Jenny Davidson

Technical Reviewer:
Jim Adams and Allen Sherrod

PTR Editorial Services Coordinator:
Erin Johnson

Interior Layout Tech:
ICC Macmillan Inc.

Cover Designer:
Mike Tanamachi

CD-ROM Producer:
Brandon Penticuff

Indexer:
Kelly D. Henthorne

Proofreader:
Sara Gullion

THOMSON

COURSE TECHNOLOGY

Professional ■ Technical ■ Reference

Thomson Course Technology PTR,
a division of Thomson Learning Inc.
25 Thomson Place
Boston, MA 02210
http://www.courseptr.com

To my children Virginia, Elizabeth, and Ian.

ACKNOWLEDGMENTS

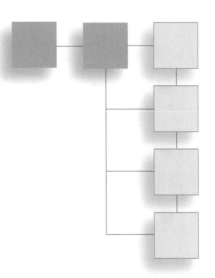

I'd like to thank Emi Smith for giving me the chance to work with Course PTR again. My experiences writing for her and Course PTR have been very rewarding. I'd also like to thank project editor Jenny Davidson for doing the editing and bringing everything together.

I'd like to take a moment to give thanks to the entire gaming industry for allowing me to be part of something so wonderful. Where else can you get paid to have fun with friends and put out some amazing products at the same time?

ABOUT THE AUTHOR

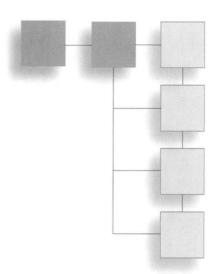

Wendy Jones devoted herself to computers the first time her eyes befell an Apple IIe in elementary school. From that point on, she spent every free moment learning BASIC and graphics programming, sketching out her ideas on graph paper to type in later. Other computer languages followed, including Pascal, C, C#, and C++.

As Wendy's career in computers took off, she branched out, teaching herself Windows programming and then jumping into the dot-com world for a bit. Although Internet companies provided a challenge, they didn't provide fulfillment, so Wendy started expanding her programming skills to games, devoting any extra energy to its pursuit.

Wendy's true passion became apparent when she got the opportunity to work for Atari's Humongous Entertainment as a game programmer. During her time at Atari, she worked on both PC and console titles, thrilled with the challenge they provided.

Wendy can now be found at Electronic Art's Tiburon studio in Orlando working with some wonderfully talented people on Next Generation consoles.

If you have any comments or questions about this book, you can reach Wendy at her website at http://www.fasterkittycodecode.com.

Contents

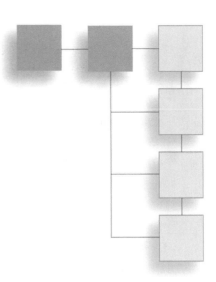

INTRODUCTION

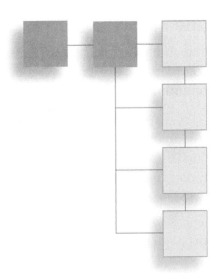

Game programming is an exciting job in the computing world. Where else do you get the chance to create virtual worlds that encompass creatures or places normally found only in dreams? You give people the ability to become anyone they want to and provide them with environments that bring their fantasies to life.

The game industry is growing by extraordinary bounds, and the technology is expanding at a rapid pace. Previously, video cards with 3D hardware were unheard of. Only expensive SGI workstations were capable of the 3D effects we take for granted today. Now it's possible to have the same computer power at home that existed only in a lab a few years ago. 3D graphics have been brought to the masses.

Microsoft Windows is riding this technology wave on the PC, competing with companies like Sony and Nintendo in the game console space. Today, most PC games on the market are built on DirectX, enabling gamers to experience the latest graphics technologies and the most realistic worlds.

Console gaming has also come under the domain of DirectX with the Xbox and the Xbox 360. The skills you learn programming DirectX are directly applicable to both PC and console platforms.

How Much Should You Know?

Even though game programming may seem like a fun way to teach yourself programming, it actually requires a more advanced understanding of programming concepts; therefore, a thorough understanding of C++ and object-oriented concepts is needed to understand all the lessons presented in this book.

Basic math skills are also a plus, although most math concepts are explained. Working knowledge of Visual Studio.NET 2005 or any product in the Visual Studio family is helpful. The opening chapters explain what you need to get started.

How to Use This Book

The first part of this book describes DirectX and how to get your first DirectX program up and running. The second part gives you the basics you need for designing and building 3D worlds, with an introduction to 3D concepts and Direct3D. The third part rounds out your DirectX knowledge with an introduction to sound processing with DirectSound and getting input from the user with DirectInput. The book wraps up with a final encompassing project that shows you how to apply the concepts you've learned.

Requirements

In order to get the full use of this book, a few things are required: A computer system running Windows Vista Retail with Visual Studio 2005 Professional installed. Additionally, you should have the June 2007 DirectX SDK installed. Later versions of the SDK may work with the samples in the book but are not guaranteed to compile as Microsoft can change the API at any time. Finally, you'll need a video card that has been certified Direct3D10 compliant. The samples and code in this book might work with the software renderer but might run slowly if at all.

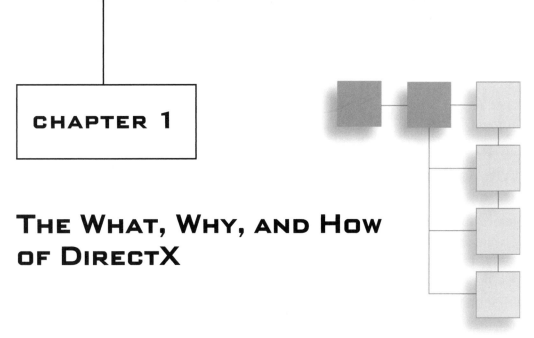

CHAPTER 1

THE WHAT, WHY, AND HOW OF DIRECTX

DirectX is the premier game API for the Windows platform. Just a few years ago, game makers were struggling with problems stemming from hardware incompatibilities, making it almost impossible for everyone to enjoy the same games. Then Microsoft came along with DirectX. It provided game makers with a single clean API to write to that would almost guarantee compatibility across different sets of PC hardware. Since DirectX's release, the number of games running under Windows has increased dramatically.

In this chapter, I'll cover the following:

- Understanding what DirectX is

- Why DirectX is useful

- How data flows through the Direct3D 10 pipeline

- What is brand new for Direct3D 10

What Is DirectX?

DirectX, Microsoft's collection of application programming interfaces (APIs), is designed to give game developers a low-level interface to the PC hardware running Windows. Each API component provides access to different aspects of the hardware, including graphics, sound, and networking, all through a standard interface. This interface allows developers to write their games using one set of functions with little worry about the hardware it's being run on.

Why Is DirectX Needed?

Before the release of the Windows operating system, developers were writing games for DOS. This single-threaded, non-GUI operating system provided developers with a direct path between their application code and the hardware it was running on. This had both its advantages and problems. For instance, because there was a direct path between the game code and the hardware, developers could pull every ounce of power out of the machine, giving them complete control of how their game performed. The down side included the need to write either directly to the hardware or use a variety of third-party libraries for any hardware they wanted their game title to support; this included even common hardware like video and sound cards.

Video cards were especially confusing since not all video cards followed the same standard. Even though most video cards supported a series of common resolutions, developers were forced to access video memory directly. This made even drawing to the screen difficult. Developers were definitely looking for a better and easier way.

When Windows 3.1 was released, it carried with it the same limitations that DOS had. Since Windows ran on top of DOS, it severely limited the resources available to games and took away the direct access developers had enjoyed for so long. Most games written to support Windows at the time consisted mainly of card and board games, while most games continued to support DOS only.

Microsoft's release of Windows 95 didn't eliminate any of these problems until the release of DirectX 1, also known as the Game SDK. It gave developers a single library to write to, placing a common layer between their game and the PC hardware; drawing graphics to the screen had just become a whole lot easier. The first version of DirectX still didn't give support for all the hardware out there, but it was a great starting point in giving game developers what they had been waiting for. Over the years, there have been multiple releases of DirectX, each one improving and adding support for new technologies such as network play, streaming audio, and new kinds of input devices. The latest version of DirectX includes Direct3D 10, which is compatible with Microsoft Windows Vista.

How DirectX Is Put Together

DirectX is based on a collection of code libraries, each providing a common set of functionality needed for games or multimedia applications. To make sure that your game only has to link to the necessary functionality, DirectX is separated into multiple components.

The Components

The DirectX API is split into multiple components, each representing a different aspect of the system. Each API can be used independently of one another, thereby only adding in the functionality your game requires.

In the latest version of DirectX, some of the components were updated, such as Direct3D, while others are now being maintained at their previous levels by Microsoft. The components within DirectX can be upgraded individually as new functionality is required.

- **DirectX Graphics.** The component that handles all graphics processing. This API provides functions for handling 2D and 3D graphic drawing, as well as initializing and setting the environment for your game.

- **DirectInput.** All user input is handled through this API. This component includes support for devices like the keyboard, mouse, gamepad, and joysticks. DirectInput also provides support for force-feedback.

- **XInput.** A new addition to the DirectX family of APIs. XInput allows for easy interfacing with the new Xbox 360 controller.

- **DirectSound.** For adding in sound effects or background music, this is the API to use. DirectSound's functionality allows for loading and playing of one or more sound files while providing complete control over how they're played.

- **DirectSetup.** After your game is complete, you'll want to show it to others. DirectSetup gives you the functionality to install the latest version of DirectX on the user's computer.

Note

In previous versions of DirectX, 2D drawing functionality was provided by a component called DirectDraw. Because DirectDraw is no longer being updated, you should perform all drawing using 3D.

The Component Object Model

The DirectX API is based on the Component Object Model (COM). COM objects consist of a collection of interfaces that expose methods that developers use to access DirectX. COM objects are normally DLL files that have been registered with the system that provide the support for the specific hardware in the machine. For DirectX COM objects, this happens during the installation of DirectX. While similar to C++ objects, COM objects require the use of an interface to access the methods within them. This is actually an advantage over standard objects because multiple versions of an interface can be present within a COM object, allowing for backwards compatibility.

For instance, each version of DirectX included a new DirectDraw interface accessible through the API, while still containing the previous version so as not to break existing code. Therefore, games created using DirectX 7 are able to work with DirectX 9 with little to no changes.

An additional advantage to COM objects is their ability to work with multiple languages, not just C++. Developers can use Visual Basic, C++, or C# and still use the same DirectX libraries. As Microsoft updates and adds new functionality to DirectX, the version numbers of each updated component will increase. You'll find when dealing with DirectX that not all the included components exist at the same version level. For instance, DirectSound remains at version 8.0 while Direct3D is now at 10.

Introducing Direct3D 10

With the latest version of Windows, called Vista, Microsoft is introducing a new version of graphic API called Direct3D 10 (D3D10). With this latest release, Direct3D has gone through a dramatic change, streamlining the API and dropping a lot of the unnecessary code. The entire desktop in Windows Vista will be based on D3D10 giving the user more than a two-dimensional workspace. Each window on the desktop will actually be a 3D object with the ability to behave as objects do in the real world. To allow this to happen, the GPU on the video card now becomes a shared resource.

Video cards are also being upgraded to provide users with the functionality that D3D10 will require. In earlier versions of DirectX, video card manufacturers had the option of providing only partial Direct3D compatibility, causing all sorts of headaches. When you bought the latest game, you were never sure that your video card could fully support the features it required. Now with D3D10, all card manufacturers must implement the full feature set to be considered compatible either within the hardware or within their driver. This will greatly benefit the buyers of video cards because companies won't be able to only support the functionality that they deem important.

Since the changes to Direct3D were extensive, the latest Direct3D will not work on earlier versions of Windows. This will be the first time that DirectX will no longer be backward compatible. You may want to keep this in mind when writing games for D3D10, because the installed base of users may take a while to migrate to Windows Vista.

Stages of Direct3D

Direct3D is more than just an API; it's a tool for transforming simple geometric shapes and images into a living, breathing world. Even though you can treat many pieces of Direct3D as a black box and not have to worry about the implementation details, it is a good idea to understand at least an overview of how it works.

Direct3D processes your scene in multiple stages, each stage performing a specific set of tasks resulting in a final image.

The first stage, called the Input-Assembler (IA) stage, can be thought of as the building block stage. This is the stage where the basic building blocks that make up your objects are put into the Direct3D pipeline.

Next, the vertices are passed into the Vertex Shader (VS) stage. Every vertex in the scene is passed into the vertex shader stage individually and transformed by the currently active shader. You'll learn about shaders later in the book. This stage is user configurable through shaders.

The third stage, the Geometry Shader (GS), is brand new to Direct3D 10. With the introduction of the Geometry shader, full primitives such as triangles and lines can be transformed as a whole. Previously, each vertex in the primitive was required to have all processing done on an individual vertex basis using the vertex shader stage. This stage is user configurable through shaders.

The fourth stage, the Rasterizer, has the job of transforming your 3D scene description into actual pixels. Any pixels that lay outside of the viewport are clipped before the image is drawn.

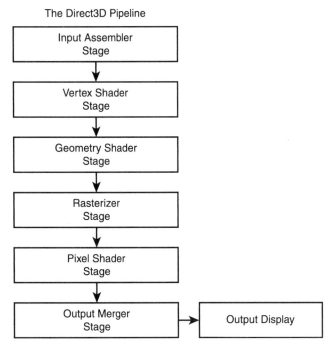

Figure 1.1
The pipeline stages of Direct3D.

The Pixel Shader (PS) stage is where pixels in your scene are processed. Like vertices, every pixel that makes up a primitive is fed into the pixel shader. Pixel shaders allow you to determine how objects in your scene are going to appear in the final image. You can apply lighting effects, handle environment mapping, or just pass the pixels through. This stage is user configurable through shaders.

The final stage, the Output Merger (OM) stage, is where it all comes together. The OM takes all of the pieces from the other stages of the pipeline and builds up the final image to send to the screen.

Figure 1.1 shows the stages of Direct3D.

Direct3D 10 Considerations

Some of you may already be familiar with writing games using DirectX, and if so, there are a few things you need to be aware of when converting your game to the latest version of Direct3D.

The biggest change is the removal of the Fixed Function pipeline. Previously you could choose one of the default ways to process your 3D scene and Direct3D would handle the clipping, lighting, and the shading. Now, with the introduction of D3D10, all this functionality needs to be specifically handled using the programmable pipeline. A brand new chapter about shaders is included to bring you up to speed.

Another of the more major changes is the removal of the CAPS bits. In previous versions of Direct3D, you had to check the capabilities of the underlying video hardware to make sure that certain functionality like pixel shaders was available to use. Now, any features not provided by the hardware are emulated by the system in software ensuring you always have the full range of functionality to play with. This will greatly simplify the initialization code for games using D3D10.

Summary

As you go through the process of learning DirectX, don't worry if things seem overwhelming at times. DirectX is a large API and covers a lot of different systems. At times it is useful to pick a system and write as many samples with it as you can. Before you know it things start to make sense and fall into place. If you ever get stuck, remember you're not alone; sites like gamedev.net and Microsoft's MSDN are great places to find help.

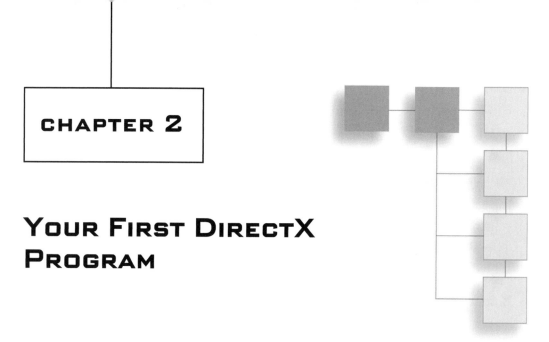

CHAPTER 2

YOUR FIRST DIRECTX PROGRAM

It's time to get into writing some actual code now. I'm going to take you step-by-step through the process of creating your very first DirectX application. Most examples that come with the DirectX Software Development Kit (SDK) rely on the sample framework, a collection of source files that take care of a lot of the tedious programming for you. In my explanations and examples that follow, I will not be using this framework so that you get an idea of everything that's needed for an actual game.

Here's what you'll learn in this chapter:

- How to create a project

- How to set up a Windows application

- How to initialize DirectX

- How to clear the screen

- How to display your scene

Creating the Project

The first step to any application is the creation of the Visual Studio project. Start by running Visual Studio .NET with no project loaded.

1. Select New > Project from the File menu to bring up the New Project dialog box, shown in Figure 2.1.

2. Change the project name to example1 and select Win32 Project from the list of project templates. Click on the OK button when this is complete. The Application Wizard dialog box appears with two option tabs available: Overview and Application Settings. This dialog box is shown in Figure 2.2.

3. Select the Applications Settings tab and make sure the Empty Project option is checked, as shown in Figure 2.3.

4. Click the Finish button.

Adding the Windows Code

At this point, Visual Studio will have created an empty project. The next step is to create the source code to initialize the main application window. You start off by adding a blank source file to the project.

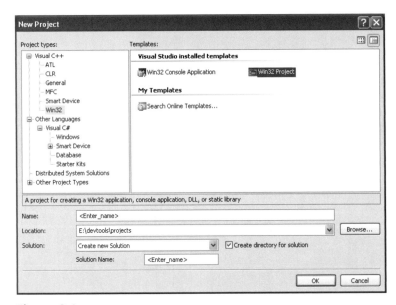

Figure 2.1
Creating a new project.

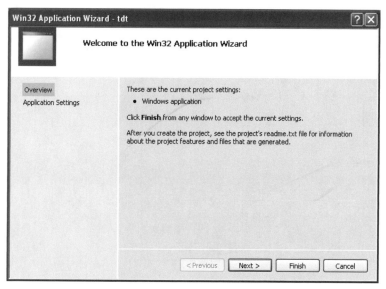

Figure 2.2
The Application Wizard dialog box.

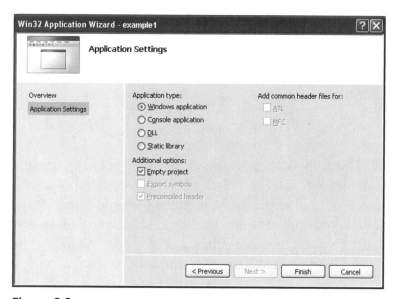

Figure 2.3
The Application Settings dialog box.

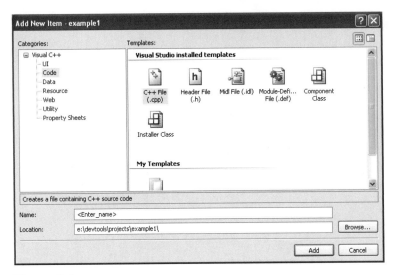

Figure 2.4
The Add New Item dialog box.

1. Select Add New Item from the Project menu. This brings up the Add New Item dialog box.

2. Select the C++ File (.cpp) from the Templates list.

3. Change the name of the file to winmain.cpp.

4. Click the Open button.

WinMain

The first part of any Windows application is always the entry point. In console applications, for example, the entry point function is called `main`, whereas the entry point function for Windows applications is called `WinMain`. The `WinMain` function is used to initialize your application, create the application window, and start the message loop. At this point, you can either type the code that follows or just load the winmain.cpp file from the Chapter2\example1 directory.

```
// Include the Windows header file, needed for all Windows applications
#include <windows.h>
#include <tchar.h>

HINSTANCE hInst;          // global handle to hold the application instance
HWND wndHandle;           // global variable to hold the window handle
```

```
int width = 640;
int height = 480;

// forward declarations
bool InitWindow( HINSTANCE hInstance, int width, int height );
LRESULT CALLBACK WndProc( HWND, UINT, WPARAM, LPARAM );

// This is winmain, the main entry point for Windows applications
int APIENTRY _tWinMain( HINSTANCE hInstance, HINSTANCE hPrevInstance,
                                LPTSTR lpCmdLine, int nCmdShow )
{
        // Initialize the window
        if ( !InitWindow( hInstance, width, height ) )
        {
            return false;
        }

        // main message loop:
        MSG msg = {0};
        while (WM_QUIT != msg.message)
        {
            while (PeekMessage(&msg, NULL, 0, 0, PM_REMOVE) == TRUE)
            {
                TranslateMessage(&msg);
                DispatchMessage(&msg);
            }
            // Additional game logic can be called from here
        }
        return (int) msg.wParam;
}
```

The most important part of this function is the main message loop. This is the part of the application that receives messages from the rest of the system, allowing the program to run in the Windows environment. In cases where your application needs to handle additional processing other than just incoming messages, it is best to use the function PeekMessage.

Most Windows applications will use a message loop with the function GetMessage. While either function is valid, there is one key difference; GetMessage waits to return to the caller until a message is available, whereas PeekMessage will return immediately.

When writing games, PeekMessage is crucial because it gives you the ability to process additional logic every time through the loop. Without this ability, the number of messages coming into the application would greatly affect how your application runs.

In either instance, if messages are available, the TranslateMessage and Dispatch Message functions are called.

After the WinMain function is complete, it's time to create the application window.

InitWindow

Before Windows allows an application to create a window on the desktop, the application must register a window class. After the class is registered, the application can create the needed window. The following code example registers a generic window with the system and then uses this class to create a default window.

```
/*****************************************************************
* InitWindow
* Inits and creates and main app window
* Inputs - application instance - HINSTANCE
           Window width - int
           Window height - int
* Outputs - true if successful, false if failed - bool
*****************************************************************/
bool InitWindow(HINSTANCE hInstance, int width, int height)
{
        WNDCLASSEX wcex;

        // Fill in the WNDCLASSEX structure. This describes how the window
        // will look to the system
        wcex.cbSize       = sizeof(WNDCLASSEX);       // the size of the structure
        wcex.style = CS_HREDRAW | CS_VREDRAW;       // the class style
        wcex.lpfnWndProc = (WNDPROC)WndProc;   // the window procedure callback
        wcex.cbClsExtra = 0;         // extra bytes to allocate for this class
        wcex.cbWndExtra = 0;         // extra bytes to allocate for this instance
        wcex.hInstance = hInstance;    // handle to the application instance
        wcex.hIcon = 0;        // icon to associate with the application
        wcex.hCursor = LoadCursor(NULL, IDC_ARROW); // the default cursor to use
        wcex.hbrBackground = (HBRUSH)(COLOR_WINDOW+1); // the background color
        wcex.lpszMenuName = NULL;              // the resource name for the menu
        wcex.lpszClassName = TEXT("DirectXExample"); // the class name being created
        wcex.hIconSm = 0;              // the handle to the small icon
        RegisterClassEx(&wcex);
```

```
        // Resize the window
        RECT rect = { 0, 0, width, height };
        AdjustWindowRect(&rect, WS_OVERLAPPEDWINDOW, FALSE);

        // create the window from the class above
        wndHandle = CreateWindow(TEXT("DirectXExample"),
    TEXT("DirectXExample"),
    WS_OVERLAPPEDWINDOW,
    CW_USEDEFAULT,
    CW_USEDEFAULT,
    rect.right - rect.left,
    rect.bottom - rect.top,
    NULL,
    NULL,
    hInstance,
    NULL);

        if (!wndHandle)
        {
            return false;
        }

        // Display the window on the screen
        ShowWindow(wndHandle, SW_SHOW);
        UpdateWindow(wndHandle);

        return true;
}
```

The preceding function is documented in every Windows programming book. I'll just give a short rundown of what this code does.

Every application that will display a window must first register a window class with the system. The window class describes certain characteristics of the window, such as the background color, the mouse cursor to use, and the icon to associate with the application. The window class is represented with the WNDCLASSEX structure. After the WNDCLASSEX structure is properly filled in, it is passed as a parameter to the function RegisterClassEx.

The RegisterClassEx function takes the information provided within the WNDCLASSEX structure and registers a window class with the system. Now that you have a valid window class registered, you are ready to create the window that your application will use.

Next, the window needs to be created, which is handled through a call to Create Window.

The CreateWindow function requires multiple parameters, each one describing to the system what the window will look like when created. Each parameter is documented in the previous code sample.

Tip

Since version Visual Studio 2005, all Win32 projects are created with Unicode support enabled by default. For this reason, _tWinMain becomes the entry point for the application. Also, all strings must be of the type LPCWSTR. The 'TEXT macro is used in places where strings are necessary to convert them to Unicode.

WndProc

The windows procedure is the final part required for a working Windows application. The windows procedure, shown in the code sample that follows as WndProc, handles events from the system that relate to your application. For instance, when a mouse click occurs within your application window, the system sends a mouse click event to your windows procedure. Your windows procedure can then decide whether the message needs handling or it can be ignored.

The windows procedure in the following example contains only the bare minimum of code needed to end the application either by clicking on the window close button or pressing the Escape key.

```
/*****************************************************************
* WndProc
* The main window procedure for the application
* Inputs - application window handle - HWND
            message sent to the window - UINT
            wParam of the message being sent - WPARAM
            lParam of the message being sent - LPARAM
* Outputs - LRESULT
*****************************************************************/
LRESULT CALLBACK WndProc(HWND hWnd, UINT message, WPARAM wParam, LPARAM lParam)
{
        // Check any available messages from the queue
        switch (message)
        {
                // Allow the user to press the Escape key to end the application
                case WM_KEYDOWN:
                    switch(wParam)
```

```
{
     // Check if the user hit the Escape key
     case VK_ESCAPE:
          PostQuitMessage(0);
     break;
}

          break;

          // The user hit the close button, close the application
          case WM_DESTROY:
              PostQuitMessage(0);
          break;
     }

     // Always return the message to the default window procedure for further
        processing
     return DefWindowProc(hWnd, message, wParam, lParam);
}
```

You should be able to compile this application and get a blank window with a white background, as shown in Figure 2.5. You will find this simple application in the chapter2\example1 directory on the CD-ROM.

Figure 2.5
The blank window application.

Time for Direct3D

Now that you know how to get a window up and running, let's add something inside of it. To do that you need to know how to set up Direct3D. All drawing with DirectX is handled through the Direct3D component. Direct3D provides you with a standard interface for accessing the graphics hardware and rendering your game to the screen.

The steps to using Direct3D are as follows:

1. Defining the swap chain.

2. Creating the Direct3D device.

3. Setting up the render target.

4. Preparing your viewport.

5. Drawing to the screen.

Sounds easy, doesn't it? Well it is; let's get started.

Initializing Direct3D

The Direct3D device is a simple interface used to provide you with access to the graphics hardware. Think of Direct3D as a middleman: You tell Direct3D what you want it to do and it will then talk to the hardware directly. For example, if you want a cube to display on the screen; you tell Direct3D the dimensions of the cube, where it should be located, and how it should look. Direct3D takes the requirements and directs the hardware on how to draw the cube.

Double Buffering

When you draw anything in Direct3D, you're not really drawing to the screen; you're drawing to an area of memory on the video card. This memory, called Video Ram (VRAM), is filled with data that represents the visual objects you see on your screen. VRAM is updated very quickly, giving objects an illusion of movement. Because of the speed at which VRAM is updated, it is possible that you're drawing to it at the same time as it is being displayed. In those instances, you will see objects flickering or visual tearing on the screen. To keep this from happening, you must use a technique called double buffering.

Double buffering is the process of drawing to an off-screen area and swapping that out with a visible area once drawing is complete. By keeping essentially two

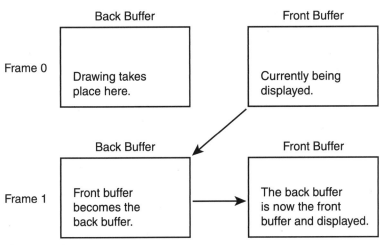

Figure 2.6
Diagram of double buffering.

copies of everything in VRAM, one can be drawn to and one can be displayed to the user. Every frame, the off-screen area is swapped with the visual area. Figure 2.6 shows an example of how double buffering works. Direct3D implements double buffering using a swap chain.

The Swap Chain

A *swap chain* is simply a series of buffers on which graphics can be drawn before being displayed to the screen. In a swap chain, one or more back buffers is available for drawing while a single front buffer is being shown. It is recommended that you create at least two buffers, one front buffer for display and a back buffer for drawing.

When creating a swap chain, you have to fill out the DXGI_SWAP_CHAIN_DESC structure. This structure contains information that describes how many buffers the swap chain will contain, as well as the buffer details. Here's an example swap chain structure:

```
DXGI_SWAP_CHAIN_DESC swapChainDesc;
// Set the width and height of the buffers in the swap chain
swapChainDesc.BufferDesc.Width = 640;
swapChainDesc.BufferDesc.Height = 480;
// Set the refresh rate. This is how often the buffers get swapped out
swapChainDesc.BufferDesc.RefreshRate.Numerator = 60;
```

```
    swapChainDesc.BufferDesc.RefreshRate.Denominator = 1;
    // Set the surface format of the buffers
    swapChainDesc.BufferDesc.Format = DXGI_FORMAT_R8G8B8A8_UNORM;
    swapChainDesc.BufferDesc.ScanlineOrdering.DXGI_MODE
    _SCANLINE_ORDER_UNSPECIFIED;
swapChainDesc.BufferDesc.Scaling.DXGI_MODE_SCALING_UNSPECIFIED;
    swapChainDesc.SampleDesc.Count = 1;
    swapChainDesc.SampleDesc.Quality = 0;
    // Set how the buffers are used. Since you are drawing to the buffers, they are
        considered a render target
    swapChainDesc.BufferUsage = DXGI_USAGE_RENDER_TARGET_OUTPUT;
    // Set the number of back buffers, 1 is the minimum and normally sufficient
    swapChainDesc.BufferCount = 1;
    // A handle to the main application window
    swapChainDesc.OutputWindow = hWnd;
    // Set whether you are running in a window or fullscreen mode
    swapChainDesc.Windowed = TRUE;
    // How the buffers are swapped. Discard allows the buffers to be overwritten
        completely when swapped.
    swapChainDesc.SwapEffect.DXGI_SWAP_EFFECT_DISCARD;
    swapChainDesc.Flags = DXGI_SWAP_CHAIN_FLAG_NONPREROTATED;
```

Many of the options in the DXGI_SWAP_CHAIN_DESC structure can be safely set to 0 and ignored. For completion I've included at least a default option in the example structure. Within the swap chain there are a few additional structures that also need to be filled out. These can easily be initialized within the swap chain structure.

In most cases the default values provided will work fine; generally you will need to only change the buffer width and height as well as the output window associated with the swap chain. Table 2.1 gives a short description of each variable in the DXGI_SWAP_CHAIN_DESC structure.

Creating the Direct3D Device

Now that you have a swap chain prepared, you create the Direct3D device. The Direct3D device, an object with the type ID3D10Device, is your main point of access to the video hardware. All Direct3D methods for drawing to the screen and accessing VRAM are handled through the ID3D10Device object.

Creating the device is handled through the function D3D10CreateDevice AndSwapChain. An example call to this function is shown next.

Table 2.1 DXGI_SWAP_CHAIN_DESC Variable Descriptions

Member	Description
BufferDesc.Width	The width of the buffers in the swap chain.
BufferDesc.Height	The height of the buffers in the swap chain.
BufferDesc.RefreshRate.Numerator	The rate at which the screen will refresh in Hz.
BufferDesc.RefreshRate.Denominator	The second piece of the refresh rate. Usually 1.
BufferDesc.Format	Every buffer has a pixel format. This describes the number of bits each pixel on the screen will have.
BufferDesc.ScanlineOrdering	Provides different methods for rendering to the screen. This comes in handy when dealing with HD resolutions.
BufferDesc.Scaling	Describes how an image is to be scaled to fit the resolution of the screen.
SampleDesc.Count	The number of multi-samples for each pixel.
SampleDesc.Quality	The level of image quality. Normally has a default value of 0.
BufferUsage	How the buffer will be used. Buffers can be used either as an output for screen display or as an input into a shader.
BufferCount	The number of back buffers.
OutputWindow	The handle to the window being used as the display.
Windowed	True if rendering to a window, False if displaying in fullscreen.
SwapEffect	This describes the method in which each back buffer is used. The buffers can either be cleared completely first or the contents from the previous frame can remain in the buffer. In most cases you will want to clear the buffer before drawing to it.
Flags	Two options are available for how the swap chain will be affected based on the orientation of the monitor. The default value works well.

```
D3D10CreateDeviceAndSwapChain( NULL,
D3D10_DRIVER_TYPE_REFERENCE,
NULL,
0,
D3D10_SDK_VERSION,
&swapChainDesc,
&pSwapChain,
&pD3DDevice );
```

In most machines, only one video adapter will be present, but in some machines more than one may be available. When only one video adapter is present, a default NULL value is passed into the D3D10CreateDeviceAndSwapChain function as the first parameter. This parameter tells Direct3D which video adapter the ID3D10Device will be created for.

The second parameter passes in D3D10_DRIVER_TYPE_REFERENCE. This is the type of driver the Direct3D device will use. If you have a video card that specifically supports Direct3D10, you can use the value D3D10_DRIVER_TYPE_HARDWARE, which will give you full hardware acceleration. If your video card only supports DirectX9 or lower, you will need to use the reference driver.

Take a look at the code below from the DirectX SDK. If you don't know at runtime which driver type you will be using, the following code attempts first to create a hardware device type followed by the reference device if that fails.

```
D3D10_DRIVER_TYPE driverType = D3D10_DRIVER_TYPE_NULL;
// define the two types of driver devices
D3D10_DRIVER_TYPE driverTypes[] =
{
    D3D10_DRIVER_TYPE_HARDWARE,
    D3D10_DRIVER_TYPE_REFERENCE,
};

UINT numDriverTypes = sizeof(driverTypes) / sizeof(driverTypes[0]);

// loop through the available type and attempt to create the hardware device first
for(UINT driverTypeIndex=0; driverTypeIndex < numDriverTypes; driverTypeIndex++ )
{
    driverType = driverTypes[driverTypeIndex];
    hr = D3D10CreateDeviceAndSwapChain(NULL,
        driverType,
        NULL,
        0,
        D3D10_SDK_VERSION,
        &swapChainDesc,
        &pSwapChain,
        &pD3DDevice );
    if( SUCCEEDED( hr ) )
        break;
}
```

Note

If your application attempts to create a Direct3D hardware device and no supporting hardware is available, then the call to D3D10CreateDeviceAndSwapChain will fail. If your application doesn't handle this gracefully the user can be confused as to why your application won't run.

All the samples in this book and on the CD-ROM assume the Direct3D10 reference device since appropriate hardware is not yet widespread.

The `D3D10CreateDeviceAndSwapChain` function is also where you use the `DXGI_SWAP_CHAIN_DESC` structure you created earlier. This helps Direct3D create the device using the options you supplied in this structure.

There are two things that are created by the `D3D10CreateDeviceAndSwapChain` function: a swap chain object and the Direct3D device.

The `D3D10CreateDeviceAndSwapChain` function will fill the `pSwapChain` variable with a valid `IDXGISwapChain` object and the `pD3DDevice` variable with a valid `ID3D10Device`.

Tip

It's always a good idea to check the return values of Direct3D functions to confirm that the objects were created correctly. Most Direct3D functions return a HRESULT value of D3D_OK if the creation was successful.

Attaching the Render Target

Direct3D does all of its drawing to what's called a render target. A render target is a type of resource considered to be an output source. The back buffer, created earlier when the swap chain was initialized, will need to be set as the render target for the final stage of the Direct3D pipeline.

Before the pipeline can use the back buffer, it has to be converted to a render target view. The back buffer at this point is considered a 2D texture resource (`ID3D10Texture2D`).

A view allows a resource to be interpreted by the stages in the pipeline in different ways. By creating different views for a resource, only a single resource needs to be held in memory and yet can be associated with multiple views. To create the render target view the pipeline needs, you use the `CreateRenderTargetView` function.

The Output Merger stage is the point at which the final image is produced from the data of the previous steps of the pipeline. The pipeline needs somewhere to write this information and that place is the render target view created from the back buffer. The function `OMSetRenderTargets` binds the render target to the pipeline. All drawing will now take place on the render target view.

```
// get the back buffer from the swap chain
ID3D10Texture2D *pBackBuffer;
HRESULT hr = pSwapChain->GetBuffer(0, __uuidof(ID3D10Texture2D), (LPVOID*)
&pBackBuffer);
```

```
if (hr != S_OK)
{
    return false;
}

// create the render target View
hr = pD3DDevice->CreateRenderTargetView(pBackBuffer, NULL,
&pRenderTargetView);

// release the back buffer
pBackBuffer->Release();

// Make sure the render target view was created successfully
if (hr != S_OK)
{
    return false;
}

// set the render target
pD3DDevice->OMSetRenderTargets(1, &pRenderTargetView, NULL);
```

The code snippet above shows how the render target is bound to the pipeline. Notice that the temporary pointer to the back buffer is released before the render target is set.

The Viewport

The viewport is used to define the properties of the viewable area on your screen. Even though the scene you're creating takes place in a 3D space, the device on which it's viewed is entirely a 2D environment. The viewport is used during the rasterizer stage of the pipeline to clip the scene to the extents defined in the D3D10_VIEWPORT structure. Any objects not within the area defined by the viewport will be clipped from the scene.

After the viewport structure is defined, it can be set using the RSSetViewports function.

```
// create and set the viewport
D3D10_VIEWPORT viewPort;
viewPort.Width = width;
viewPort.Height = height;
viewPort.MinDepth = 0.0f;
viewPort.MaxDepth = 1.0f;
```

```
viewPort.TopLeftX = 0;
viewPort.TopLeftY = 0;

// Set the viewport
pD3DDevice->RSSetViewports(1, &viewPort);
```

Clearing the Screen

Now that the Direct3D device has been created, you can render to the screen, be it with an image or a bunch of polygons. The first thing you have to do during each pass of the main game loop is clear the screen. Clearing the screen gives you a clean slate to render to each frame.

Clearing the screen is done with the function `ClearRenderTargetView`.

```
// clear the target buffer
pD3DDevice->ClearRenderTargetView(pRenderTargetView, D3DXCOLOR(0.0f, 0.0f,
0.0f, 0.0f));
```

When the screen is cleared, you can use any color available to Direct3D. The `D3DXCOLOR` function lets you create a 32-bit color from RGBA values in the range from 0.0f to 1.0f. In most cases, black is used as the clear color but any color can be used.

Displaying the Scene

Now that you've cleared the frame, it's time to display it to the screen. Direct3D uses the `Present` function to do this. All the drawing that you've been doing up to this point has been to the back buffer. The `Present` function performs the page flipping of the buffers in the swap chain.

Note

Page flipping refers to the swapping of the buffers in the swap chain. For instance, drawing to the back buffer requires a page flip to occur before its contents can be seen on the screen.

Tip

It is a good idea to make sure the Direct3D object is valid before trying to render anything. If the Direct3D object is NULL, then skip all rendering.

```
// Page flip and display the next buffer in the swap chain
pSwapChain->Present(0, 0);
```

The first parameter to the Present function gives you the ability to control how drawing is synced. Sending a default value of 0 will present the next buffer in the swap chain to the screen immediately.

The second parameter gives you a way of testing the swap chain before actually presenting anything to the screen. Passing a value of DXGI_PRESENT_TEST performs the test and the HRESULT can be checked for any problems. A default value of 0 will go ahead and perform the swap.

The example in the chapter2\example2 directory on the CD-ROM contains the code for setting up Direct3D, clearing the screen, and presenting a scene.

Cleaning Up

The final thing to do in any Direct3D application is to clean up and release the objects that you've created. For instance, at the beginning of your program, you created a Direct3D object, a swap chain, and a render target view. When the application closes, you need to release these objects so the resources are returned to the system for reuse.

COM objects keep a reference count that tells the system when it's safe to remove objects from memory. By using the Release function, you decrement the reference count for an object. When the reference count reaches 0, the system reclaims these resources.

```
// release the rendertarget
if (pRenderTargetView)
{
    pRenderTargetView->Release();
}

// release the swapchain
if (pSwapChain)
{
    pSwapChain->Release();
}

// release the D3D Device
if (pD3DDevice)
{
    pD3DDevice->Release();
}
```

The if statement first checks to make sure that the variable pD3DDevice, which was assigned to the device earlier, is not NULL and then calls the Release function. It's a good idea to release the objects in the reverse order in which they were created.

Formats

Occasionally you'll be required to specify a DXGI format. Formats can be used to describe the layout of an image, the number of bits used for each color, or the layout of vertices for a vertex buffer. Most commonly, DXGI formats are used to describe the layout of the buffers in the swap chain. DXGI formats are not specific to any type of data, only the format in which it comes.

An example DXGI format, DXGI_FORMAT_R8G8B8A8_UNORM says that the data coming in will use 8 bits for each of the RGBA components. When defining vertices, formats like DXGI_FORMAT_R32G32B32_FLOAT are used where 32 bits are available for the three components. Even though a format may specify RGB, it's only a description of how the data is laid out, not what the data is used for.

Occasionally you'll see formats that specify the same number of bits for each component but have a different extension to them. For instance, both DXGI_FORMAT_R32G32B32A32_FLOAT and DXGI_FORMAT_R32G32B32A32_UINT reserve the same number of bits for each component but also specify the type of data contained in those bits. These are considered fully typed formats.

Formats that don't declare a type are called typeless formats. They reserve the same number of bits for each component, but don't care what type of data is contained, such as DXGI_FORMAT_R32G32B32A32_TYPELESS. Here is an abbreviated list of common formats:

DXGI_FORMAT_R32G32B32A32_TYPELESS
128-bit format consisting of four typeless RGBA components.

DXGI_FORMAT_R32G32B32A32_FLOAT
128-bit format consisting of four float RGBA components.

DXGI_FORMAT_R32G32B32A32_UINT

128-bit format consisting of four unsigned integer RGBA components.

DXGI_FORMAT_R32G32B32A32_SINT

128-bit format consisting of four signed integer RGBA components.

DXGI_FORMAT_R8G8B8A8_TYPELESS

32-bit format consisting of four typeless RGBA components.

DXGI_FORMAT_R8G8B8A8_UINT

32-bit format consisting of four unsigned integer RGBA components.

DXGI_FORMAT_R8G8B8A8_SINT

32-bit format consisting of four signed integer RGBA components.

Updating the Code

Now that you've seen how to get DirectX up and running, it's time to add the code to do it yourself. These code additions should be made to the winmain.cpp file that was created earlier.

The first step when writing any DirectX-enabled application is adding the Direct3D header.

```
#include <d3d10.h>
#include <d3dx10.h>
```

The following three variables need to be added into the globals section at the top of the code.

```
// Direct3D global vars
ID3D10Device*            pD3DDevice = NULL;
IDXGISwapChain*          pSwapChain = NULL;
ID3D10RenderTargetView*  pRenderTargetView = NULL;
```

There are three pointers being created, one for the D3D10 device, one for the swap chain, and finally, one for the render target view.

Next, you add a call to the InitDirect3D function, which you'll be defining a bit further down in the code. This call should be placed right after the InitWindow call within the WinMain function. Notice that the InitDirect3D takes three parameters, the handle to the application window and the width and height.

```
// called after creating the window
if ( !InitDirect3D( mainhWnd, width, height) )
{
    return 0;
}
```

If the function fails for any reason, the application will end.

Changing the Message Loop

The message loop needs to only change slightly. The loop is already set up to process the normal application messages, but now it has to change to also perform the game processing that's needed.

The only difference in the message loop is the addition of a call to the Render function. This function, which will be defined in a bit, handles drawing everything to the screen.

```
// Main message loop
MSG msg = {0};
while (WM_QUIT != msg.message)
{
    while (PeekMessage(&msg, NULL, 0, 0, PM_REMOVE) == TRUE)
    {
        TranslateMessage(&msg);
        DispatchMessage(&msg);
    }

    // Call the render function
    Render();
}
```

The Init Function

The InitDirect3D function creates the Direct3D object and the device.

```
/*************************************************************
* InitDirect3D
* Initializes Direct3D
* Inputs - Parent window handle - HWND,
            Window width - int
            Window height - int
```

```
* Outputs - true if successful, false if failed - bool
**********************************************************************/
bool InitDirect3D(HWND hWnd, int width, int height)
{
    // Create the clear the DXGI_SWAP_CHAIN_DESC structure
    DXGI_SWAP_CHAIN_DESC swapChainDesc;
    ZeroMemory(&swapChainDesc, sizeof(swapChainDesc));

    // Fill in the needed values
    swapChainDesc.BufferCount = 1;
    swapChainDesc.BufferDesc.Width = width;
    swapChainDesc.BufferDesc.Height = height;
    swapChainDesc.BufferDesc.Format = DXGI_FORMAT_R8G8B8A8_UNORM;
    swapChainDesc.BufferDesc.RefreshRate.Numerator = 60;
    swapChainDesc.BufferDesc.RefreshRate.Denominator = 1;
    swapChainDesc.BufferUsage = DXGI_USAGE_RENDER_TARGET_OUTPUT;
    swapChainDesc.OutputWindow = hWnd;
    swapChainDesc.SampleDesc.Count = 1;
    swapChainDesc.SampleDesc.Quality = 0;
    swapChainDesc.Windowed = TRUE;

    // Create the D3D device and the swap chain
    HRESULT hr = D3D10CreateDeviceAndSwapChain(NULL,
        D3D10_DRIVER_TYPE_REFERENCE,
        NULL,
        0,
        D3D10_SDK_VERSION,
        &swapChainDesc,
        &pSwapChain,
        &pD3DDevice);

    // Error checking. Make sure the device was created
    if (hr != S_OK)
    {
        return false;
    }

    // Get the back buffer from the swapchain
    ID3D10Texture2D *pBackBuffer;
    hr = pSwapChain->GetBuffer(0, __uuidof(ID3D10Texture2D), (LPVOID*)
    &pBackBuffer);
    if (hr != S_OK)
    {
        return false;
    }
```

```
// create the render target view
hr = pD3DDevice->CreateRenderTargetView(pBackBuffer, NULL,
&pRenderTargetView);

// release the back buffer
pBackBuffer->Release();

// Make sure the render target view was created successfully
if (hr != S_OK)
{
    return false;
}

// set the render target
pD3DDevice->OMSetRenderTargets(1, &pRenderTargetView, NULL);

// create and set the viewport
D3D10_VIEWPORT viewPort;
viewPort.Width = width;
viewPort.Height = height;
viewPort.MinDepth = 0.0f;
viewPort.MaxDepth = 1.0f;
viewPort.TopLeftX = 0;
viewPort.TopLeftY = 0;
pD3DDevice->RSSetViewports(1, &viewPort);

    return true;
}
```

At the beginning of this function, you're creating and filling in the DXGI_ SWAP_CHAIN_DESC structure. This structure defines the properties of the swap chain that gets created with the D3D10CreateDeviceAndSwapChain function. This function will return with a valid ID3D10Device and a IDXGISwapChain object.

Next, the back buffer from the swap chain is set up as the render target. Finally, the viewport that is used by the Rasterizer stage is defined.

The Render Function

The Render function is where the actual drawing takes place. As you recall from earlier, this function is called from within the main loop and is called once per frame.

```
/****************************************************************
* Render
* All drawing happens in the Render function
* Inputs - void
* Outputs - void
****************************************************************/
void Render()
{
    if (pD3DDevice != NULL)
    {
        // clear the target buffer
        pD3DDevice->ClearRenderTargetView(pRenderTargetView, D3DXCOLOR
        (0.0f, 0.0f, 0.0f, 0.0f));

        // All drawing will go here.

        // display the next item in the swap chain
        pSwapChain->Present(0, 0);
    }
}
```

This is a simple example of a Render function. First, you check to make sure that you have a valid ID3D10Device device by checking it against NULL. If this object has been released before calling the Render function, you don't want further code in here to execute.

First, you need to make use of the ClearRenderTargetView function presented earlier. This clears the render target with the defined color. The color is defined using the D3DXCOLOR macro.

Next, you add in the code that performs the drawing for your application. Since nothing is being drawn, the screen will just be cleared to the specified color.

Lastly, flip the buffers in the swap chain with the Present function.

The ShutdownDirect3D Function

Of course, after the application ends, you need to release the objects that were created. This is handled with the following code.

```
/****************************************************************
* ShutdownDirect3D
* Closes down and releases the resources for Direct3D
```

```
* Inputs - void
* Outputs - void
*******************************************************************/
void ShutdownDirect3D()
{
    // release the rendertarget
    if (pRenderTargetView)
    {
        pRenderTargetView->Release();
    }

    // release the swapchain
    if (pSwapChain)
    {
        pSwapChain->Release();
    }

    // release the D3D Device
    if (pD3DDevice)
    {
        pD3DDevice->Release();
    }
}
```

First, the objects are checked to make sure they are still valid; if so, then they are released. The preceding function should be added right before the return call at the end of the WinMain function.

Adding the DirectX Libraries

At last, you have all the code you need to create your first DirectX application. Before you can compile and run this, you have to do one more thing: link in the DirectX libraries. For this simple example, you only need to link with D3D10.lib.

1. Select the Properties option from the Project menu. The Project Properties dialog box appears. This dialog box is shown in Figure 2.7.

2. Click the Linker option in the left pane. This expands to show the included options.

3. Next, select the Input option. The dialog box changes and should reflect what's shown in Figure 2.8.

4. Type **D3D10.lib** into the Additional Dependencies field and click OK.

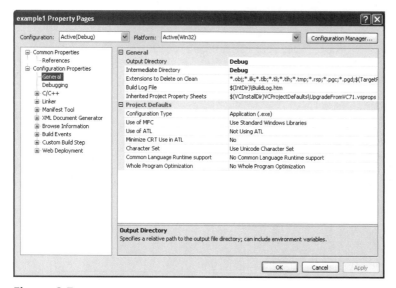

Figure 2.7
The Project Properties dialog box.

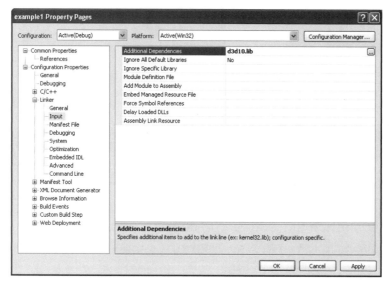

Figure 2.8
Changing the Linker option in the Project Properties dialog box.

Compile and run the application. Unlike the white window from before, this window should now display a black background color. Although this application doesn't show the depth of what DirectX can do, it does give you the basics to start with.

Note

Multiple libraries are needed for different DirectX functionality. You only need to link to those specific libraries within which you are accessing functions.

Summary

This chapter covered a lot of information, ranging from the beginnings of a project to a workable DirectX application. These examples might not show much, but they are the building blocks for everything you will do going forward.

What You Have Learned

In this chapter, you learned the following:

- How the Direct3D 10 object is created

- The proper method for clearing the screen each frame

- The changes to a standard message loop that need to be made for games

- How to add the DirectX libraries to your game projects

- What a swap chain is and how it's used

The next chapter introduces some 2D concepts including texture loading and animated sprites.

Review Questions

You can find the answers to Review Questions in Appendix A, "Answers to End-of-Chapter Exercises."

1. What is the main difference between the `GetMessage` and `PeekMessage` functions in a message loop?

2. What's the first DirectX object that needs to be created in any application?

3. How many buffers can be created in a swap chain?

4. The `DXGI_FORMAT_R32G32B32A32_TYPELESS` defines how many bits for each color?

5. What DirectX function is required to blank the screen to a specific color?

On Your Own

1. Change example 2 on the CD-ROM to clear the screen to a green color instead of blue.

2. Update example 3 on the CD-ROM to use more than one back buffer.

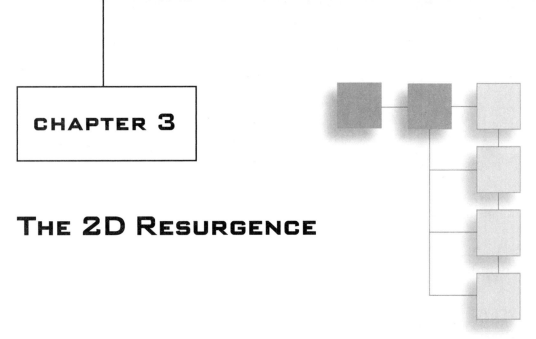

CHAPTER 3

THE 2D RESURGENCE

Two-dimensional (2D) games, immensely popular in the early days of video games, are having a revival. Due to the relative ease of development, thousands of casual games are being brought to life using 2D techniques like vector- and sprite-based graphics. Using Microsoft's Xbox Live Arcade as an example, a number of the most popular games available are strictly 2D. In addition, web games based on Macromedia's Flash are increasingly popular with gamers. Developers are quickly being reminded that games don't have to have the most expensive budgets or the latest 3D technology; they just have to be fun. Larger game development companies like Microsoft and Sony have taken notice and are allowing more 2D console games onto the market through their online services.

Here's what you'll learn in this chapter:

- How to take advantage of 2D techniques needed to build a game

- What textures are and how they can be used

- How to draw directly to the back buffer

- An easy way to load in a texture

- How to create and use sprites

- How to animate sprites

- How to use timers for smooth animation

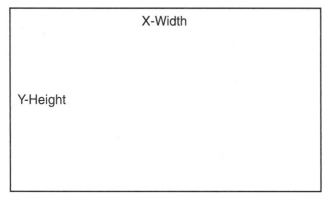

Figure 3.1
A 2D representation.

2D Game Development

2D games take place in a grid-like area having only width and height. If you look at your computer monitor, you'll see a perfect representation of a 2D area. Objects in your game can be placed anywhere in this two-dimensional world, but they remain on the same plane. Figure 3.1 shows how a 2D world is laid out.

2D game development hasn't changed much since the first video games. There are still a few key pieces needed for every 2D game:

- ■ Textures

- ■ Sprites

- ■ Animation

Textures

Textures are a core piece of any 2D game. Textures are simply the graphics your game uses. For instance, any graphics for a character, weapon, or house would use a texture. Textures are created through the use of applications like Photoshop, Paint Shop Pro, or even Windows paint. Figure 3.2 shows examples of textures.

Figure 3.2
Example textures.

The graphics you use in your game don't have to be elaborate; they can even just be programmer art. Any artwork you do can easily be replaced later by just swapping out the textures.

Loading a Texture

Textures, like other data your game needs, will usually be loaded at runtime. Since textures are an integral part of Direct3D, a few built-in functions are available to you for handling textures. The function `D3DX10CreateTextureFromFile` is used to load in textures from disk. This function supports a variety of popular graphics formats, such as .BMP, .PNG, and .DDS.

The `D3DX10CreateTextureFromFile` function takes six parameters.

The first parameter is a pointer to the active `ID3D10Device`; this was created when Direct3D was initialized.

The second and most key parameter is the filename of the texture to load. This is the full path and filename to the texture.

The third parameter contains a `D3DX10_IMAGE_LOAD_INFO` structure. This structure is used by the `D3DX10CreateTextureFromFile` function to determine how to load the texture. The area of memory to load the texture and the texture dimensions are just some of the information contained in this structure. Passing `NULL` to this parameter allows Direct3D to determine this behavior on its own.

Parameter four is a pointer to a thread pump interface. The thread pump interface is used to asynchronously load resources in a background thread. Passing `NULL` to this parameter will cause the resource to block until the texture is loaded.

The fifth parameter is the `ID3D10Resource` interface, which will receive the loaded texture. The `ID3D10Resource` object is used to manage image data.

The final parameter is a pointer to an `HRESULT` object. If you use the `HRESULT` passed back from the `D3DX10CreateTextureFromFile`, you can pass `NULL` as this parameter.

The following code snippet demonstrates how to use the `D3DX10CreateTexture-FromFile` function.

```
ID3D10Resource*  pD3D10Resource = NULL;

// Loads the texture into a temporary ID3D10Resource object
HRESULT hr = D3DX10CreateTextureFromFile(pD3DDevice,
    "C:\\test.bmp",
    NULL,
    NULL,
    &pD3D10Resource,
    NULL);

// Make sure the texture was loaded successfully
if (FAILED(hr))
{
    return NULL;
}
```

NULL values were passed into the D3DX10_IMAGE_LOAD_INFO and thread pump parameters.

Before the texture can be used, it needs to be converted to use the appropriate texture resource interface.

Note

Texture sizes should be a power of two for the best support across video cards.

Texture Interfaces

Texture interfaces are used to manage image data of a certain type. Within Direct3D there are three main types of texture interfaces:

- **ID3D10Texture1D**—Handles a 1D or image strip type of texture.

- **ID3D10Texture2D**—2D image data. This is the most common type of texture resource.

- **ID3D10Texture3D**—Image data used to represent volume textures.

Each of these texture resources contains one or more subresources. The subresources represent the different mip levels of the texture. *Mip levels* are decreasingly lower resolution versions of the same texture. Mip levels allow the system to swap in the proper texture resolution based on an object's distance. Objects further away need a lower texture applied to them since they are not close enough to see all the detail anyway.

Most of the textures you use in your game will be of the 2D variety and will need to be converted to `ID3D10Texture2D` resources.

Converting a *ID3D10Resource* to a Texture Resource

Converting between resource types is actually fairly easy using the COM function `QueryInterface`. The following code shows how to use the `QueryInterface` function to convert between the two resource types.

```
// Translates the ID3D10Resource object into a ID3D10Texture2D object
ID3D10Texture2D* texture2D = NULL;
pD3D10Resource->QueryInterface(__uuidof( ID3D10Texture2D ),
 (LPVOID*) &texture2D);
pD3D10Resource->Release();
```

The code to load in and convert a texture to the correct resource type can be contained in a single helper function called `GetTexture2DFromFile`.

```
/******************************************************************
* GetTexture2DFromFile
* Loads a texture from a file into a ID3D10Texture2D object
* Inputs - LPCSTR the path and filename of the texture
* Outputs - pointer to an ID3D10Texture2D object
******************************************************************/
ID3D10Texture2D* GetTexture2DFromFile(LPCSTR filename)
{
    ID3D10Texture2D* texture2D = NULL;
    ID3D10Resource*   pD3D10Resource = NULL;

    // Loads the texture into a temporary ID3D10Resource object
    HRESULT hr = D3DX10CreateTextureFromFile(pD3DDevice,
        LPCSTR(filename),
        NULL,
        NULL,
        &pD3D10Resource,
        NULL);

    // Make sure the texture was loaded in successfully
    if (FAILED(hr))
    {
        return NULL;
    }
```

```
    // Translates the ID3D10Resource object into a ID3D10Texture2D object
    pD3D10Resource ->QueryInterface(__uuidof( ID3D10Texture2D),
(LPVOID*)&texture2D);
    pD3D10Resource ->Release();

    // returns the ID3D10Texture2D object
    return texture2D;
}
```

Texture Details

Occasionally you'll need to get certain information from a texture such as its dimensions or pixel format. This information is available using ID3D10Texture2D's GetDesc function. This function fills in a D3D10_TEXTURE2D_DESC structure with all the details.

```
// srcTexture must be a valid ID3D10Texture2D object
D3D10_TEXTURE2D_DESC desc;
srcTexture->GetDesc(&desc);
```

D3D10_TEXTURE2D_DESC is just one of the texture description structures available and is specifically for 2D textures. Direct3D also has the structures D3D10_TEXTURE1D_DESC and D3D10_TEXTURE3D_DESC available for 1D and 3D textures respectively. The content of the structure for 2D textures is shown next.

```
typedef struct D3D10_TEXTURE2D_DESC {
    SIZE_T Width;
    SIZE_T Height;
    UINT MipLevels;
    UINT ArraySize;
    DXGI_FORMAT Format;
    DXGI_SAMPLE_DESC SampleDesc;
    D3D10_USAGE Usage;
    UINT BindFlags;
    UINT CPUAccessFlags;
    UINT MiscFlags;
} D3D10_TEXTURE2D_DESC, *LPD3D10_TEXTURE2D_DESC;
```

The D3D10_TEXTURE2D_DESC structure will give you additional information such as the format of the texture, stored in the Format variable. For more details regarding this structure, see the DirectX SDK documentation.

Viewing a Texture

Direct3D doesn't provide a built-in way to view a texture once it's loaded. An easy way to view a texture though is to copy it directly to the back buffer.

The back buffer can just be considered another texture resource and Direct3D provides functions for copying data between textures. The function `CopyResource` allows the full contents from one resource to be copied into another. This is useful when you need a background image copied in full.

Direct3D also provides the `CopySubresourceRegion` function. This function allows for the copying of rectangular image chunks between resources. The `CopySubresourceRegion` function takes eight parameters.

The first parameter is the pointer to the destination texture resource. In this instance, this will be the back buffer. The second parameter is the destination subresource. You enter the index of the mip level you want the image data copied to. The third, fourth, and fifth parameters are the location in the destination resource to copy the image data to. The sixth and seventh parameters are the source resource and the source subresource index. The final parameter is a `D3D10_BOX` structure. This structure gives the boundary of the image data to copy.

The following code sample shows how to use the `CopySubresourceRegion` function to copy image data from a source texture to the back buffer.

```
// Get a pointer to the back buffer texture
ID3D10Texture2D *pBackBuffer;
HRESULT hr = pSwapChain->GetBuffer(0, __uuidof(ID3D10Texture2D),
 (LPVOID*)&pBackBuffer);
if(hr != S_OK)
{
    return;
}

D3D10_BOX sourceRegion;
sourceRegion.left = 0;
sourceRegion.right = 640;
sourceRegion.top = 0;
sourceRegion.bottom = 480;
sourceRegion.front = 0;
sourceRegion.back = 1;

// Copy part of a texture resource to the back buffer texture
// The last parameter is a D3D10_BOX structure which defines the rectangle to
```

Figure 3.3
Texture viewed on the back buffer.

```
copy to the back
// buffer. Passing in 0 will copy the whole buffer.
pD3DDevice->CopySubresourceRegion(pBackBuffer, 0, 0, 0, 0, srcTexture, 0,
&sourceRegion);
```

To get access to the back buffer, your code must access the swap chain that you
created when Direct3D was initialized. The back buffer is then converted to an
`ID3D10Texture2D` object for use by the `CopySubresourceRegion` function. Figure 3.3
shows a texture being displayed.

Note

Texture files, such as DDS and bitmaps can be viewed in the DirectX Texture Tool (dxTex.exe found
in the Utilities\bin directory).

The `CopySubresourceRegion` function passed in all zeroes for the location variables causing the texture to be placed in the top-left corner of the screen. A full
code example is in the Chapter3/example1 directory on the CD-ROM.

Sprites

2D games just wouldn't be the same without sprites. Before you start thinking
soda or fairies, *sprites* are 2D graphical representations of characters or objects
within a game. Every tree, treasure chest, or dungeon creature you encounter is

Figure 3.4
An example of a sprite.

presented on-screen using a sprite. Sprites are one of the most widely used and easily understood aspects of 2D game programming. Figure 3.4 shows an example of a sprite created from a colored rectangle.

Sprites come in all different sizes, but tend to come in only one shape, rectangular. Because of their shape, sprites need only a width and height to define their area and are more easily controlled from a programmer's perspective. Since your game is taking place in a 2D area consisting of only width and height, it only takes two variables to describe the sprite's location. These two variables are commonly referred to as X and Y. The X variable controls the horizontal position with Y controlling the vertical.

Moving a character sprite along a straight line from one side of the screen to the other is simple. The sprite's location need only change horizontally, without any concern for depth. Because of the lack of actual depth in sprite-based games, depth is normally faked by a technique called Z ordering.

Z Ordering

Z ordering is the process in which objects are sorted before being drawn. Each sprite you create can be given a different Z-order value designating the depth at which it should be drawn. Sprites with a lower Z-order value are drawn behind those sprites with a higher value, giving the illusion of depth. Figure 3.5 shows how Z ordering works.

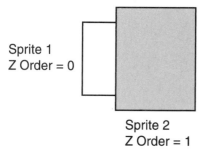

Figure 3.5
A diagram demonstrating Z ordering.

Sprite Image

The most important aspect of a sprite is its image. Each sprite needs an image to be associated with it both from a gameplay perspective and a technical one. The image is what the sprite uses to convey its purpose to the player. For instance, your main character sprite in an RPG game may be the image of a knight or even a spaceship in a space battle. You can choose any image you'd like, but your sprite can't be displayed without an image.

Earlier you learned how to load a texture from the disk; now you'll learn how textures can be used with sprites.

Shader Resource Views

Before a texture can be attached to a sprite, it needs to be configured into a format the sprite can use. The way resources are accessed in Direct3D differs based on how the resource is going to be used. Resources, such as textures, are commonly stored linearly in a buffer within memory. While this is an easy way to load the texture, it isn't always in the format that is most efficient for the video hardware. Direct3D solves this problem by using resource views.

A resource view allows data to be accessed differently based on part of the Direct3D pipeline using it. When creating a sprite, the D3DX10_SPRITE structure expects the texture to be accessed through an ID3D10ShaderResourceView object, which helps the shader know how to use a particular resource.

The ID3D10ShaderResourceView is created using the CreateShaderResourceView function.

The CreateShaderResourceView function takes three parameters.

The first parameter is a pointer to the texture resource from which to create the view. The second parameter is a pointer to a D3D10_SHADER_RESOURCE_VIEW_DESC structure. This structure is used to define the type of resource view being created. The final parameter is the newly created ID3D10ShaderResourceView.

Before the shader resource view can be created, you need to create and fill out the D3D10_SHADER_RESOURCE_VIEW_DESC structure.

```
typedef struct D3D10_SHADER_RESOURCE_VIEW_DESC {
    DXGI_FORMAT Format;
    D3D10_SRV_DIMENSION ViewDimension;
```

```
    union {
        D3D10_BUFFER_SRV Buffer;
        D3D10_TEX1D_SRV Texture1D;
        D3D10_TEX1D_ARRAY_SRV Texture1DArray;
        D3D10_TEX2D_SRV Texture2D;
        D3D10_TEX2D_ARRAY_SRV Texture2DArray;
        D3D10_TEX2DMS_SRV Texture2DMS;
        D3D10_TEX2DMS_ARRAY_SRV Texture2DMSArray;
        D3D10_TEX3D_SRV Texture3D;
        D3D10_TEXCUBE_SRV TextureCube;
    };
} D3D10_SHADER_RESOURCE_VIEW_DESC;
```

Although the size of the `D3D10_SHADER_RESOURCE_VIEW_DESC` structure may look imposing, there are only a few variables that need to be filled out.

The `DXGI_FORMAT` is simply the texture format. This information is available in the `D3D10_TEXTURE2D_DESC` structure by calling the `GetDesc` function.

The `D3D10_SRV_DIMENSION` lets the resource view know the type of texture it is representing. This will most commonly be a 2D texture.

The last piece is to fill out the variables that pertain to the type of texture resource. In the case of 2D textures, this includes information like the number of mip levels.

The following code sample shows how to create and complete the `D3D10_SHADER_ RESOURCE_VIEW_DESC` structure.

```
// Load the texture for the sprite
ID3D10Texture2D* texture = GetTexture2DFromFile(TEXT("../brick.bmp"));

// Make sure there's a valid texture
if (texture != NULL)
{
    // Get the texture details
    D3D10_TEXTURE2D_DESC desc;
    texture->GetDesc( &desc );

    // Create a shader resource view of the texture
    D3D10_SHADER_RESOURCE_VIEW_DESC SRVDesc;
    // Clear out the shader resource view description structure
    ZeroMemory( &SRVDesc, sizeof(SRVDesc) );
```

```
    // Set the texture format
    SRVDesc.Format = desc.Format;
    // Set the type of resource
    SRVDesc.ViewDimension = D3D10_SRV_DIMENSION_TEXTURE2D;
    SRVDesc.Texture2D.MipLevels = desc.MipLevels;
}
```

Once you have a completed `D3D10_SHADER_RESOURCE_VIEW_DESC` structure, you can call the `CreateShaderResourceView` function. The following code shows how to use this function to create a resource view.

```
ID3D10ShaderResourceView *gSpriteTextureRV = NULL;
pD3DDevice->CreateShaderResourceView(texture, &SRVDesc, &gSpriteTextureRV);
```

When the call is complete, the `gSpriteTextureRV` function will contain a valid shader resource view usable to create a sprite.

Creating a Sprite

Now that you have your image data ready, it's time to create the sprite. Direct3D has built-in support for sprites so there won't be a need to mess with the textures directly like you did in the first example.

There are a few easy steps you need to follow to create a sprite. First, define each of your sprites using a `D3DX10_SPRITE` structure. Second, use the `ID3DX10Sprite` interface to manipulate and draw the sprites. The steps are detailed in the following sections.

The D3DX10_SPRITE Structure

Direct3D has a special object reserved specifically for representing sprites: the `D3DX10_SPRITE` structure. This structure contains variables for specifying everything Direct3D needs to know in order to draw the sprite, including its position, texture, resource, and color. By filling in this structure, you're detailing how and where you want your sprite drawn by Direct3D. Each sprite your game displays will need one of these structures filled out with the sprite's appropriate data.

```
typedef struct D3DX10_SPRITE {
    D3DXMATRIX matWorld;
    D3DXVECTOR2 TexCoord;
    D3DXVECTOR2 TexSize;
    D3DXCOLOR ColorModulate;
    ID3D10ShaderResourceView * pTexture;
```

```
    UINT TextureIndex;
} D3DX10_SPRITE;
```

The first member of the D3DX10_SPRITE structure is the matWorld variable. This variable contains the transform used to specify where the sprite should be drawn.

The second member is TexCoord; this is the sprite's texture coordinate. The texture coordinate describes the location of the sprite's top-left corner in its image data. This value ranges from 0 to 1.

TexSize details the size of the texture used for the sprite. This value, ranging from 0 to 1, will tell the sprite just how much of the image data it uses.

The fourth member is ColorModulate. Whichever color is specified in this variable will be applied to the sprite before it's drawn. If the sprite is being drawn at full brightness and color, this variable is normally white.

pTexture is a pointer to the shader resource view that represents the texture the sprite will use.

Lastly, TextureIndex is the index into an array of textures. If the texture being used for the sprite is not a texture array, this value should be 0.

The following small code sample shows how to create and initialize a sprite using the D3DX10_SPRITE structure.

```
// Create a new sprite variable
D3DX10_SPRITE testSprite;

// Set the sprite's shader resource view
testSprite.pTexture = gSpriteTextureRV;

// top-left location in U,V coords
testSprite.TexCoord.x = 0;
testSprite.TexCoord.y = 0;

// Determine the texture size in U,V coords
testSprite.TexSize.x = 1.0f;
testSprite.TexSize.y = 1.0f;

// Set the texture index. Single textures will use 0
testSprite.TextureIndex = 0;

// The color to apply to this sprite, full color applies white.
testSprite.ColorModulate = D3DXCOLOR(1.0f, 1.0f, 1.0f, 1.0f);
```

The preceding code assumed that the sprite was using the entire contents of the image by specifying 0 for the texture coordinates and 1.0 for the texture size.

The Direct3D Sprite System

Direct3D includes an interface for managing and drawing the sprites defined in the D3DX10_SPRITE structures. This interface, ID3DX10Sprite, is the main work-horse of sprite drawing. The ID3DX10Sprite interface expects the application to create one or more sprite structures for it to manage. It takes the structures, sorts them, and sends them to the graphics hardware to be drawn.

You can create an ID3DX10Sprite object using the D3DX10CreateSprite function. The D3DX10CreateSprite function takes only three parameters.

The first parameter is a pointer to the D3DX10Device you created when Direct3D was initialized.

Second is the number of sprites to be rendered at any one time. Specifying 0 for this parameter will cause Direct3D to default to 4096.

The final parameter is a pointer to an ID3DX10Sprite interface waiting to be initialized.

The following code sample shows how to create and initialize the sprite system.

```
ID3DX10Sprite  *spriteObject = NULL;

// create the sprite object
HRESULT hr = D3DX10CreateSprite(pD3DDevice, 0, &spriteObject);

// Make sure the sprite creation was successful
if (hr != S_OK)
{
    // Handle failure
}
```

Remember to release the ID3DX10Sprite interface after you're done using it. Failure to do so will cause a memory leak.

```
// spriteObject contains a valid ID3DX10Sprite object
if (spriteObject)
{
    spriteObject->Release();
    spriteObject = NULL;
}
```

Getting the Sprite to the Screen

When drawing sprites, the sprite object needs to know a few things about the environment in which it's drawing. Not only does it need to know the position of each and every sprite, but it needs to know the specifics about the area in which it's drawing. This means the sprite object must be aware of the boundaries of the area where the sprites will be drawn. Normally, the size of this area is determined by the viewport associated with the Direct3D device. Figure 3.6 shows how a viewport is laid out.

The area in which the sprites are drawn, in this case, will consist of the entire viewport. The SetProjectionTransform function is used to set the available drawing area for the sprite object. The SetProjectionTransform function takes one parameter, a D3DXMATRIX structure called the projection matrix, which defines the dimensions of the drawing area. Because matrices are explained in more detail in Chapter 5, I'll just describe how the projection matrix is created.

The function D3DXMatrixOrthoOffCenterLH is used to create the projection matrix. The first parameter for this function is a pointer to a D3DXMATRIX structure where the resulting projection matrix is placed. D3DXMatrixOrthoOffCenterLH creates a left-handed projection matrix that is used for setting up the viewport for sprite drawing. This function is used specifically to offset the coordinates used causing the top-left corner to be at 0, 0.

The second, third, fourth, and fifth parameters define the drawing area.

Figure 3.6
Viewport example.

The last two parameters determine the depth of the scene. Even though sprites have no depth, the projection matrix needs valid depth values. The depth values are used by the system to figure out when to clip pieces of the scene.

The following code sample shows how to create a projection matrix based on the viewport.

```
The projection matrix
D3DXMATRIX matProjection;

// Create the projection matrix using the values in the viewport
D3DXMatrixOrthoOffCenterLH(&matProjection,
    (float)viewPort.TopLeftX,
    (float)viewPort.Width,
    (float)viewPort.TopLeftY,
    (float)viewPort.Height,
    0.1f,
    10);


// Set the projection matrix
HRESULT hr = spriteObject->SetProjectionTransform(&matProjection);
```

The projection matrix lets the system know the size of the grid on which the sprites will be placed. In the previous code sample, if the viewport is 640 pixels wide and 480 pixels tall, then the projection matrix would restrict visible sprite drawing to that area. Sprites positioned outside of this area would not be visible on the screen.

The projection matrix only needs to be changed if the size of the viewport changes.

Positioning and Scaling the Sprite

Now that the sprites know the extent of their environment, positioning them within it is possible. The act of moving an object within a space is called translation. Sprites being two dimensional in nature can be translated in two directions, X and Y. If you want to position a sprite in the center of a 640 × 480 display area, you would translate the sprite to an X, Y position of (320, 240). This in effect, moves the sprite 320 pixels horizontally and 240 pixels vertically. When sprites are translated, they're moved based on an internal point called the translation point. The translation point on a sprite is by default in the sprite's center. You can see an example of a sprite's translation point in Figure 3.7.

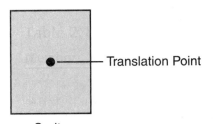

Translation Point

Sprite

Figure 3.7
A sprite's translation point. This point defaults to the sprite's center.

Because the default translation point for the sprite was in its center, the sprite appears correctly centered on the screen. When using sprites for characters within a game, it is common for the translation point to be moved to the top-left corner of the sprite.

When translating a sprite it is necessary to create another matrix called the translation matrix. The translation matrix, once defined, is used by Direct3D to position the sprite. The translation matrix can be created by using the function D3DXMatrix Translation. The D3DXMatrixTranslation function uses four parameters.

The first parameter is a pointer to the output translation matrix.

The second and third parameters are the X and Y position where the sprite should be moved.

The final parameter is the depth at which the sprite should be placed.

The following code sample shows how to use this function.

```
// these variables describe the dimensions of the sprite
// and where it should be located.
float spritePosX = 320;
float spritePosY = 240;
float spriteWidth = 64;
float spriteHeight = 64;

// The translation matrix to be created
D3DXMATRIX matTranslation;

// Create the translation matrix
D3DXMatrixTranslation( &matTranslation,
    spritePosX,
    (windowHeight - spritePosY),
    0.1f);
```

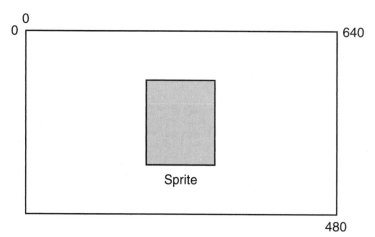

Figure 3.8
A centered sprite.

When positioning a sprite vertically, it is necessary to subtract the destination Y position from the height of the application window. This allows the sprite to be positioned based on the top-left corner of the window. Figure 3.8 shows a diagram of a sprite centered in the viewport area.

By default, Direct3D will draw your sprites only 1 pixel tall and 1 pixel wide. To make sure your sprite gets drawn at its correct size, the sprite must be scaled. Scaling the sprite requires the use of one more matrix, the scaling matrix.

The scaling matrix is created using the D3DXMatrixScaling function.

The D3DXMatrixScaling function takes four parameters.

The first parameter is a pointer to the output scaling matrix. The second and third parameters are the values by which to scale the sprite in the X and Y directions, respectively. Passing in the sprite's width and height values will make sure the sprite is sized correctly.

The final parameter is the amount to scale the sprite's depth. Since the sprite shouldn't be scaled in this direction, you should pass 1.0f as the default value.

The following code sample shows how to use the D3DXMatrixScaling function to create the scaling matrix.

```
// Scale the sprite to its correct width and height
D3DXMATRIX matScaling;
D3DXMatrixScaling(&matScaling, spriteWidth, spriteHeight, 1.0f );
```

So now that you have the translation matrix and the scaling matrix, what do you do with them? Do you remember the matWorld parameter of the D3DX10_SPRITE structure? This parameter is the world transform, which positions the sprite. The translation and scaling matrices need to be multiplied together to get the correct value for the matWorld parameter. This code snippet shows how this is accomplished.

```
// The sprite structure, the rest of the parameters should be filled in as well.
D3DX10_SPRITE  testSprite;

// Setting the sprite's position and size
testSprite.matWorld = (matScaling * matTranslation);
```

You've come a long way so far; there's only one more step, drawing.

Drawing the Sprite

The drawing of a sprite takes place within your render function. Previously, you had used the Render function to clear the render target. Now, you're going to add the drawing of the sprite as well.

To draw the sprite, you need some functionality provided by the sprite object (ID3DX10Sprite). All drawing of sprites takes place between two calls, Begin and End. Seems simple enough. The Begin call prepares Direct3D to draw sprites, setting up the proper internal states. The End call finalizes the drawing. Table 3.1 shows the possible flags that can be sent to the Begin function.

Table 3.1 Sprite Flags

Flag	Description
D3DX10_SPRITE_SORT_TEXTURE	Sort the sprites by texture.
D3DX10_SPRITE_SORT_DEPTH_BACK_TO_FRONT	Sort the sprites from back to front based on Z order.
D3DX10_SPRITE_SORT_DEPTH_FRONT_TO_BACK	Sort the sprites from front to back based on Z order.
D3DX10_SPRITE_SAVE_STATE	Makes sure the render state before sprite drawing is restored when the End function is called.
D3DX10_SPRITE_ADDREF_TEXTURES	Causes the reference count for each sprite texture to be incremented.

Tip

Sprites can be made to have transparent areas by giving their textures an alpha layer in your paint program and applying a Direct3D blend state.

The key function for sprite drawing is the DrawSpritesImmediate function. This is the function that takes the sprite and sends it to the video card to be drawn. The DrawSpritesImmediate function takes four parameters.

The first parameter is the sprite structure you created earlier, testSprite.

The second parameter is the number of sprites that DrawSpritesImmediate is expected to draw. In this example, only one sprite is needed.

The third parameter is the size of the D3DX10_SPRITE structure. Passing 0 will default to the proper size.

The final parameter is reserved and should be set to 0.

The DrawSpriteImmediate function has the capability of drawing more than one sprite. This functionality will be explained in the next section.

```
/*******************************************************************
* Render
* All drawing happens in the Render function
* Inputs - void
* Outputs - void
*******************************************************************/
void Render()
{
    if (pD3DDevice != NULL)
    {
        // clear the target buffer
        pD3DDevice->ClearRenderTargetView(pRenderTargetView, D3DXCOLOR (0.0f,
        0.0f, 0.0f, 0.0f));

        // start drawing the sprites
        spriteObject->Begin(D3DX10_SPRITE_SORT_TEXTURE);

        // Draw all the sprites
        spriteObject->DrawSpritesImmediate(testSprite, 1, 0, 0);

        // Finish up and send the sprites to the hardware
        spriteObject->End();
```

```
            // display the next item in the swap chain
            pSwapChain->Present(0, 0);
        }
}
```

A full code example is in the Chapter3/example2 directory on the CD-ROM.

Handling Multiple Sprites

So far you've been shown how to create and draw a single sprite. Unless you want a very boring game, you're probably going to need more sprites—quite a few more actually. Drawing more than one sprite and keeping the code clean is going to require a change to the way the sprite information is stored. Previously, the sprite's position and size were stored in a series of global variables.

```
float spritePosX = 320;
float spritePosY = 240;
float spriteWidth = 64;
float spriteHeight = 64;
```

Since you're going to need this information for multiple sprites, this information is going to be moved to a structure.

Defining a GameSprite Structure

The GameSprite structure contains the sprite's position and dimensions and is a much cleaner way of storing this information. Additionally, a new Boolean variable called visible is added. The visible variable is used to track whether the sprite is currently able to be seen on the screen. This enables the sprites to be shown or hidden. This is useful if sprites were being used for bullets or other items that have a limited lifetime.

```
// Sprite structure
typedef struct
{
    // sprite dimensions
    float width;
    float height;

    // sprite position
    float posX;
    float posY;

    BOOL visible;
} GameSprite;
```

Since you'll need multiple sprites, an array of GameSprite structures should be created. The small snippet below creates an array of ten GameSprite structures.

```
#define MAX_SPRITES 10
GameSprite sprites[MAX_SPRITES] = {0};
```

Initializing the GameSprite Structures

Initializing the sprite data in the GameSprite structure is very similar to how you set up one sprite. Create a loop to allow all the sprites to be set up at one time.

In the following code, the ten GameSprite structures are initialized with a size of 64×64 and a random screen position. Each of the sprites also has its visible variable set to TRUE.

```
// Loop through and init the active sprites
for (int curSprite = 0; curSprite < MAX_SPRITES; curSprite++)
{
    // Set the width and height of the sprite
    sprites[curSprite].width = 64;
    sprites[curSprite].height = 64;

    // Create and set a random x, y position
    sprites[curSprite].posX = (float)(rand()%600);
    sprites[curSprite].posY = (float)(rand()%450);

    // This sprite is visible
    sprites[curSprite].visible = TRUE;
}
```

The Sprite Pool

Instead of associating a single D3DX10_SPRITE structure with each GameSprite, you're going to employ a sprite pool. A sprite pool is an array of D3DX10_SPRITE structures where each structure is used on an as-needed basis. The structures are filled dynamically with information from the GameSprite objects each frame. These sprites are updated using the Update function. By using a sprite pool, the amount of dynamic allocations is kept down and places a restriction on the memory sprites can use.

Because the pool is pre-allocated, the size of the sprite pool array needs to be large enough to hold all the possible sprites that may be visible at one time. In the following code, there is enough space for thirty-two sprites to be allocated. An additional variable, numActiveSprites, is also being declared here. Since the number of sprites visible on the screen will be less than the number of available slots in the sprite pool, it is best to keep track of the number of sprites to be drawn. This variable comes in handy later when the function to draw the sprites is called.

```
// Maximum number of sprites possible in the pool
#define NUM_POOL_SPRITES 32

// Create the sprite pool array
D3DX10_SPRITE  spritePool[NUM_POOL_SPRITES];

// the number of active sprites
int numActiveSprites = 0;
```

Tip

Separating the game logic contained in the GameSprite from the rendering of the sprites in the pool allows for the drawing method to be changed without affecting the game logic.

The previous code uses a definition to specify the number of possible sprites in the pool instead of hard-coding the value. This allows the number of sprites to change easily.

Clearing the Sprites in the Pool

It is always a good idea to clear out all the items in the sprite pool to a default value before they're used. Doing so keeps you from accidentally using garbage data.

```
// Loop through and set the defaults for the
// sprites in the pool
for (int i = 0; i < NUM_POOL_SPRITES; i++)
{
    // Texture for this sprite to use
    spritePool[i].pTexture = gSpriteTextureRV;
    spritePool[i].TextureIndex = 0;

    // top-left location in U,V coords
    spritePool[i].TexCoord.x = 0;
    spritePool[i].TexCoord.y = 0;

    // Determine the texture size in U, V coordinates
    spritePool[i].TexSize.x = 1;
    spritePool[i].TexSize.y = 1;

    spritePool[i].ColorModulate = D3DXCOLOR(1.0f, 1.0f, 1.0f, 1.0f);
}
```

All the sprites in the pool default to using the same texture in the pTexture variable.

Updating the Sprites

During the main loop, the information contained in each of the GameSprite structures needs to be copied to available sprites available in the sprite pool. Since the GameSprites do not have a specific sprite associated with them, they must be updated dynamically each frame. The UpdateScene function below sets up each sprite in the sprite pool with the correct information and keeps a running total of the number of sprites currently active.

In the following code sample, only sprites that have their visible variable set to TRUE are being updated.

```
/*********************************************************************
* UpdateScene()
* Updates the scene with the current sprite information
* Inputs - void
* Outputs - void

*********************************************************************/
void UpdateScene()
{
    D3DXMATRIX matScaling;
    D3DXMATRIX matTranslation;

    int curPoolIndex = 0;

    // Loop through the sprites
    for (int i = 0; i < MAX_SPRITES; i++)
    {
        // only update visible sprites
        if (sprites[i].visible)
        {
            // set the proper scale for the sprite
    D3DXMatrixScaling(&matScaling, sprites[i].width, sprites[i].height,
1.0f);

            // Move the sprite to spritePosX, spritePosY
            // SpriteWidth and SpriteHeight are divided by 2 to move the
            // translation point to the top-left sprite corner instead of
            // the center of the sprite.
            D3DXMatrixTranslation(&matTranslation,
```

```
            (float)sprites[i].posX + (sprites[i].width/2),
            (float)(windowHeight - sprites[i].posY - (sprites[i].
            height/2)), 0.1f);

        // Update the sprites position and scale
        spritePool[curPoolIndex].matWorld = matScaling * matTranslation;
        // Increment the pool index
        curPoolIndex++;
    }
}

    // set the number of active sprites
    numActiveSprites = curPoolIndex;
}
```

The UpdateScene function should be called before the Render function in the main game loop.

Drawing More Than One Sprite

Now that you have multiple sprites created and updating, how do you draw them? Well, you remember before where I mentioned that DrawSpritesImmediate was capable of drawing more than one sprite? The first parameter to the DrawSpritesImmediate function is a pointer to an array of D3DX10_SPRITE structures. Because the sprite pool is an array of this type, it can be passed directly into the DrawSpritesImmediate function.

Previously, a value of 1 had been passed into this function to draw only a single sprite. Now that there's an array of sprites to draw, the number of active sprites should be passed in. The variable numActiveSprites contains the current number of valid sprites in the array.

The DrawSpritesImmediate function isn't the only available function for drawing sprites. The ID3DX10Sprite object also includes the function DrawSpritesBuffered. The behavior of the two functions is slightly different.

The DrawSpritesImmediate function sends the sprites to the video hardware as soon as it is called.

The DrawSpritesBuffered function builds up a list of sprites to be drawn before actually sending them to the card. This is useful if you have functions where one or only a few sprites are needed each time. Once you're ready to finally draw the sprites, calling the function Flush sends the sprites to the video card.

The following code sample shows an example usage of the DrawSpritesBuffered function.

```
/****************************************************************
* Render
* All drawing happens in the Render function
* Inputs - void
* Outputs - void

****************************************************************/
void Render()
{
    if (pD3DDevice != NULL)
    {
        // clear the target buffer
pD3DDevice->ClearRenderTargetView(pRenderTargetView, D3DXCOLOR(0.0f, 0.0f,
    0.0f, 0.0f));

        if (spriteObject != NULL)
        {
            HRESULT hr = spriteObject->SetProjectionTransform(&matProjection);

            // start drawing the sprites
            spriteObject->Begin(D3DX10_SPRITE_SORT_TEXTURE);

            // Draw all the sprites in the pool
            spriteObject->DrawSpritesBuffered(spritePool,
            numActiveSprites);

            // Finish up and send the sprites to the hardware
            spriteObject->Flush();
            spriteObject->End();
        }

        // display the next item in the swap chain
        pSwapChain->Present(0, 0);
    }
}
```

An example of buffer sprite drawing is available in the chapter3\example3 directory on the CD-ROM.

Getting the Sprites Moving

Getting the sprites to move around within the window isn't very difficult. The position of each sprite, updated every frame, is stored in the posX and posY variables within the GameSprite structure. These variables are used during the Update function to correctly position the sprite on the screen. By manipulating the values in these variables before the Update function is called, the sprite's position can be changed.

Changing the Sprite's Position

Since each sprite can be moved around at a different rate, you're going to add movement variables to the GameSprite structure so movement can be controlled on a per-sprite basis; these variables are called moveX and moveY.

The updated GameSprite structure is shown here:

```
// Sprite structure
typedef struct
{
    // sprite dimensions
    float width;
    float height;

    // sprite position
    float posX;
    float posY;

    // sprite movement
    float moveX;
    float moveY;

    BOOL visible;
} GameSprite;
```

The moveX and moveY variables store the current amount that each sprite should be moved in both the X and Y directions each frame. By changing the value in these two variables and how often these variables are applied, it will appear as though the sprites are moving around the screen.

The posX and posY variables, which control the actual sprite location, need to be updated each frame with the values contained in the moveX and moveY variables.

A function called MoveSprites, which not only updates the location of a sprite but makes sure it remains within the confines of the game window, is shown next.

```
/****************************************************************
* MoveSprites
* Moves the sprites around the screen
* Inputs - void
* Outputs - void

****************************************************************/
void MoveSprites()
{
    // Loop through and update all sprites
    for (int i = 0; i < MAX_SPRITES; i++)
    {
        // only update visible sprites
        if (sprites[i].visible)
        {
            // clamp the sprite position to the current window
            if ((sprites[i].posX > windowWidth) || (sprites[i].posX <= 0))
            {
                sprites[i].moveX = -sprites[i].moveX;
            }
            // move the sprite in the X direction
            sprites[i].posX += sprites[i].moveX;

            // clamp the sprite position to the current window
            if ((sprites[i].posY > windowHeight) || (sprites[i].posY <= 0))
            {
                sprites[i].moveY = -sprites[i].moveY;
            }
            // move the sprite in the Y direction
            sprites[i].posY += sprites[i].moveY;
        }
    }
}
```

Using Sprites with Transparent Areas

Most game characters aren't square, and they don't normally take up the entire area of a sprite's image. Up until now all the sprites you've been drawing were square and completely opaque, but take a look at sprites in use in games. They have transparent areas around the characters allowing you to see what's behind them. Implementing transparent areas when drawing sprites isn't difficult, but it does take some explanation to describe how it happens.

The blending state dictates how Direct3D draws overlapping objects. Without blending, the object closest to the viewer is completely opaque, obscuring anything beneath it. When blending is enabled, overlapping objects can be made to be partly translucent or have completely transparent areas. Blending works by merging the colors of multiple overlapping objects to determine the final output drawn to the screen.

Different areas of a sprite can contain alpha components, which affect the amount of transparency a sprite has. Areas with an alpha value of 0 have no transparency at all and are drawn completely opaque. Areas with an alpha value of 1 are drawn as see through. Alpha values between 0 and 1 give the sprite a partial see-through appearance.

Whether Direct3D pays attention to the alpha component of an image is determined by the current blend state.

N o t e

The alpha component is applied to a sprite's image when the source texture is created in your art tool.

Creating and Setting a New Blend State

Before a new blend state can be applied, you have to describe how it will behave. The behavior of a blend state is defined by the criteria set in a D3D10_BLEND_DESC structure.

The D3D10_BLEND_DESC structure defines the criteria of how a blend operation between a source and a destination will work. The source is the object being applied, whereas the destination is the color already existing at that pixel. Blending works by merging the color values of the two. For instance, blending the red component of a source and destination will create a final red output. How these two components are blended is up to you.

The D3D10_BLEND_DESC structure is shown here:

```
typedef struct D3D10_BLEND_DESC {
    BOOL AlphaToCoverageEnable;
    BOOL BlendEnable[8];
    D3D10_BLEND SrcBlend;
```

```
        D3D10_BLEND DestBlend;
        D3D10_BLEND_OP BlendOp;
        D3D10_BLEND SrcBlendAlpha;
        D3D10_BLEND DestBlendAlpha;
        D3D10_BLEND_OP BlendOpAlpha;
        UINT8 RenderTargetWriteMask[8];
} D3D10_BLEND_DESC;
```

The BlendEnable variable is an array of BOOL values, each one representing a rendertarget. In most cases, you'll be dealing with only the first item in the array.

The D3D10_BLEND_DESC structure splits the full RGBA components of an object into two pieces. The first piece, controlled by the SrcBlend and DestBlend variables, dictates how the RGB components are blended. The second piece, using SrcBlendAlpha and DestBlendAlpha, controls the blending of the A (alpha) component.

As I mentioned earlier, you get to control how the components are blended; this is controlled through the BlendOp and BlendOpAlpha variables. These variables, of type D3D10_BLEND_OP, allow you to add, subtract, or otherwise manipulate how the components are blended.

An example of a completed D3D10_BLEND_DESC structure is shown next. This one blends on the sprite's alpha component only, allowing a sprite to be drawn with transparency.

```
// The variable  that will contain the new blend state.
ID3D10BlendState*      pBlendState10 = NULL;

// Initialize the blend state for alpha drawing
D3D10_BLEND_DESC StateDesc;
ZeroMemory(&StateDesc, sizeof(D3D10_BLEND_DESC));
StateDesc.AlphaToCoverageEnable = FALSE;
StateDesc.BlendEnable[0] = TRUE;
StateDesc.SrcBlend = D3D10_BLEND_SRC_ALPHA;
StateDesc.DestBlend = D3D10_BLEND_INV_SRC_ALPHA;
StateDesc.BlendOp = D3D10_BLEND_OP_ADD;
StateDesc.SrcBlendAlpha = D3D10_BLEND_ZERO;
StateDesc.DestBlendAlpha = D3D10_BLEND_ZERO;
StateDesc.BlendOpAlpha = D3D10_BLEND_OP_ADD;
StateDesc.RenderTargetWriteMask[0] = D3D10_COLOR_WRITE_ENABLE_ALL;
pD3DDevice->CreateBlendState(&StateDesc, &pBlendState10);
```

The creation of a new blend state is handled using the function `CreateBlendState`. The `CreateBlendState` function simply takes a pointer to the D3D10_ BLEND_DESC structure you created earlier and returns an `ID3D10BlendState` object.

```
ID3D10BlendState*  pBlendState10 = NULL;
// Create the new    blend state
pD3DDevice->Create BlendState(&StateDesc, &pBlendState10);
```

The `ID3D10BlendState` object then needs to be applied before it can take affect. Applying a blend state object happens using the `OMSetBlendState` function. `OMSetBlendState` uses the blend state you created, as well as two more parameters, a blend factor color and a sample mask.

The blend factor color is a default color used in the instance where either the source or destination color is set as D3D10_BLEND_BLEND_FACTOR or D3D10_BLEND_ INVBLEND_FACTOR.

The sample mask is used to determine which samples get updated when using multisampling. By default, this value should be set to 0xffffffff.

Because of the simple nature of the blend state, default values for the blend factor and sample mask are used.

```
FLOAT NewBlendFactor[4] = {0,0,0,0};
pD3DDevice->OMSetBlendState(pBlendState10, NewBlendFactor, 0xffffffff);
```

At this point the blend state is applied and active in the scene. When the sprite is drawn, any areas with an alpha value above 0 will appear to be slightly or completely transparent.

Storing the Current Blend State

Before you change the blend state, it is a good idea to save the previous state so it can be restored when the new one is no longer needed. The `OMGetBlendState` function is used to collect the current state. There are three parameters that `OMGetBlendState` requires.

The first parameter is a pointer to an `ID3D10BlendState` object. This object will be the one holding the original state.

The second parameter is a pointer to an array holding four float values. This array will be used to store the original blend factor.

The final parameter is an unsigned integer that will hold the original sample mask.

The following small example shows how to save the original blend state so it can be restored later.

```
ID3D10BlendState* pOriginalBlendState10 = NULL;
FLOAT OriginalBlendFactor[4];
UINT  OriginalSampleMask = 0;

// Save the current blend state
pD3DDevice->OMGetBlendState(&pOriginalBlendState10, OriginalBlendFactor,
&OriginalSampleMask);
```

Restoring the original blend state when you're done is a simple matter of calling the OMSetBlendState function with the values you stored.

```
// Restore the previous blend state
pD3DDevice->OMSetBlendState(pOriginalBlendState10, OriginalBlendFactor,
OriginalSampleMask);
```

An updated Render function supporting sprites with transparent areas is shown next.

```
/******************************************************************
* Render
* All drawing happens in the Render function
* Inputs - void
* Outputs - void

******************************************************************/
void Render()
{
    FLOAT OriginalBlendFactor[4];
    UINT  OriginalSampleMask = 0;

    if (pD3DDevice != NULL)
    {
        // clear the target buffer
        pD3DDevice->ClearRenderTargetView(pRenderTargetView,D3DXCOLOR(0.0f,
        0.0f, 0.0f, 0.0f));

        if (spriteObject != NULL)
        {
            HRESULT hr = spriteObject->SetProjectionTransform(&matProjection);

            // start drawing the sprites
            spriteObject->Begin(D3DX10_SPRITE_SORT_TEXTURE);
```

```
        // Draw all the sprites in the pool
        spriteObject->DrawSpritesBuffered(spritePool, numActiveSprites);

        // Save the current blend state
        pD3DDevice->OMGetBlendState(&pOriginalBlendState10,
        OriginalBlendFactor, &OriginalSampleMask);

        // Set the blend state for alpha drawing
        if(pBlendState10)
        {
            FLOAT NewBlendFactor[4] = {0,0,0,0};
            pD3DDevice->OMSetBlendState(pBlendState10, NewBlendFactor,
            0xffffffff);
        }

        // Finish up and send the sprites to the hardware
        spriteObject->Flush();
        spriteObject->End();
    }

    // Restore the previous blend state
    pD3DDevice->OMSetBlendState(pOriginalBlendState10,
    OriginalBlendFactor, OriginalSampleMask);

    // display the next item in the swap chain
    pSwapChain->Present(0, 0);
    }
}
```

Figure 3.9 shows a series of sprites with a transparent area at their center.

A full example utilizing sprite movement with transparent areas can be found in the Chapter3\example4 directory on the CD-ROM.

Sprite Animation

The preceding version of the sprite structure allowed for the display of the sprites on the screen, but sprites that don't animate aren't that exciting. The sprites are constantly displaying the same static image the whole time. Sprites are commonly animated using a technique called frame-based animation. *Frame-based animation* is equivalent to a movie reel, where the individual images or frames are displayed in rapid succession giving the appearance of movement. Sprite

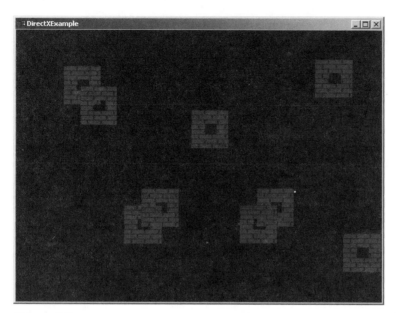

Figure 3.9
Multiple sprites with a transparent area.

animation uses the same idea, quickly changing the image that the sprite displays to give the illusion of movement.

The first part of sprite animation is updating your sprites to support more than one image.

The Updated GameSprite Structure

Animating a sprite requires that the sprite support the ability to cycle through multiple frames; currently, the GameSprite structure supports only a single frame. Adding animation support is actually quite simple. The sprite needs to be able to track which image it is currently displaying, as well as know how many images it can cycle through.

The GameSprite structure needs to be updated by adding two new variables.

First, an integer called numFrames keeps track of the number of frames the sprite has available.

Second, an integer called curFrame is used to hold the current frame being displayed.

You can see an updated GameSprite structure next; the new variables are shown in bold.

```
// Sprite structure
typedef struct
{
    // sprite dimensions
    float width;
    float height;

    // sprite position
    float posX;
    float posY;
    // sprite movement
    float moveX;
    float moveY;

    BOOL visible;

    // animation information
    int curFrame;          // the current frame of animation
    int numFrames;         // the number of frames in this animation
} GameSprite;
```

Now that you have two new variables in the GameSprite structure, you need to set them to their default values when the sprites are initialized. In the following code sample, the current frame is set to 0 and the number of frames for the sprite is set to 4. In most sprite systems, the sprites will be able to handle more than a single series of animations; only a simple example is shown here.

```
// Loop through and init the active sprites
for (int curSprite = 0; curSprite < MAX_SPRITES; curSprite++)
{
    // Set the width and height of the sprite
    sprites[curSprite].width = 64;
    sprites[curSprite].height = 64;

    // Create and set a random x,y position
    sprites[curSprite].posX = (float)(rand()%600);
    sprites[curSprite].posY = (float)(rand()%450);

    // This sprite is visible
    sprites[curSprite].visible = TRUE;
```

```
    // Set up the animation information
    sprites[curSprite].curFrame = 0;
    sprites[curSprite].numFrames = 4;
}
```

Updating the Sprite's Animation

When displaying the previous sprites, special image processing wasn't necessary. Now that the sprites have multiple frames that need to be managed, an Update Sprites function is needed.

The UpdateSprites function handles the incrementing of the current frame of animation, as well as checking against the number of frames. If the current frame were constantly incremented without comparing against the number of frames, the sprite would quickly run out of images and cause an error in your application. When the current frame reaches the maximum number of frames, the current frame needs to be reset to 0 and the whole process starts over again. This causes the sprite's animation to loop indefinitely.

The following UpdateSprites function loops through the sprites and updates their animations.

```
/******************************************************************
* UpdateSprites
* Updates the sprite's animation information
* Inputs - none
* Outputs - void

******************************************************************/
void UpdateSprites()
{
    // Loop through the sprites and update the animation info
    for (int i = 0; i < MAX_SPRITES; i++)
    {
        // only update visible sprites
        if (sprites[i].visible)
        {
            // increment the current frame
            sprites[i].curFrame++;

            // if the current frame is past the number of frames
            // reset to 0
```

```
            if (sprites[i].curFrame >= sprites[i].numFrames)
            {
                sprites[i].curFrame = 0;
            }
        }
    }
}
```

The UpdateSprites function can be inserted into the main application loop right after the Render function.

```
// Main message loop
MSG msg = {0};
while (WM_QUIT != msg.message)
{
    // Process Windows messages first
    while (PeekMessage(&msg, NULL, 0, 0, PM_REMOVE) == TRUE)
    {
        TranslateMessage(&msg);
        DispatchMessage(&msg);
    }

    // update and render the current frame
    UpdateScene();
    Render();

    // Update the sprites for the next frame
    UpdateSprites();
}
```

Displaying the Animated Sprites

At this point the sprites are animating within the GameSprite structure but will still be displayed using only a single image. To remedy this, the UpdateScene function will need to be changed. If you recall, the job of the UpdateScene function is to update the sprites in the sprite pool. Currently, those sprites are constantly pointing to the same frame in their source texture. The texture coordinates associated have to be updated based on the current frame of animation.

When animating sprites, it is common for the all the frames of an animation to appear in the same texture. The frames are laid out horizontally in the texture, as displayed in Figure 3.10.

Figure 3.10
Multiple frames for a sprite in a single texture.

When using this type of texture, the texture coordinates in the X direction reference the correct frame. The new X texture coordinate can be calculated in the `UpdateScene` function by dividing the current frame number by the number of frames in the animation. This will yield a value between 0 and 1.

Also, the texture size should be updated to reflect the current frame. Not all frames are the same size. The texture size is calculated by dividing the current frame width by the width of the whole texture. In the following example, the width of the texture is determined by multiplying the sprite width by the number of frames. This only works because all frames in the sample animation are the same size.

```
/****************************************************************
* UpdateScene()
* Updates the scene with the current sprite information
* Inputs - void
* Outputs - void

****************************************************************/
void UpdateScene()
{
    D3DXMATRIX matScaling;
    D3DXMATRIX matTranslation;

    int curPoolIndex = 0;

    // Loop through the sprites
    for (int i = 0; i < MAX_SPRITES; i++)
    {
        // only update visible sprites
        if (sprites[i].visible)
        {
            // set the proper scale for the sprite
            D3DXMatrixScaling(&matScaling, sprites[i].width, sprites[i].height,
            1.0f);
```

```
// Move the sprite to spritePosX, spritePosY
// SpriteWidth and SpriteHeight are divided by 2 to move the
// translation point to the top-left sprite corner instead of
// the center of the sprite.
D3DXMatrixTranslation(&matTranslation,
    (float)sprites[i].posX + (sprites[i].width/2),
    (float)(windowHeight - sprites[i].posY - (sprites[i].height/2)),
    0.1f);

// Update the sprite's position    and scale
spritePool[curPoolIndex].matWorld = matScaling * matTranslation;

// determine the texture coordinates for the current frame
spritePool[curPoolIndex].TexCoord.x = (float)(sprites[i].curFrame /
sprites[i].numFrames);

spritePool[curPoolIndex].TexCoord.y = 0.0f;

// Set the texture size for this frame
spritePool[curPoolIndex].TexSize.x = (float)(sprites[i].width /
(sprites[i].width * sprites[i].numFrames));

// Increment the pool index
curPoolIndex++;
    }
  }

  // set the number of active sprites
  numActiveSprites = curPoolIndex;
}
```

A full example of sprite animation can be found in the chapter3\example5 directory on the CD-ROM.

Timers: How to Animate on Time

You've probably noticed that the sprites tend to go through their four frames of animation rather quickly. This is due to the use of the brute-force animation technique that was used. Because there is no way to speed up or slow down the animations, they are completely machine dependent. For example, on faster computers the sprites will animate more quickly than on a machine with a slower processor.

Creating smooth animations within your game should be a top priority. Using a timer, animation movement can be set up to occur at fixed intervals. For example, if you want to run an animation at 30 frames per second (fps) but your game's current frame rate is 60fps, you'll need to slow down the update of animation to keep it from playing through twice in one second. In this instance, you'd use a timer that updates the animation only half as often, resulting in keeping your 30fps rate.

Timing under Windows

There are multiple functions for tracking time within Windows, `GetTickCount` and `QueryPerformanceCounter`.

`GetTickCount`, based on the system timer, is limited in its usefulness when it comes to game programming. `GetTickCount` retrieves the number of milliseconds that have elapsed since the system was started and has a limited granularity, being updated every 10 milliseconds. Because of its limitations, a higher performance timer is needed; the `QueryPerformanceCounter` function fills that need.

`QueryPerformanceCounter` has a higher resolution than its `GetTickCount` counterpart. The `QueryPerformanceCounter` function, based on a hardware counter instead of a software solution, allows for timing in microseconds. This is useful in games where functions for animation normally require a more detailed timer to keep the animation smooth.

Using QueryPerformanceCounter

The QueryPerformanceCounter function is defined as:

```
BOOL QueryPerformanceCounter(
    LARGE_INTEGER *lpPerformanceCount
);
```

The above function takes only one parameter, a pointer to a `LARGE_INTEGER` type. After this function completes, the `lpPerformanceCount` variable will contain the current value from the hardware performance counter.

Below is a small code example that uses the `QueryPerformanceCounter` function.

```
LARGE_INTEGER timeStart;
QueryPerformanceCounter(&timeStart);
```

The `timeStart` variable is being used to hold the value returned from the `QueryPerformanceCounter` function.

Getting the Time for Each Frame

To accurately time your animations, you need to call the `QueryPerformance-Counter` function twice within the game loop. Once before you start any drawing, and once after all drawing has completed. Both values returned will contain the number of counts from the system at the time the function was called. Since the performance counter has such a high resolution, both of these values should be unique. You can use the difference between these two values to determine the number of counts that have passed between the calls.

For example, you could write the following code:

```
LARGE_INTEGER timeStart;
LARGE_INTEGER timeEnd;
// Get the start time
QueryPerformanceCounter(&timeStart);
// Draw the scene
Render( );
// Get the end time
QueryPerformanceCounter(&timeEnd);
LARGE_INTEGER numCounts = ( timeEnd.QuadPart - timeStart.QuadPart )
```

After this code executes, the `numCounts` variable will contain the number of timer counts that have elapsed between the two calls to `QueryPerformanceCounter`. The `QuadPart` portion of the `LARGE_INTEGER` type tells the system that you want the full 64-bit value returned from the counter.

Once you have the number of counts stored in a variable, there is one more step that is required before you have a useful number with which to time your animations. The value in the `numCounts` variable needs to be divided by the frequency of the performance counter.

Note

The performance counter frequency is a value that represents the number of times per second the counter is incremented.

The function `QueryPerformanceFrequency` is used to get the frequency of the counter from the system.

The `QueryPerformanceFrequency` function takes only one parameter, a pointer to a `LARGE_INTEGER` that will hold the returned frequency. An example call to this function is shown here:

```
LARGE_INTEGER timerFrequency;
QueryPerformanceFrequency(&timerFrequency);
```

After you have the frequency of the timer, it can be used along with the value in the numCounts variable to give you a rate of movement for your animation. The animation rate is found by dividing the number of counts that have passed by the frequency of the timer. The following code sample performs this task:

```
float anim_rate = numCounts / timerFrequency.QuadPart;
```

Changing the Animation to Be Time Based

I'm going to show you how to take the information you learned in the preceding section and apply it to make your sprites use time-based animation.

Additional variables need to be defined to keep track of the animation timing.

```
// timer variables
LARGE_INTEGER timeStart;
LARGE_INTEGER timeEnd;
LARGE_INTEGER timerFreq;
float         anim_rate;

// Variable to hold how long since last frame change
float         lastElapsedFrame = 0;
// How long should the frames last
float         frameDuration = 0.5;
```

The variables that keep track of the animation timing, timeStart, timeEnd, and timerFreq, need to be updated each time through the game loop. The variable timeStart gets updated before anything is drawn and contains the timer count as the frame starts. timeEnd is set after drawing is complete and contains the timer count at the end of the frame.

The updated game loop is shown here.

```
// Main message loop
MSG msg = {0};
while (WM_QUIT != msg.message)
{
    // Process Windows messages first
    while (PeekMessage(&msg, NULL, 0, 0, PM_REMOVE) == TRUE)
    {
        TranslateMessage(&msg);
        DispatchMessage(&msg);
    }
```

```
    // Get the start timer count
    QueryPerformanceCounter(&timeStart);

    // update and render the current frame
    UpdateScene();
    Render();

    // Update the sprites for the next frame
    UpdateSprites();

    // Get the end timer count
    QueryPerformanceCounter(&timeEnd);

    // Set the animation rate
    anim_rate = ( (float)timeEnd.QuadPart - (float)timeStart.QuadPart ) /
timerFreq.QuadPart;
}
```

Since the sprite's animation will no longer be updated once a frame, the system needs a way of determining if enough time has passed before incrementing to the next frame; the variables lastElapsedFrame and frameDuration are used to keep track of this.

lastElapsedFrame is incremented each frame with the amount of time the previous frame took to draw.

The variable frameDuration contains the amount of time that is required to pass between frames. Each time through the game loop, the frameDuration variable is compared to the value in lastElapsedFrame to see if the animation needs to progress to the next frame. If lastElapsedFrame is greater than the value in frame Duration, it is time to continue the animation. Once the animation is incremented one frame, the lastElapsedFrame value is reset to 0 and starts counting again.

The UpdateSprites function shown next increments the animation based on the timer count.

```
/*****************************************************************
* UpdateSprites
* Updates the sprite's animation information
* Inputs - none
* Outputs - void
```

```
**********************************************************************/
void UpdateSprites()
{
    lastElapsedFrame += anim_rate;

    // test if its time to increment the frame
    if (lastElapsedFrame < frameDuration)
    {
    return;
    }

    // reset the frame counter
    lastElapsedFrame = 0;

    // Loop through the sprites and update the animation info
    for (int i = 0; i < MAX_SPRITES; i++)
    {
        // only update visible sprites
        if (sprites[i].visible)
        {
            // increment the current frame
            sprites[i].curFrame++;

            // if the current frame is past the number of frames
            // reset to 0
            if (sprites[i].curFrame >= sprites[i].numFrames)
            {
                sprites[i].curFrame = 0;
            }
        }
    }
}
```

The rest of the manner in which the animation is performed remains the same as frame-based animation. You can change the value contained in frameDuration to speed up or slow down the time it takes to animate between frames.

The full source listing can be found in the chapter3\example6 directory on the CD-ROM.

Summary

At this point you should have a basic understanding of how sprites, textures, and animation work. Using the information presented in this chapter, it's now possible to create a sprite-based demo or screen saver.

What You Have Learned

In this chapter, you learned the following:

- How textures are loaded

- What a sprite is and how it's used

- How to create a sprite pool to conserve resources

- The difference between time-based and frame-based animation

- How timers can be used for animation

Review Questions

You can find the answers to Review Questions in Appendix A, "Answers to End-of-Chapter Exercises."

1. Which function is used to load textures?

2. Which structure is used to represent sprites?

3. Sprites are commonly used to represent what in a video game?

4. What is a sprite's translation point used for?

5. What is the process of moving a sprite called?

On Your Own

1. Show how to use the scaling matrix to double the size of a sprite.

2. Show how the animation rate can be used to control a sprite's speed of movement.

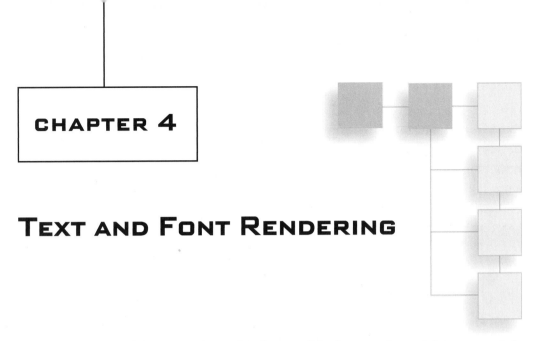

CHAPTER 4

TEXT AND FONT RENDERING

Text doesn't seem like it is going to be that useful when you're writing games; it is a minor feature that doesn't really affect the game, or is it? Text is used for more than just the title screen. You have to give the player instructions, designate the goals of the game, or let the user know how many gold coins he has in his inventory. Text can be thought of as the glue that holds graphics and gameplay together.

From a programmer's standpoint, text can be your best debugging tool. You can add any number of real-time metrics that can be accessible at runtime, such as frame count. Many games implement what is essentially a debug console in the game itself, giving them a way to track and manipulate different areas of the game.

Here's what you'll learn in this chapter:

- Why fonts and text are useful to game developers

- How a font system works

- How to create a simple font system from scratch

- How to use the Direct3D font system

- How to draw text to the screen

Adding Text

Over the years, game text has been implemented in multiple ways—texture blits to the screen, vector drawing, and even just the use of message boxes. In modern development, most game libraries support the concept of text rendering, removing the burden of having to implement this yourself. DirectX does support a method of text rendering, but it still requires a bit of work on your part for it to be useful. The following sections describe how font systems are commonly put together.

Textured Fonts

When using text in your game, it is best that all the text appears in a consistent manner. Using a single font style will help in this regard. A *font* is a series of letters and symbols written in a certain style. In both 2D and 3D games, text is commonly drawn using textured fonts.

Textured fonts, or bitmapped fonts, are based on letters pre-drawn into a texture. The letters are arranged in a grid with a single letter occupying each section of the grid. When it comes time to write out words, the words are built dynamically by drawing the textured letters on the screen. This allows a single series of letters to be used to create any word or phrase you require. Because of the simplistic nature in which the font is used, text rendering can be quite fast. Also, because the fonts are pre-drawn on a texture, the look and feel of the text can be changed by altering the applied texture.

Textured fonts do have some downsides though:

- They don't scale well. Because they are pieces of a texture, they can only grow or shrink so much before they become ugly and unreadable.

- The texture must support every possible letter or symbol you may use. If your game contains only a language such as English, this may not be a problem, but translating your game to a language such as Japanese may make your texture too large.

- Because there are different amounts of spacing preceding and following each letter, textured fonts sometimes appear odd when writing certain words.

Textured fonts allow for the build-up of words as they're needed and are managed through a font system.

ABCDEFGHIJKLMNOPQRSTUVwXYZ

Figure 4.1
A font layout.

Figure 4.1 shows how the letters of a font can be laid out in a texture.

A Font System Explained

Occasionally there are instances when it makes sense to hardcode any text in the game into preexisting graphics; a font system is used when the text that you need to draw needs to be drawn dynamically. Imagine that you're playing an RPG and you need to talk to a resident in the village. In a hardcoded text system, what the character says is pre-generated into a texture and pulled up at the appropriate time. Depending on the amount of text, that could potentially mean hundreds of textures needing to be loaded just for standard conversations. A dynamic font system allows for the building up of these strings by loading in only a single texture containing all the letters in the font. This method saves load times and a huge amount of otherwise wasted memory.

Font systems commonly use sprites to do the actual text drawing. Each letter uses a single sprite and is drawn in a sequence to spell out words or phrases.

Creating a Font System Using Sprites

A sprite-based font system is drawn in a similar way that multiple sprites were drawn in the last chapter. The input string comes into the system and is broken up into multiple sprites. These sprites are then positioned correctly and passed to Direct3D to be drawn.

The following sections show how to implement a sprite-based font system.

The FontSprite Structure

The first step is the creation of a FontSprite structure. The FontSprite structure is needed to describe the properties of every letter sprite.

A simple font system requires a simple FontSprite structure. The FontSprite structure is very similar to the GameSprite structure used in the last chapter. The most important difference is the inclusion of a new variable called letterIndex. Each letter in the font texture has an index associated with it, with the first letter 'A' being 0, 'B' is 1, and so on.

The FontSprite structure is shown here:

```
// FontSprite structure
typedef struct
{
    // sprite details
    float width;
    float height;

    // sprite position
    float posX;
    float posY;

     int letterIndex;

    BOOL visible;
}FontSprite;
```

Translating a String to Sprites

A new function called UpdateText needs to be created to translate the input string into FontSprite structures. For each letter in the string, a FontSprite structure needs to be filled in. Since the string coming through is dynamic, the UpdateText function needs to be able to pick up on the text it contains and generate valid FontSprites. Because of the number of sprites being created, the font system will use sprites from a sprite pool.

The following code sample shows the UpdateText function.

```
// The string that will be output in sprites
char *message = "HELLO WORLD";
/******************************************************************
* UpdateText
* Updates the sprites being used for text rendering
* Inputs - void
* Outputs - void
******************************************************************/
void UpdateText()
{
    int curLetterCount = 0;

    // loop through the letters in the message string
    for (unsigned int i = 0; i < strlen(message); i++)
```

```
    {
        // set the position of the letter
        sprites[curLetterCount].posX = (curLetterCount * letterWidth);

        // save off the letter index
        sprites[curLetterCount].letterIndex = (message[i] - 'A');

        // go to the next letter
        curLetterCount++;
    }

    numberOfLetters = curLetterCount;
}
```

The UpdateText function loops through the input string looking at each letter. The function then determines the letter's index by subtracting the ASCII value from 'A'. This index is then stored in the letterIndex variable for passage to the function that updates the sprites in the sprite pool. The posX variable is also set based on the current letter in the string. Because this is a simplified example, only capital letters are supported in the input string.

The function sets a variable called numberOfLetters, which is used during the Render function to tell Direct3D how many sprites are to be drawn in the batch.

Updating the Sprite Pool

After the FontSprite structures are filled out, the system will convert these over to sprite objects within the sprite pool. If you remember from the last chapter, a sprite pool is a collection of general D3DX10_SPRITE structures that can be dynamically repurposed each frame.

Since the sprites in the sprite pool can be used for any letter in the input string, the texture coordinate needs to be constantly changed to reflect the current letter. The texture coordinate for each letter is calculated with the help of the letterIndex variable set during the UpdateText function. The letterIndex is used to reference the letter's position in the font texture.

```
spritePool[curPoolIndex].TexCoord.x = (float)((sprites[i].letterIndex *
letterWidth) / fontTextureWidth);
```

The only change to the Render function is the use of the numberOfLetters variable set within the UpdateText function. This keeps extra sprites in the sprite pool

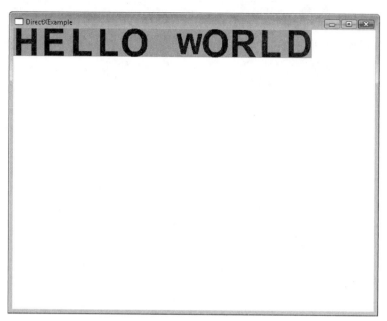

Figure 4.2
A font system's Hello World.

from being drawn when they're not in use. Figure 4.2 shows the output of the simple font system.

A full example of a sprite-based font system is included in the chapter4\example1 directory on the CD-ROM. This system is set up to draw a single string and is not meant as a reusable general purpose component. The font system also doesn't support alpha blending, causing the letters to appear within rectangles.

Direct3D Fonts

Even though it may seem like a fairly simple matter to implement your own font system, there are multiple problems that would take a while to overcome; luckily, you don't have to worry because Direct3D already has a font system built in. The Direct3D font system, while sprite-based, doesn't require you to create your own font texture. The fonts used by Direct3D are created using the fonts installed under Windows. This system also allows for the text to be drawn at multiple point sizes without the need to scale the sprites. This gives a crisper, cleaner look to the text.

The Direct3D font system is based upon functionality provided by the ID3DX10Font interface. This interface provides all the functions needed for text drawing.

Creating the Font Object

Before you can use the functionality in the ID3DX10Font object, it has to be instantiated; this is done using the D3DX10CreateFont function. During the font creation process, a texture is created that contains the letters and symbols in the font. When calling the D3DX10CreateFont function, you specify the font face, size, and weight that will be contained in the texture.

```
HRESULT D3DX10CreateFont(
    ID3D10Device* pDevice,
    INT Height,
    UINT Width,
    UINT Weight,
    UINT MipLevels,
    BOOL Italic,
    UINT CharSet,
    UINT OutputPrecision,
    UINT Quality,
    UINT PitchAndFamily,
    LPCSTR pFaceName,
    ID3DX10Font** ppFont
);
```

The D3DX10CreateFont function requires twelve parameters.

The first parameter is a pointer to the Direct3D device in use. The second and third parameters dictate the width and height of each of the letters in the font. The width and height are changeable only when the font is first created.

The fourth parameter is the font weight. The font weight is the thickness of the lines. Direct3D provides the following weights:

- FW_DONTCARE

- FW_THIN

- FW_EXTRALIGHT

- FW_LIGHT

- FW_NORMAL

- FW_MEDIUM

- FW_SEMIBOLD

- FW_BOLD

- FW_EXTRABOLD

- FW_HEAVY

The fifth parameter, MipLevels, allows you to designate the number of levels the resulting font texture will have. More mip levels increase the readability when the text is further away.

The sixth parameter allows you to create an italic font. This variable is either true if italic or false otherwise.

The seventh parameter dictates the character set the font will use. By specifying anything other than DEFAULT_CHARSET, you can create fonts based on character sets from other languages such as Chinese.

The next three parameters determine the precision, quality, and font pitch. The precision and quality help map the selected font size to existing Windows fonts. Default options are available for each of these settings.

The most important parameter passed to the D3DX10CreateFont function is pFace Name. This variable is used to set up the actual font to be used. Examples of font face names are Helvetica, Verdana, and Times New Roman.

The last parameter is the actual output variable. When the call to D3DX10Create Font completes, this last parameter is used as a pointer to the ID3DX10Font object.

Note

Most of the options available to be sent into the D3DX10CreateFont function can be found in the wingdi.h header file.

The following example shows how to use the D3DX10CreateFont function.

```
/*****************************************************************
* InitFont
* Initialize the font object
* Inputs - void
```

```
* Outputs - bool - true/success, false/failure
*************************************************************/
bool InitFont()
{
    HRESULT hr = D3DX10CreateFont(pD3DDevice,
        35,     // the font height
        0,      // the font width
        FW_BOLD,     // the weight of the font
        1,      // number of mip levels
        FALSE,      // this is not an italic font
        DEFAULT_CHARSET,     // default character set
        OUT_DEFAULT_PRECIS,      // default size mapping
        DEFAULT_QUALITY,     // default quality mapping
        DEFAULT_PITCH | FF_DONTCARE,     // default pitch
        L"Helvetica",     // use Helvetica as the basis for this font
        &pFont);     // the output

    // make sure the font was created correctly
    if (FAILED(hr))
    {
        return false;
    }

    return true;
}
```

DrawText

Drawing text to the screen using the ID3DX10Font object functionality is simple; the member function DrawText does all the work. DrawText takes the string you provide and creates a series of sprites containing the text. The sprites use the font texture you created previously.

The DrawText function is simple to use; its parameters and usage are explained next.

Since the text is rendered using a series of sprites, the first parameter to the DrawText function is a pointer to the ID3DX10Sprite object that should be used. If you want DrawText to create and use its own sprite object, pass in NULL.

The next two parameters specify the string and its length. You can either pass in the number of characters in the string or pass –1 if the string is null terminated.

The fourth parameter is a pointer to a RECT structure detailing the draw area. The RECT structure lets DrawText know the extents of the area the text will be drawn to.

The fifth parameter, Format, is the most confusing. This parameter specifies how the text should be aligned when drawn. Options such as left align, centered, and top justify are available. The text formatting options are as follows:

DT_TOP	Top justify the text.
DT_BOTTOM	Bottom justify the text.
DT_CENTER	Center the text horizontally.
DT_VCENTER	Center the text vertically.
DT_LEFT	Left justify the text.
DT_RIGHT	Right justify the text.

Format also contains some options that aren't specifically used to position the text.

- DT_CALCRECT—By setting the format to use this option, the RECT structure passed to the fourth parameter will be set with the correct size values for the text. When using this option, the text is not actually drawn. This is a great way to determine the size of the rectangle needed though.

- DT_NOCLIP—No matter the size of the rectangle passed to the DrawText function, all the text will be drawn. This disables clipping of text that would normally fall outside the draw rectangle area.

- DT_WORDBREAK—Words are split onto multiple lines if they extend past the draw area.

- DT_SINGLELINE—Even if the text contains line feeds, this draws the text on a single line.

The final parameter to the DrawText function is the color in which the text should be drawn.

An updated Render function and helper function—GetFontRectangle, which demonstrates the DrawText functionality, are shown next.

```
/**********************************************************************
* Render
* All drawing happens in the Render function
* Inputs - void
```

```
* Outputs - void
*****************************************************************/
void Render()
{
    if (pD3DDevice != NULL)
    {
        // clear the target buffer
        pD3DDevice->ClearRenderTargetView(pRenderTargetView, D3DXCOLOR(0.0f,
        0.0f, 0.0f, 0.0f));

        // Create and Initialize the destination rectangle
        RECT rc;
        SetRectEmpty(&rc);

        // Use the GetFontRectangle helper function to get the proper size of
        // the rectangle.
        GetFontRectangle(TEXT("This is a test string"), &rc);

        // Draw the text to the screen
        HRESULT hr = pFont->DrawText( NULL,
            TEXT("This is a test string"),
            -1,
            &rc,
            DT_LEFT,
            D3DXCOLOR( 1.0f, 1.0f, 1.0f, 1.0f ) );

        // display the next item in the swap chain
        pSwapChain->Present(0, 0);
    }
}

/*****************************************************************
* GetFontRectangle
* Resizes the font's destination rectangle
* Inputs - LPCWSTR, the text that will be drawn
*          RECT, pointer to the rectangle to return
* Outputs - void
*****************************************************************/
void GetFontRectangle(LPCWSTR text, RECT *rect)
{
    // Using DT_CALCRECT causes the rectangle to be determined but
    // not to be drawn
    pFont->DrawText(NULL,
```

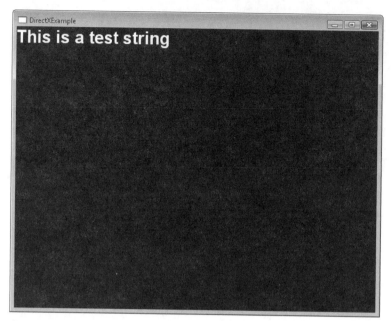

Figure 4.3
Direct3D font drawing.

```
            text,
            -1,
            rect,
            DT_CALCRECT | DT_LEFT,
            D3DXCOLOR(1.0f, 1.0f, 1.0f, 1.0f));
}
```

The GetFontRectangle function is used to calculate the proper rectangle size for the text. This requires two calls to the DrawText function, but makes sure the rectangle is always accurate. Figure 4.3 shows an example of Direct3D font drawing.

A full example of text rendering using Direct3D is available in the Chapter4\ example2 directory on the CD-ROM.

Optimized Drawing

Allowing the DrawText function to create and use its own ID3DX10Sprite object is costly if you're planning on drawing more than one line of text. It is more efficient for you to create the sprite object yourself, allowing it to be reused for each line of text. This keeps the number of sprite objects being created and destroyed to a minimum.

Using a Sprite Object

The first parameter to the DrawText function is a pointer to the sprite object. In the previous section, you passed NULL to this parameter; to utilize your own sprite, a valid ID3DX10Sprite object needs to be created.

The sprite object can be created anytime before the first DrawText function call is made. To keep similar functionality together, the sprite object can be created right after the font object. The InitFont function can be updated to include both tasks.

```
/*************************************************************
* InitFont
* Initialize the font object
* Inputs - void
* Outputs - bool - true/success, false/failure
*************************************************************/
bool InitFont()
{
    HRESULT hr = D3DX10CreateFont(pD3DDevice,
        35,     // the font height
        0,      // the font width
        FW_BOLD,     // the weight of the font
        1,      // number of mip levels
        FALSE,     // this is not an italic font
        DEFAULT_CHARSET,     // default character set
        OUT_DEFAULT_PRECIS,     // default size mapping
        DEFAULT_QUALITY,     // default quality mapping
        DEFAULT_PITCH | FF_DONTCARE,     // default pitch
        L"Helvetica",     // use Helvetica as the basis for this font
        &pFont);     // the output

    if (FAILED(hr))
    {
        return false;
    }

    // Create the sprite that fonts will use to draw with
    D3DX10CreateSprite(pD3DDevice, 512, &pFontSprite);

    return true;
}
```

Remember to release both the font and sprite objects when the program ends.

```
// Release the font
if (pFont != NULL)
{
    pFont->Release();
    pFont = NULL;
}

// Release the font sprite
if (pFontSprite != NULL)
{
    pFontSprite->Release();
    pFontSprite = NULL;
}
```

Text Drawing

The DrawText function is still the workhorse of text drawing; the major difference now is the text is being drawn to objects you specify.

There are only a few changes needed to draw the text using your own sprites. The DrawText function call needs to be updated to pass in a pointer to your sprite object. Because sprites are being drawn here, the DrawText function needs to be placed between calls to the sprite object's Begin and End calls. This prepares the system for sprite drawing. An updated Render function follows, showing which changes should be made.

```
/******************************************************************
* Render
* All drawing happens in the Render function
* Inputs - void
* Outputs - void
******************************************************************/
void Render()
{
    if (pD3DDevice != NULL)
    {
        // clear the target buffer
        pD3DDevice->ClearRenderTargetView(pRenderTargetView, D3DXCOLOR(0.0f,
        0.0f, 0.0f, 0.0f));
        // Create and Initialize the destination rectangle
        RECT rc;
        SetRectEmpty(&rc);
```

```
    // Use the GetFontRectangle helper function to get the proper size
    // of the rectangle.
    GetFontRectangle(TEXT("This is a test string"), &rc);

    // Start font drawing
    pFontSprite->Begin(D3DX10_SPRITE_SORT_TEXTURE);

    // Draw the text to the screen
    HRESULT hr = pFont->DrawText( pFontSprite,
        TEXT("This is a test string"),
        -1,
        &rc,
        DT_LEFT,
        D3DXCOLOR( 1.0f, 1.0f, 1.0f, 1.0f ) );

    pFontSprite->End();

    // display the next item in the swap chain
    pSwapChain->Present(0, 0);
    }
}
```

While this may seem like a simple change, the results won't quite be what you were expecting. The text being drawn shows up as a series of color-filled rectangles. Figure 4.4 shows the result of using your own sprites to draw text. The proceeding code is a shortened and modified version of the Render() function found in the Chapter4\example3 directory on the CD-ROM.

The rectangles contain an alpha channel that is not being drawn correctly. To solve this problem, the Render function needs to be updated to change the current blend state. The blend state follows the same process as the sprites in the previous chapter.

The Render function shown next correctly updates the blend state for font drawing.

```
/******************************************************************
* Render
* All drawing happens in the Render function
* Inputs - void
* Outputs - void
******************************************************************/
void Render()
```

Figure 4.4
A font that's not quite right.

```
{
    FLOAT OriginalBlendFactor[4];
    UINT  OriginalSampleMask = 0;

    if (pD3DDevice != NULL)
    {
        // clear the target buffer
        pD3DDevice->ClearRenderTargetView(pRenderTargetView, D3DXCOLOR(0.0f,
        0.0f, 0.0f, 0.0f));

        // Create and Initialize the destination rectangle
        RECT rc;
        SetRectEmpty(&rc);

        // Use the GetFontRectangle helper function to get the proper size
        // of the rectangle.
        GetFontRectangle(TEXT("This is a test string"), &rc);

        // Start font drawing
        pFontSprite->Begin(D3DX10_SPRITE_SORT_TEXTURE);
```

```
// Draw the text to the screen
HRESULT hr = pFont->DrawText( pFontSprite,
    TEXT("This is a test string"),
    -1,
    &rc,
    DT_LEFT,
    D3DXCOLOR( 1.0f, 1.0f, 1.0f, 1.0f ) );

// Save the current blend state
pD3DDevice->OMGetBlendState(&pOriginalBlendState10,
    OriginalBlendFactor,
    &OriginalSampleMask);

// Set the blend state for font drawing
if(pFontBlendState10)
{
    FLOAT NewBlendFactor[4] = {0,0,0,0};
    pD3DDevice->OMSetBlendState(pFontBlendState10, NewBlendFactor,
    0xffffffff);
}

pFontSprite->End();

// Restore the previous blend state
pD3DDevice->OMSetBlendState(pOriginalBlendState10,
OriginalBlendFactor, OriginalSampleMask);

// display the next item in the swap chain
pSwapChain->Present(0, 0);
    }
}
```

Summary

Knowing how to draw text to the screen can be one of the more useful skills to have. You should be able to easily implement font rendering using the Direct3D font object. By manipulating where the text is placed, it can be used for debugging or part of your UI.

What You Have Learned

In this chapter, you learned the following:

- What a font system is and how it's used

- How to create your own textured font system

- The benefits of Direct3D's font system

- How to optimize font drawing

Review Questions

You can find the answers to Review Questions in Appendix A, "Answers to End-of-Chapter Exercises."

1. What is another term for textured fonts?

2. What is a font?

3. What are some uses for text in a game?

4. Which text formatting parameter value is used to measure a string and return a properly sized rectangle?

5. What happens when text is drawn to a rectangle area too small to contain it and the value DT_NOCLIP is not specified?

On Your Own

1. Add alpha blending to the sprite-based font system.

2. Write a Render function that is capable of drawing multiple lines of text.

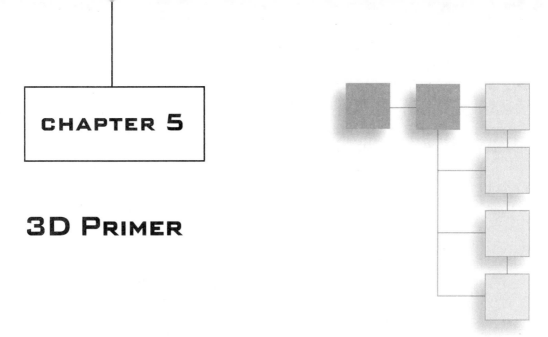

CHAPTER 5

3D PRIMER

Everything you've done up to this point has happened in a flat two-dimensional environment. Your sprites have moved either horizontally or vertically, but there's another dimension you have yet to explore—the third dimension, depth. Sure, some great games can be made that take advantage of only the technology you've explored so far, but the latest cutting-edge games take place in a 3D world. In this chapter, you're going to be introduced to the concepts and math you'll need to build a 3D world.

Here's what you'll learn in this chapter:

- What coordinate systems are and how they're used

- How to define points within 3D space

- What vectors are

- The wonderful world of matrices

- How to position and move objects

3D Space

The basis to any three-dimensional world is the space it takes place in. Look around you. The keyboard and monitor on your desk, the chair on the floor, all of these items exist in a 3D space. If you had to describe the location of one of these objects to someone over the phone, how would you do it? Would you describe your desk as located in front of you or would you say it was near a certain wall? If the person on the phone knew absolutely nothing about the room you were in, from that description, would they understand? Probably not, they're missing a point of reference.

A *point of reference* is a location that both you and the other person understand. For instance, if the point of reference was a doorway, you could then explain that the desk was located about ten feet from the door on the left hand side. When you're building a 3D world, a point of reference is crucial.

You need to be able to place objects in relation to a point of reference that both you and the computer understand. When working with 3D graphics, this point of reference is the coordinate system. A *coordinate system* is a series of imaginary lines that run through space and are used to describe locations within it. The center of this coordinate system is called the origin; this is the core of your point of reference. Any location within this space can be described precisely in relation to the origin.

For example, you can describe the location of an object by saying it is four units up from the origin and two units to the left. By using the origin as the point of reference, any point within the defined space can be described.

If you remember from working with sprites, any point on the screen can be explained using an X and Y coordinate. The X and Y coordinates determine the sprite's position in a coordinate system consisting of two perpendicular axes, a horizontal and a vertical. Figure 5.1 shows an example of a 2D coordinate system.

When working with three dimensions, a third axis will be needed, called the Z axis. The Z axis extends away from the viewer, giving the coordinate system a way to describe depth. So now you have three dimensions, width, height, and depth as well as three axes. Figure 5.2 shows a 3D coordinate system.

When dealing with 3D coordinate systems, you have to be aware that they come in two flavors, left-handed and right-handed. The handedness of the system determines the direction the axes face in relation to the viewer.

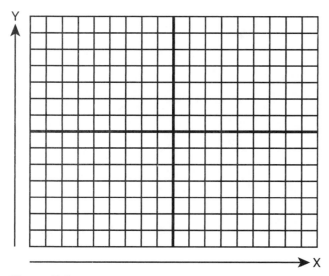

Figure 5.1
How a 2D coordinate system is laid out.

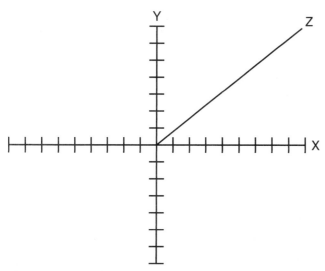

Figure 5.2
An example of a 3D coordinate system.

Left-Handed Coordinate Systems

A left-handed coordinate system extends the positive X axis to the right and the positive Y axis upward. The major difference is the Z axis. The Z axis in a left-handed system is positive in the direction away from the viewer, with the negative portion extending toward them. Figure 5.3 shows how a left-handed coordinate system is set up.

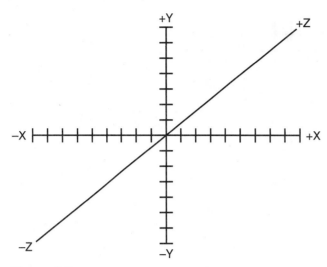

Figure 5.3
A left-handed coordinate system.

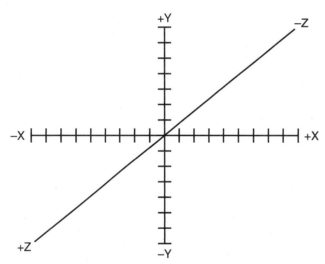

Figure 5.4
A right-handed coordinate system.

Right-Handed Coordinate Systems

The right-handed coordinate system extends the X and Y axes in the same direction as the left-handed system, but it reverses the Z axis. The positive Z values extend toward the viewer, whereas the negative values continue away. Figure 5.4 shows a right-handed system.

Points

Now that you're familiar with the coordinate system, let's go over how to place objects within it. Any position within a coordinate system can be represented using a point. A *point* is simply an infinitely small location in space. When locating a point in space, it is described using a single value for each axis. This value is the offset from the origin along each respective axis.

For example, a point located in 2D space would need two values, an X and a Y value, to describe its location, such as <1, 3>. Figure 5.5 shows how this point would look.

For each axis added, it takes one additional value to represent the point. In 3D space, three values, X, Y, and Z, are needed to describe a point, such as <1, 2, 4>.

Points can be used in many ways in the creation of a game, from player position to the location of a planet. Even though each point is tiny, that one point can be used to represent the location of any object in your game.

Finding the Distance between Two Points

Occasionally you will need to determine the distance between two points. These points can be either the origin and a fixed location or two completely arbitrary points.

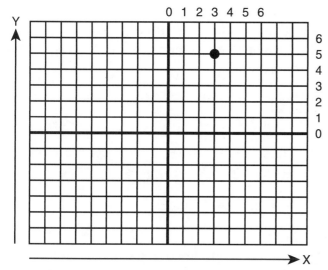

Figure 5.5
A point located in 2D space.

For example, imagine you're creating a real-time strategy game. Each of the monsters of the opposing army has the opportunity to move towards a common goal. During the turn of the AI it can choose to move one of these monsters toward the goal, but which one? This is where the ability to figure out distance comes in handy. By calculating the relative distance between each monster and the common goal, the AI can choose which one of the creatures is more advantageous to move.

Whether you are determining the distance within a 2D or 3D space, the calculation is essentially the same.

```
X Distance = x2 - x1
Y Distance = y2 - y1
Final Distance = Square root (X Distance * X Distance + Y Distance * Y Distance)
```

1. First, calculate the distance between the two X values. You can do this by subtracting the X value from point 1 from the X value of point 2.

2. Next, figure out the distance for the Y value. The Y value is calculated the same way as the X value.

3. Add the squares of the X and Y values.

4. Take the square root of the resulting value.

The final result will be a single value that represents the distance between the two points. When determining the distance between two points in 3D space, make sure to take the Z value into account as well.

```
X Distance = x2 - x1
Y Distance = y2 - y1
Z Distance = z2 - z1
Final Distance = Square root( (X Distance * X Distance) + (Y Distance * Y Distance)
+ (Z Distance * Z Distance) )
```

Vectors

Vectors have multiple uses in 3D graphics, from describing distance and direction to speed. Unlike a point, which has only a position, a vector has both a direction and a length (magnitude), allowing it to be utilized to determine which direction a polygon is facing, which direction an object or particle is heading or

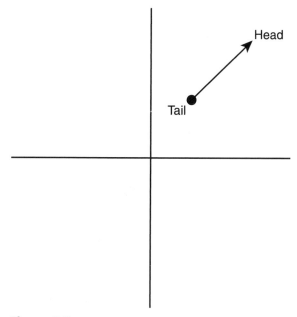

Figure 5.6
An example vector.

just describe its position. Typically, vectors are designated as arrows with a head and tail showing the direction and magnitude. Figure 5.6 shows an example of a vector within a coordinate system.

Vectors typically fall into two categories, free vectors and fixed vectors. The vector shown in Figure 5.6 is an example of a free vector.

A free vector is a vector that can be placed in an arbitrary location within a coordinate system and its meaning doesn't change.

A fixed vector remains fixed to the origin of the coordinate system. This places the tail of these vectors at the origin while the head is placed at a location in space. Because fixed vectors are centered on the origin, it allows them to be used to designate a position. This position is comprised of three scalar values called components. The number of components within the vector corresponds to the number of axes. For example, if the coordinate system is describing 3D space, then three components are needed to describe a position within it. For example, the vector <3, 2, 7> corresponds to a position 3 units away from the origin on the X axis, 2 units away on the Y axis, and 7 units away on the Z axis.

Direct3D has a few types defined in the D3DX library that are useful when working with vectors.

The D3DXVECTOR2 type is a structure containing two components, an X and a Y.

```
typedef struct D3DXVECTOR2 {
    FLOAT x;
    FLOAT y;
} D3DXVECTOR2;
```

The D3DXVECTOR3 type contains three components, an X, Y, and a Z, within its structure.

```
typedef struct D3DXVECTOR3 {
    FLOAT x;
    FLOAT y;
    FLOAT z;
} D3DXVECTOR3;
```

While you could define these types yourself, the Direct3D structures contain more than just the definitions of the embedded components. The structures contain functions and operator overloads relevant to the specific vector type, allowing the vectors to be manipulated easily.

Note

If you want to see all the functionality provided the vector types by D3DX, look at the D3DX10math.h header file in the DirectX SDK.

When using vectors you're bound to come across a few different types; here's a small list:

- **Position Vector**—A type of vector that is used to describe a position within a coordinate system, with the tail being at the origin and the head at a point.

- **Normal Vector**—A vector that is perpendicular to a plane. This is useful for determining whether a polygon is front or back facing.

- **Unit Vectors**—A vector that has a length of 1. Not all vectors require a large length. When creating a directional light, only the direction of the vector is important.

- **Zero Vectors**—A vector with a length of 0.

Determining the Length of a Vector

Occasionally it is useful to know the length of a vector—since the length or magnitude of the vector can be used as acceleration or velocity when applied to a game object. The length is also used as an input when normalizing the vector.

To calculate the length of a vector, each of the components must be first squared and then added together. Finally, the square root of this number is taken to give the output length.

```
sqrt(vectorX * vectorX + vectorY * vectorY + vectorZ * vectorZ);
```

Direct3D provides a function called D3DXVec3Length that can be used to calculate a vector length.

```
FLOAT D3DXVec3Length( CONST D3DXVECTOR3 *pV );
```

Normalize a Vector

Normalizing a vector is the process of reducing any length vector into a unit vector. This is best done when only the direction of a vector is needed and the length is unimportant. Vectors can be normalized simply by dividing each of the components by the vector's length.

```
vectorX = (vectorX / length);
vectorY = (vectorY / length;
vectorZ = (vectorZ / length);
```

The final vector will still point in the same direction, but the length of the vector is reduced to 1.

Direct3D offers a function to perform this for you called D3DXVec3Normalize.

```
D3DXVECTOR3 * D3DXVec3Normalize(
    D3DXVECTOR3 *pOut,
    CONST D3DXVECTOR3 *pV
);
```

This function takes two parameters. The first parameter is a pointer to the D3DXVECTOR3 object to be filled with the normalize vector. The last parameter is the original vector.

Cross Product

A cross product of a vector is used to calculate a normal vector. A normal vector or normal is used when performing lighting to determine the orientation of a particular polygon. The polygon's orientation is used to figure out how much light the polygon is receiving.

Normals can be calculated on a polygon or vertex basis and have vastly different visual results. Because there are more vertices in an object than polygons, calculating normals on a per-vertex basis is more complicated but yields much better visual results. For the sake of simplicity, I'll describe the method for determining a polygon normal; vertex normals will be covered in the chapter on shaders.

Calculating the normal vector using the cross product requires two vectors from an existing polygon. The resulting vector will be perpendicular to the input vectors.

```
newVectorX = (vector1Y * vector2Z) - (vector1Z * vector2Y);
newVectorY = (vector1Z * vector2X) - (vector1X * vector2Z);
newVectorZ = (vector1X * vector2Y) - (vector1Y * vector2X);
```

Direct3D provides the D3DXVec3Cross function for calculating the cross product.

```
D3DXVECTOR3* D3DXVec3Cross( D3DXVECTOR3 *pOut,
    CONST D3DXVECTOR3 *pV1,
    CONST D3DXVECTOR3 *pV2 );
```

The D3DXVec3Cross function takes three parameters. The first parameter is the output vector for the calculation. The second and third parameters are the existing polygon vectors.

Dot Product

The final vector calculation I'll go over is the dot product. The dot product is used to determine the angle between two vectors and is commonly used for back-face culling. Back-face culling is the process by which polygons that are not visible are removed to reduce the number of polygons being drawn. If two vectors have an angle less than 90 degrees, then the dot product is a positive value; otherwise, the dot product is negative. The sign of the dot product is what's used to determine whether a polygon is front or back facing. Polygons facing away from the viewer are not shown.

The dot product is calculated based on two existing vectors of a polygon. The components of the two vectors are multiplied and then added together to create the dot product. Before calculating the dot product, always normalize the two input vectors.

```
Float dotProduct = Vector1X * vector2X + vector1Y * vector2Y + vector1Z *
vector2Z;
```

Direct3D contains the function D3DXVec3Dot for calculating the dot product.

```
FLOAT D3DXVec3Dot( CONST D3DXVECTOR3 *pV1, CONST D3DXVECTOR3 *pV2 );
```

The D3DXVec3Dot function takes the two input vectors as parameters.

The Geometry Pipeline

3D models are for the most part created outside of your game code. For instance, if you're creating a racing game, you'll probably create the car models in a 3D art package. During the creation process, these models will be working off of the coordinate system provided to them in the modeler. This causes the objects to be created with a set of vertices that aren't necessarily going to place the car model exactly where and how you want it in your game environment. Because of this, you will need to move and rotate the model yourself. You can do this by using the geometry pipeline. The *geometry pipeline* is a process that allows you to transform an object from one coordinate system into another. Figure 5.7 shows the transformations a vertex goes through.

When a model first starts out, it is centered on the origin. This causes the model to be centered in the environment with a default orientation. Not every model you load needs to be at the origin, so how do you get models where they need to be? The answer to that is through transformations.

Transformations refer to the actions of translating (moving), rotating, and scaling an object. By applying these actions, you can make an object appear to move around. These actions are handled as your objects progress through the stages of the geometry pipeline.

When you load a model, its vertices are in a local coordinate system called model space. *Model space* refers to a coordinate system where the parts of an object are relative to a local origin. For instance, upon creation, a model's vertices are in reference to the origin point around which they were created. A cube that is

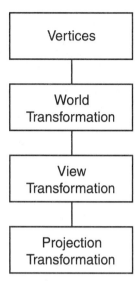

Figure 5.7
The stages of vertex transformations.

2 units in size centered on the origin would have its vertices 1 unit on either side of the origin. If you then wanted to place this cube somewhere within your game, you would need to transform its vertices from model space into the global system used by all the objects in your world. This global coordinate system is called *world space*, where all objects are relative to a single fixed origin. The process of transforming an object from model space into world space is called *world transformation*.

World Transformation

The world transformation stage of the geometry pipeline takes an existing object with its own local coordinate system and transforms that object into the world coordinate system. The world coordinate system is the system that contains the position and orientation of all objects within the 3D world. The world system has a single origin point that all models, transformed into this system, become relative to.

The next stage of the geometry pipeline is the view transformation. Because all objects at this point are relative to a single origin, you can only view them from this point. To allow you to view the scene from any arbitrary point, the objects must go through a view transformation.

View Transformation

The *view transformation* transforms the coordinates from world space into view space. *View space* refers to the coordinate system that is relative to the position of a virtual camera. When you choose a point of view for your virtual camera, the coordinates in world space get reoriented in respect to the camera. For instance, the camera remains at the origin while the world itself is moved into the camera's view.

Note

> I've been saying virtual camera instead of camera because the concept of a camera in 3D doesn't really exist. By either moving the virtual camera up along the Y axis or by moving the entire world down along that same axis, you obtain the same visual results.

At this point, you have the camera angle and view for your scene and you're ready to display it to the screen.

Projection Transformation

The next stage in the geometry pipeline is the projection transformation. The projection transformation is the stage of the pipeline where depth is applied. When you cause objects that are closer to the camera to appear larger than those farther away, you create an illusion of depth.

Finally, the vertices are scaled to the viewport and projected into 2D space. The resulting 2D image appears on your monitor with the illusion of being a 3D scene. Table 5.1 shows the types of transformations within the geometry pipeline and the types of spaces each affects.

Transforming an Object

Now that you're aware of the transformations, what are they really used for? As an example, say you were modeling a city. This city is made up of houses, office buildings, and a few cars here and there. Now, you load in a model of a new car

Table 5.1 Coordinate System Transformations

Transformation Type	From Space	To Space
World transformation	Model space	World space
View transformation	World space	View space
Projection transformation	View space	Projection space

and need to add it to your existing scene. When the model comes in though, it's centered on the origin and facing the wrong way. To get the car to the correct spot and orientation in the scene, the car model will have to be rotated properly and then translated to its world space location.

When putting an object through the transformation pipeline, you're really transforming each vertex individually. In the case of the car, every vertex that makes up the car will be moved individually by a certain amount and then rotated. After each vertex is complete, the object appears in the new position. These transformations take place by multiplying each vertex in the model by a transformation matrix.

What Are Matrices?

You've probably come across matrices in a math class along the way and wondered what they would ever be used for; well, here it is: game programming. Matrices are used to transform objects from one coordinate system to another. By applying a matrix to an existing point, it is transformed from its original coordinate system to the new one. For example, most objects start out in their own local coordinate system. This means that all the points that make up that object are relative to a local origin. To convert those points into a common world coordinate system, they must be transformed using a matrix.

You will probably find matrices to be the single-most confusing concept to wrap your thoughts around when just starting out with 3D graphics. Matrices and the math involved can feel very daunting and overwhelming at the start. The important thing to take away from this section on matrices isn't necessarily how they work, but what they're for and how to use them. No one should expect you to be able to perform all the math required right off the bat; luckily, Direct3D provides optimized functionality to do a lot of this work for you. If you ever want to know all the details behind matrices, there are a ton of good math resources available on the web.

Mathematically, a matrix is a 4×4 grid of numbers that are arranged in columns and rows. Shown here is a simple matrix with the individual cells numbered 1 through 16.

1	2	3	4
5	6	7	8
9	10	11	12
13	14	15	16

Each row in the matrix corresponds to the three major axes. The first row is used for the X axis, the second row for the Y axis, and the third row for the Z axis. The final row is used to contain the translation offset values.

If you wanted to create your own matrix in code, you could define it as a simple 4×4 array of float values.

```
float matrix [4][4] = {
    1.0f, 0.0f, 0.0f, 0.0f,
    0.0f, 1.0f, 0.0f, 0.0f,
    0.0f, 0.0f, 1.0f, 0.0f,
    0.0f, 0.0f, 0.0f, 1.0f
};
```

Like vectors, Direct3D provides its own matrix type to work with called D3DMATRIX.

```
typedef struct _D3DMATRIX {
    union {
        struct {
            float  _11, _12, _13, _14;
            float  _21, _22, _23, _24;
            float  _31, _32, _33, _34;
            float  _41, _42, _43, _44;
        };
        float m[4][4];
    };
} D3DMATRIX;
```

The D3DMATRIX type creates a structure that allows the enclosed matrix to be accessed either as a 4×4 array or a series of sixteen float values. Additional functionality is provided by the D3DXMATRIX type which inherits from D3DMATRIX, giving you the built-in functionality for matrix calculations. You can look up D3DXMATRIX in the DirectX SDK documentation to see all the functionality it provides.

The Identity Matrix

There is a special matrix that you should be aware of. It's called the *identity matrix*. This is the default matrix. It contains values that reset scaling to 1, with no rotations and no translation taking place. The identity matrix is created by zeroing out all sixteen values in the matrix and then applying 1s along the diagonal. The Identity Matrix can be used as a starting point of all matrix operations.

Following is an identity matrix.

```
float IdentityMatrix [4][4] = {
    1.0f, 0.0f, 0.0f, 0.0f,
    0.0f, 1.0f, 0.0f, 0.0f,
    0.0f, 0.0f, 1.0f, 0.0f,
    0.0f, 0.0f, 0.0f, 1.0f
};
```

Creating an identity matrix in Direct3D is as simple as calling the D3DXMatrixIdentity function. This function takes a single parameter, a pointer to an output D3DXMATRIX object. This will initialize or reset a matrix to contain the identity values.

```
D3DXMATRIX * D3DXMatrixIdentity(
    D3DXMATRIX * pOut
);
```

Tip

The Direct3D function D3DXMatrixIsIdentity can be used to check if a matrix contains the identity values. Also, be aware that not all matrix functions available in Direct3D10 appear in the SDK documentation, but they can be found by perusing the DirectX SDK header files.

Initializing a Matrix

For the most part, you'll be using the functions defined by Direct3D to initialize and populate values within your matrices, but you don't have to. If you feel like ever getting your hands dirty, the values contained in the matrix are open and available for you to look at and change individually. As you saw earlier, the D3DXMATRIX type holds the matrix values in a union, allowing them to be accessed either using array notation or by single floats. The following code snippet shows how to create and fill a new matrix manually to contain the identity matrix.

```
D3DXMATRIX matrix;
// first row
matrix._11 = 1.0f;
matrix._12 = 0.0f;
matrix._13 = 0.0f;
matrix._14 = 0.0f;
```

```
// second row
matrix._21 = 0.0f;
matrix._22 = 1.0f;
matrix._23 = 0.0f;
matrix._24 = 0.0f;

// third row
matrix._31 = 0.0f;
matrix._32 = 0.0f;
matrix._33 = 1.0f;
matrix._34 = 0.0f;

// fourth row
matrix._41 = 0.0f;
matrix._42 = 0.0f;
matrix._43 = 0.0f;
matrix._44 = 1.0f;
```

Matrix Scaling

One of the transformations you can apply to an object is scaling. Scaling is the ability to shrink or grow an object by a certain factor. For instance, if you have a square centered on the origin that was two units wide and two units tall and you scaled it twice its size, you would have a square that now went four units in each direction. Figure 5.8 shows an example of the scaling effect.

Remember the 1s that were placed into the identity matrix? Those 1s control the scaling on each of the three axes. When vertices are transformed using this matrix, their X, Y, and Z values are altered based on the scaling values. By changing the X axis value to a 2 and the Y axis to a 3, the objects will be scaled twice their size in the X direction and three times their size in the Y. An example ScaleMatrix array is shown next. The variables scaleX, scaleY, and scaleZ show where the appropriate scaling values would go.

```
float ScaleMatrix [4][4] = {
    scaleX, 0.0f,   0.0f,   0.0f,
    0.0f,   scaleY, 0.0f,   0.0f,
    0.0f,   0.0f,   scaleZ, 0.0f,
    0.0f,   0.0f,   0.0f,   1.0f
};
```

Direct3D has a function called D3DXMatrixScaling that will generate a matrix for you based on scaling values you pass in.

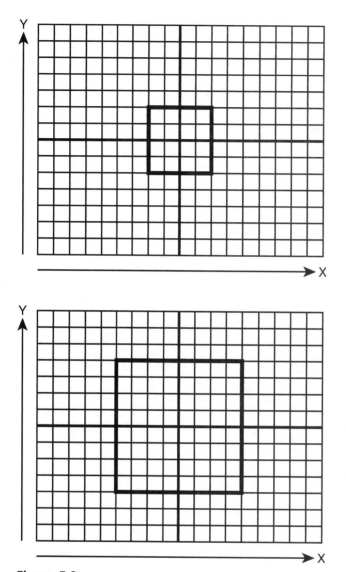

Figure 5.8
A square scaled in both the X and Y directions.

```
D3DXMATRIX * D3DXMatrixScaling (
    D3DXMATRIX * pOut,
    FLOAT sx,
    FLOAT sy,
    FLOAT sz
);
```

Matrix Translation

The act of moving an object is called translation. Translation allows for an object to be moved along any of the three axes by specifying the amount of movement needed. For example, if you want to move an object right along the X axis, you would need to translate that object an appropriate number of units in the positive X direction. To do so, you would need to create a translation matrix. This matrix will then cause any objects it affects to be moved to the right. Figure 5.9 shows an example of a square being translated.

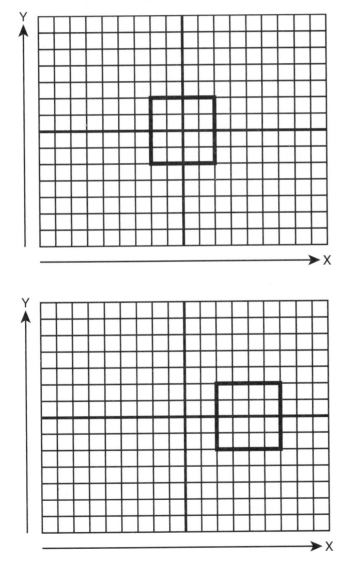

Figure 5.9
A square translated to the right along the X axis.

Again, I'll start with the identity matrix and change it to add in the variables that affect translation. Take a look at the following translation matrix; the variables moveX, moveY, and moveZ show you where the translation values would go. If you wanted to translate an object 4 units to the right, you would replace moveX with the value 4.

```
float TranslationMatrix [4][4] = {
    1.0f,  0.0f,  0.0f,  0.0f,
    0.0f,  1.0f,  0.0f,  0.0f,
    0.0f,  0.0f,  1.0f,  0.0f,
    moveX, moveY, moveZ, 1.0f
};
```

The Direct3D function D3DXMatrixTranslation is used to easily create a translation matrix with any values you specify.

```
D3DXMATRIX* D3DXMatrixTranslation(
  D3DXMATRIX *pOut,
  FLOAT x,
  FLOAT y,
  FLOAT z
);
```

Matrix Rotation

The final effect I'm going to describe is rotation. *Rotation* is the act of turning an object around a certain axis. This allows objects to change their orientation within space. For instance, if you wanted to rotate a planet, you would create a rotation matrix and apply it to the planet.

Rotation matrices take a little more explanation because the matrix needs to change based on the axis you're trying to rotate around.

Rotate around the X Axis

When rotating around any axis, it will require you to convert the angle of rotation into both a sine and cosine value. These values are then plugged into the matrix to cause the proper amount of rotation.

When rotating around the X axis, the sine and cosine values are placed into the matrix in the following manner.

```
float RotateXMatrix [4][4] = {
    1.0f, 0.0f,      0.0f,     0.0f,
    0.0f, cosAngle,  sinAngle, 0.0f,
    0.0f, -sinAngle, cosAngle, 0.0f,
    0.0f, 0.0f,      0.0f,     1.0f
};
```

The Direct3D function D3DXMatrixRotationX will create a rotation matrix along the X axis.

```
D3DXMATRIX * D3DXMatrixRotationX(
  D3DXMATRIX * pOut,
  FLOAT Angle
);
```

Rotate around the Y Axis

Rotating around the Y axis (see Figure 5.10) requires only that the sine and cosine values be moved to different positions within the matrix. In this instance, the values are moved to affect the X and Z axes.

```
float RotateYMatrix [4][4] = {
    cosAngle, 0.0f, -sinAngle, 0.0f,
    0.0f,     1.0f, 0.0f,      0.0f,
    sinAngle, 0.0f, cosAngle,  0.0f,
    0.0f,     0.0f, 0.0f,      1.0f
};
```

The D3DXMatrixRotationY function will generate a rotation matrix around the Y axis.

```
D3DXMATRIX * D3DXMatrixRotationY(
  D3DXMATRIX * pOut,
  FLOAT Angle
);
```

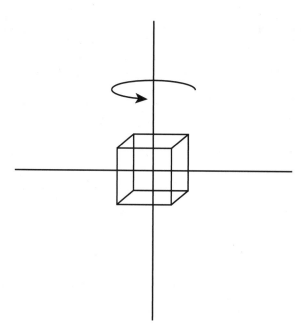

Figure 5.10
A cube rotated 45 degrees around the Y axis.

Rotate around the Z Axis

The final rotation matrix allows for rotation around the Z axis. In this instance, the sin and cosine values affect the X and Y axes.

```
float RotateZMatrix [4][4] = {
    cosAngle,  sinAngle, 0.0f, 0.0f,
    -sinAngle, cosAngle, 0.0f, 0.0f,
    0.0f,      0.0f,     1.0f, 0.0f,
    0.0f,      0.0f,     0.0f, 1.0f
};
```

The D3DXMatrixRotationZ function will generate a rotation matrix around the Z axis.

```
D3DXMATRIX * D3DXMatrixRotationZ(
  D3DXMATRIX * pOut,
  FLOAT Angle
);
```

Multiply Matrices

The last thing you need to learn about matrices is how to combine them. Most of the time, you won't need to only translate an object, you'll need to scale it or maybe rotate it all in one go. Multiple matrices can be multiplied, or concatenated, together to create a single matrix that is capable of containing the previously single calculations. This means that instead of needing a matrix for rotation as well as one for translation, these two can be combined into one.

Because the D3DXMatrix type overrides the multiplication operator, the act of multiplying two D3DXMatrix objects together is easy. The following single line of code demonstrates this.

```
D3DXMatrix finalMatrix = rotationMatrix * translationMatrix;
```

A new matrix called finalMatrix is created, which now contains both the rotation and translation. This new matrix can then be applied to any object going through the pipeline. One thing to mention though is to watch out for the order in which you multiply matrices. Using the previous line of code, objects will be rotated first and then translated away from that position. For example, rotating the object 90 degrees around the Y axis and then translating it four units along the X axis would cause the object to be rotated in place at the origin and then moved four units to the right.

If the translation came first, the object would be translated four units to the right of the origin first and then rotated 90 degrees. Think what would happen if you extended your hand to your right and then turned your body 90 degrees—where would your hand end up? Not exactly in the same place as before; you need to make sure that the order in which you multiply the matrices is the order you really want them applied.

If you don't like using the multiplication operator to combine matrices, you can use the Direct3D function D3DXMatrixMultiply instead.

```
D3DXMATRIX * D3DXMatrixMultiply(
    D3DXMATRIX * pOut,
    CONST D3DXMATRIX *pM1,
    CONST D3DXMATRIX *pM2
);
```

The D3DXMatrixMultiply function takes three parameters. The first parameter is a pointer to the output matrix to be created. The second and third parameters are the matrices you want to multiply. Using this function may make your code slightly easier to follow.

Note

Matrix multiplication is not cumulative. Multiplying Matrix A by Matrix B does not result in the same output matrix as multiplying Matrix B by Matrix A. The order in which matrices are multiplied is important.

Primitive Types

When drawing geometry, Direct3D has the option of interpreting the points you send in multiple ways. By connecting these points in different ways, it affects how your geometry is drawn. For instance, you could declare a series of three points; depending on the primitive type you select, these points could be drawn as either three individual dots or as a line-connected triangle.

Based on the primitive type you select, the number of points necessary to draw your object can be greatly reduced. You'll learn more about primitive types in the next chapter. In the meantime, here's a short introduction to the different types available.

Direct3D offers the following primitive types:

- Point lists
- Line lists
- Line strips
- Triangle lists
- Triangle strips
- Triangle fans

Point Lists

A *point list* consists of a series of points that are not connected in any way. Figure 5.11 shows a grid containing four distinct points. Each point is defined using X, Y, and Z coordinates. For example, the top-left point would be defined as (1, 6, 0).

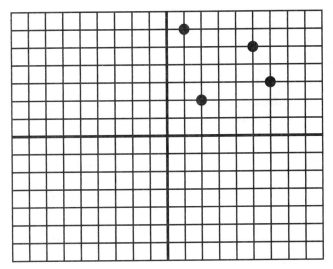

Figure 5.11
An example of rendered points using a point list.

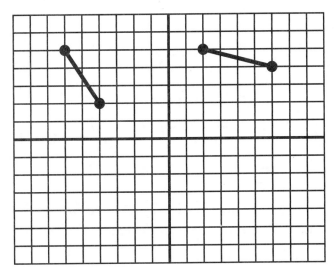

Figure 5.12
Lines rendered using a line list.

Line Lists

Line lists consist of lines constructed by two points, one at each end. The lines within a line list are not connected. Figure 5.12 shows two lines rendered using a line list. This particular line list is constructed from four vertices. The line on the left is formed using (−6, 5, 0) for the upper coordinate and (−4, 2, 0) for the bottom coordinate.

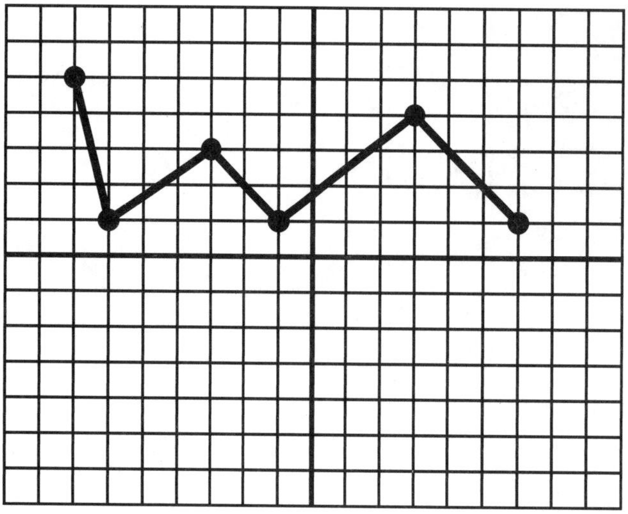

Figure 5.13
Lines rendered using a line strip.

Line Strips

Line strips are a series of connected lines where each additional line is defined by a single vertex. Each vertex in the line strip is connected to the previous vertex for a line. Figure 5.13 shows how a line list is constructed and rendered. The line list in this figure is constructed using a series of six vertices creating five lines.

Triangle Lists

Triangle lists contain triangles that are not connected in any way and can appear anywhere within your world. Figure 5.14 shows two individual triangles constructed from six vertices. Each triangle requires three vertices to construct a complete triangle.

Triangle Strips

Triangle strips are a series of triangles connected to one another where only one vertex is required to define each additional triangle. Figure 5.15 shows four triangles created using only six vertices.

Triangle strips are constructed first by creating three vertices to define the first triangle. If an additional vertex is defined, lines are drawn between the two

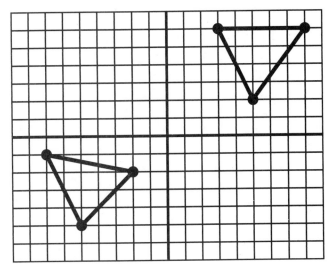

Figure 5.14
Triangles rendered using a triangle list.

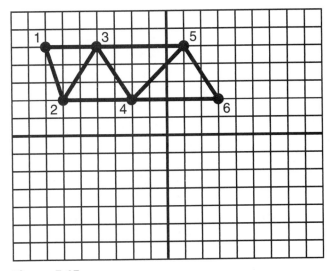

Figure 5.15
Triangles rendered using a triangle strip.

previously created vertices, forming another triangle. Within Figure 5.15, the order in which the vertices are created is shown.

Triangle Fans

Triangle fans are a series of triangles that share a common vertex. After the first triangle is created, each additional vertex creates another triangle with one of its points being the first vertex defined.

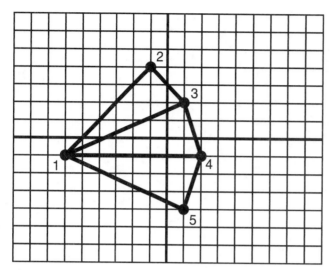

Figure 5.16
Triangles rendered using a triangle fan.

Figure 5.16 shows how a triangle fan consisting of three triangles is created using only five vertices. The order of the vertices controls what the triangle fan looks like. Figure 5.16 shows the order in which the vertices are created to construct the displayed fan.

Summary

You should now understand the basis on which all 3D systems are built. No matter how complicated a 3D system or game you come across, they all have their start in the theories and calculations explained in this chapter. In the next chapter, you'll get the chance to use what you've learned so far and try out the 3D concepts.

What You Have Learned

In this chapter, you learned the following:

- The differences between 2D and 3D coordinate systems

- What vectors and matrices are

- How to create and use matrices

- The different primitive types available

Review Questions

You can find the answers to the Review Questions in Appendix A, "Answers to End-of-Chapter Exercises."

1. How is a point defined in a 3D coordinate system?

2. What does normalizing a vector do?

3. What is the purpose of the dot product calculation?

4. What primitive type consists of a series of connected lines?

5. What is the identity matrix?

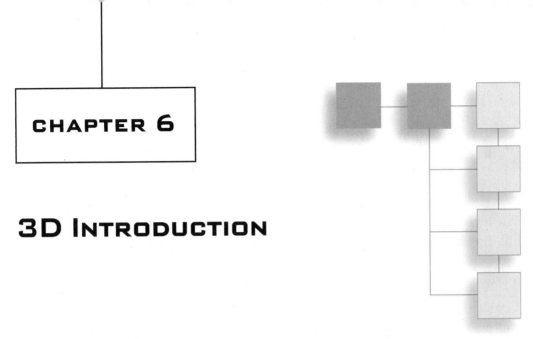

CHAPTER 6

3D INTRODUCTION

Now that you've learned the theory and math behind 3D, it's time to dive into using it. Direct3D offers a variety of functionality that will help you take the concepts you've already learned and turn those into something you can see and interact with. Before you can jump into creating the next big game, you're going to have to start a bit smaller with a single triangle.

Here's what we'll cover in this chapter:

- What vertices are and how they're defined

- A small glimpse into the world of shaders

- How to create and fill a vertex buffer

- How to optimize your drawing with indices

- How to rotate an object

The Triangle

You've probably realized that most examples start out with drawing a single triangle and you might wonder why. Like most programming languages, even Direct3D has its own "Hello World" example in the form of a triangle. It's the most simple and straightforward way to describe all the steps needed for 3D drawing without introducing a bunch of extra code; things that at this point would only help to confuse and take away from the lesson.

After you've endured the triangle, you'll build on this simple example, adding complexity but always understanding why and how it all comes together.

Vertices

The most basic element making up any 3D object is the vertex. Vertices are the building blocks from which all other primitives are constructed. Even a triangle relies on three vertices to make up its simple shape. The vertices dictate the exact location in space where the sides of the triangle come together.

Vertices, at their most simple form contain at least a position coordinate. This coordinate contains the same number of components as the space has axes. For a 2D coordinate system, a vertex will define its position by using only X and Y component values. When moving into a 3D space, a third component, Z, is needed.

Vertices are commonly defined in Direct3D using either the D3DXVECTOR2 or D3DXVECTOR3 structure types. Both of these types contain multiple float values, each one referring to a separate axis. Below you can see an example of how the D3DXVECTOR3 structure is defined. As you can see, there are three components allowing for positioning within 3D space.

```
typedef struct D3DXVECTOR3 {
    FLOAT x;
    FLOAT y;
    FLOAT z;
} D3DXVECTOR3;
```

An individual D3DXVECTOR3 structure can represent a single vertex; because triangles have three sides, three of these structures must be filled out. Direct3D also has a D3DXVECTOR4 type, which is useful when storing vertex colors.

Custom Vertex Structure

As you progress into the world of 3D, you'll find that all the objects you create will be made up of different types of vertices. Vertices can have any number of properties associated with them, from position, color, texture coordinates, and normals. Because of the dynamic nature of vertices, Direct3D requires you to define the properties of the vertices you'll be using. Vertices are defined using a structure, allowing you to group all the properties needed together. An example vertex structure containing only the property for position is shown here:

```
struct VertexPosStruct
{
    D3DXVECTOR3 Pos;
};
```

The vertex structure is then used to declare an array of vertices, containing all the vertices that are needed to make up an object. To demonstrate, a triangle can be defined using the vertices in the array below.

```
// Define the vertices for  a triangle
VertexPosStruct vertices[] =
{
    D3DXVECTOR3(0.0f, 0.5f, 0.5f),
    D3DXVECTOR3(0.5f, -0.5f, 0.5f),
    D3DXVECTOR3(-0.5f, -0.5f, 0.5f),
};
```

Most of the objects you create will be much more complicated than a simple triangle, but even this one triangle requires the same set up and rendering path as a complicated 3D monster.

Vertex Input Layout

Now that you've defined what your vertex structure will look like, it's time to put it into a format that Direct3D can understand: the input layout.

The input layout defines how the vertices will be fed through the pipeline. As vertices are passed through the pipeline, Direct3D needs to know how to access the properties contained within each vertex. The input layout defines not only the order of the vertex properties, but also their size and type.

When defining an input layout, each property of a vertex can be described using a D3D10_INPUT_ELEMENT_DESC structure.

```
typedef struct D3D10_INPUT_ELEMENT_DESC {
    LPCSTR SemanticName;
    UINT SemanticIndex;
    DXGI_FORMAT Format;
    UINT InputSlot;
    UINT AlignedByteOffset;
```

```
        D3D10_INPUT_CLASSIFICATION InputSlotClass;
        UINT InstanceDataStepRate;
} D3D10_INPUT_ELEMENT_DESC;
```

Each vertex property needs one of these input element structures filled out. The structures are then included in an array and used by Direct3D to create the input layout.

The following code shows an example of how to define a layout for a vertex with both a position and a color.

```
// The vertex input layout
D3D10_INPUT_ELEMENT_DESC layout[] = {
{ "POSITION", 0, DXGI_FORMAT_R32G32B32_FLOAT, 0, 0, D3D10_INPUT_PER_VERTEX_DATA,
0 },
{ "COLOR", 0, DXGI_FORMAT_R32G32B32A32_FLOAT, 0, 12,
D3D10_INPUT_PER_VERTEX_ DATA, 0 },
};

// Calculate the number of elements in the layout array
UINT numElements = ( sizeof(layout) / sizeof(layout[0]) );
```

A few of the members of the D3D10_INPUT_ELEMENT_DESC structure are detailed next.

SemanticName is the name that the property will be referenced by within a shader. Most properties in a vertex have a default semantic name that can be used.

The member Format describes the size of the data this property represents. The position property uses the DXGI_FORMAT_R32G32B32_FLOAT value. This gives each position a 32-bit long float variable to use as storage.

AlignedByteOffset is the number of bytes that this property is offset from the start of the layout. For instance, position is first in the input layout so it has an AlignedByteOffset of 0. Color, which follows the position, has an offset of 12. This says that position requires 12 bytes at the front of the input layout. As it may be a bit confusing as to where the value of 12 came from, each member of the vertex position requires 32 bits or 4 bytes to store their value. Since there are three values needed to store a vertex position, it would take 12 bytes to hold this information.

Now that you've described the vertex properties, you can create the input layout object. The input layout object allows the input stage of the pipeline to know beforehand the format of the data it is ingesting. For more details on the input stage of the pipeline, refer back to Chapter 1. The input layout object is based on the `ID3D10InputLayout` interface and is created using the `CreateInputLayout` function. The following code shows how this function is called.

```
// Get the pass description
D3D10_PASS_DESC PassDescription;
pTechnique->GetPassByIndex(0)->GetDesc(&PassDescription);

// Create the vertex input layout
hr = pD3DDevice->CreateInputLayout(layout,
    numElements,
    PassDescription.pIAInputSignature,
    PassDescription.IAInputSignatureSize,
    &modelObject->pVertexLayout);

if(FAILED(hr))
{
    return false;
}
```

You'll notice that a call was made to fill in a `D3D10_PASS_DESC` object. `D3D10_PASS_DESC` is used to gather information about the shader that will be used when drawing this object, specifically the input signature. This makes sure that the vertex format used to define the object is the same format the shader expects later when drawing the object.

Note

Each object within a scene may be based on a different layout of vertex properties. Some may need only position, while others may require position and color. Not all objects are the same, so you'll need to define a vertex input layout for objects using unique vertex properties.

Right before an object is drawn, the input layout for the object needs to be set. Since multiple items with different layouts can be drawn sequentially, Direct3D needs a way of knowing the layout of the next item it is about to draw. The `IASetInputLayout` function is used to do this. It takes the input layout object you created and makes it the active layout.

```
// Set the input layout
pD3DDevice->IASetInputLayout( pVertexLayout );
```

A Small Shader Introduction

Because Direct3D no longer supports the fixed function pipeline, it falls to you to designate the behavior of how vertices and pixels are handled. The fixed function pipeline previously had a set way of processing vertices as they passed through on their way to being drawn. This restricted the options you had to fully control the pipeline, limiting you to the functionality the pipeline supported. There was a single method for handling lighting and a set maximum value of textures you could work with. This severely limited the effects you could achieve using Direct3D. With Direct3D 10 that all changed. The fixed pipeline is no more and how objects are drawn is completely within your hands.

As each vertex is processed by the system, you get the opportunity to manipulate it or to allow it to pass through unchanged. The same can be said for pixels. Any pixel being rendered by the system also is provided to you to be changed before going to the screen. The functionality to change vertices and pixels is contained within Direct3D's shader mechanism.

Shaders are Direct3D's way of exposing pieces of the pipeline to be dynamically reprogrammed by you. Direct3D supports three types of shaders: vertex, pixel, and geometry.

Vertex shaders operate on just what you'd expect, vertices. Every vertex going through the pipeline is made available to the current vertex shader before being outputted. Likewise, any pixel being rendered must also pass through the pixel shaders. Geometry shaders are a new special type of shader introduced with Direct3D 10. Geometry shaders allow for multiple vertices to be manipulated simultaneously, giving the option of controlling entire pieces of geometry. Since shaders are required for even the simplest 3D drawing, I'll explain how shaders are loaded and applied. How to write and use shaders will be explained in more detail in the next chapter.

Loading an Effect File

Shaders are bundled together in what's called an effect. Most of the time, you'll be using a combination of vertex and pixel shaders together to create a certain behavior called a technique. Because the different types of shaders depend on each other, their functionality is combined into one file. The effect file contains the code for vertex and pixel shaders and now with Direct3D10, geometry shaders as well.

The simplest form of effect contains a technique with a vertex shader that allows the incoming data from the vertex structure to just pass through. This means the vertex position and other properties will not be changed in any way and are passed on to the next stage in the pipeline.

A simple pixel shader will perform no calculations and return only a single color. Geometry shaders are optional and can be NULL. The contents of a basic effect file are shown next.

```
// PS_INPUT - input variables to the pixel shader
// This struct is created and filled in by the
// vertex shader
struct PS_INPUT
{
    float4 Pos : SV_POSITION;
    float4 Color : COLOR0;
};


/////////////////////////////////////////////
// Vertex Shader - Main Function
/////////////////////////////////////////////
PS_INPUT VS (float4 Pos : POSITION)
{
    PS_INPUT psInput;

    psInput.Pos = Pos;
    psInput.Color = float4 (1.0f, 1.0f, 0.0f, 1.0f);

    return psInput;
}


/////////////////////////////////////////////
// Pixel Shader
/////////////////////////////////////////////
float4 PS(PS_INPUT psInput) : SV_Target
{
    return psInput.Color;
}

// Define the technique
technique10 Render
{
    pass P0
```

```
    {
        SetVertexShader( CompileShader( vs_4_0, VS() ) );
        SetGeometryShader( NULL );
        SetPixelShader( CompileShader( ps_4_0, PS() ) );
    }
}
```

Go ahead and look at the code within the effect file. You probably won't understand much of the syntax yet, but it should give you an idea as to what to expect.

Effects are usually loaded in from a file using the D3DX10CreateEffectFromFile
function. I'll only go over the use of the function now because effect files and
their components will be explained in more detail later. An example of how to
use the D3DX10CreateEffectFromFile function is shown next.

```
// The name of the effect file to load
LPCWSTR effectFilename = L"..\\simple.fx";
// The effect object
ID3D10Effect* pEffect = NULL;

// Load the effect file and create the effect object
HRESULT hr = D3DX10CreateEffectFromFile (effectFilename,
    NULL,
    NULL,
    "fx_4_0",
    D3D10_SHADER_ENABLE_STRICTNESS,
    0,
    pD3DDevice,
    NULL,
    NULL,
    &pEffect,
    NULL);

if (FAILED(hr))
{
    return false;
}
```

The file name contained in the effectFilename variable is loaded and the resulting effect is created and placed into the pEffect variable. If the loading of the
effect was successful, the effect can now be used. One important parameter to
take note of is the fourth parameter; this parameter specifies the shader model the
shader should be compiled with upon load. Under Direct3D10, the new shader
model 4.0 is used.

The Technique

Effects files also include a section called the technique. The technique is a way for the effect file to declare a method of shading behavior.

Each technique has a set of vertex and pixel shaders that it uses as vertices and pixels are passed through the pipeline. Effects allow for multiple techniques to be defined but you must have at least one technique defined. Each technique can also contain multiple passes. Most techniques you come across will contain only one pass but just be aware that multiple passes are possible for more complicated effects. Each pass uses the available shader hardware to perform different kinds of special effects.

After loading the effect file, you need to gain access to its technique in order to use it. The technique is then stored in an ID3D10EffectTechnique object for use later when rendering or defining a vertex layout. A small code sample showing how to create the technique object from an effect is shown here:

```
// The name of the technique in the effect file
LPCSTR effectTechniqueName = "Render";
// The technique object
ID3D10EffectTechnique*  pTechnique;


// Obtain the technique
pTechnique = pEffect->GetTechniqueByName( effectTechniqueName );
```

You now have a technique object ready to use when drawing your objects. Techniques are used by looping through the available passes and calling your draw functions. Before drawing using the shader technique in a pass, the technique is applied preparing the hardware for drawing. The Apply function is used to set the current technique.

```
// Render an object
D3D10_TECHNIQUE_DESC techniqueDescription;
pTechnique->GetDesc(&techniqueDescription);

// Loop through the technique passes
for(UINT p=0; p < techniqueDescription.Passes; ++p)
{
    pTechnique->GetPassByIndex(p)->Apply(0);

    // Draw function
}
```

Note

The Apply function takes only a single parameter that is currently unused for Direct3D. 0 is always passed in for this value.

Vertex Buffers

A vertex buffer is at its most basic, an array of vertices. This array is contained within a single chunk of memory ready to be passed to the video card for drawing. The entire job of the vertex buffer is to hold a collection of vertices that Direct3D will use to create 3D objects with. All vertices for an object must live in a vertex buffer so they can be drawn.

Creating a Vertex Buffer

Vertex buffers are based on the ID3D10Buffer interface and are created using the function CreateBuffer. The CreateBuffer function has multiple uses; it can create both vertex and index buffers. Because the function can be used in multiple ways, you have to define what you want it to do by filling out a D3D10_BUFFER_DESC structure. This structure describes not only the type of buffer you want, but the size and type of the data it will contain.

```
typedef struct D3D10_BUFFER_DESC {
    UINT ByteWidth;
    D3D10_USAGE Usage;
    UINT BindFlags;
    UINT CPUAccessFlags;
    UINT MiscFlags;
} D3D10_BUFFER_DESC;
```

The D3D10_BUFFER_DESC structure encompasses five variables.

The first variable, ByteWidth, is the number of bytes required for all the vertices the buffer will contain. This can be calculated by multiplying the number of vertices by the size of the custom vertex structure.

```
sizeof(VertexPosStruct) * numVertices;
```

The Usage variable details how the buffer will be used by the system. In most cases using a value of D3D10_USAGE_DEFAULT is acceptable, letting the system know the buffer will be updated only occasionally. If you absolutely will not be changing the data contained in the buffer, use the value D3D10_USAGE_IMMUTABLE. This will allow the system to optimize the access of the vertex buffer. If you will be changing the information in the buffer regularly, the value D3D10_USAGE_DYNAMIC is for you. The system will make sure the buffer is accessible to you for updates.

The BindFlags variable dictates the type of buffer being created. In the case of vertex buffers, a value of D3D10_BIND_VERTEX_BUFFER should be used.

CPUAccessFlags specifies whether the CPU should have access to the data in the buffer. If you want to be able to update a buffer quite often, use the value D3D10_CPU_ACCESS_WRITE. Otherwise, a value of 0 can be used.

The final variable, MiscFlags, should have a value of 0 if you have a single Direct3D device. Setting a value of D3D10_RESOURCE_MISC_SHARED allows the buffer to be shared across multiple devices.

Now that you've described what type of buffer you want to create, you have the opportunity to fill that buffer with some data during the buffer creation process using the D3D10_SUBRESOURCE_DATA structure.

The D3D10_SUBRESOURCE_DATA structure builds a subresource filled with your vertex data that is then assigned to the buffer.

Since you're creating a vertex buffer, the initial data will be filled with vertices. The D3D10_SUBRESOURCE_DATA structure contains a variable called pSysMem whose purpose is to point to an array of data; in this instance, an array of vertices.

```
D3D10_SUBRESOURCE_DATA InitData;
InitData.pSysMem = vertices;
```

You now know the type of buffer you're creating and have a subresource created to pass into; those were the two items you needed before creating the buffer. You can now call the CreateBuffer function, passing in the buffer description and subresource structures. The CreateBuffer function fills in the pVertexBuffer variable with the newly created vertex buffer.

```
ID3D10Buffer* pVertexBuffer;

// Do the creation of the actual vertex buffer
hr = pD3DDevice->CreateBuffer(&bufferDescription, &InitData, &pVertexBuffer);
```

The following code sample shows the steps necessary to create a vertex buffer.

```
ID3D10Buffer* pVertexBuffer;

// Create vertex buffer
VertexPosStruct vertices[] =
```

```
{
    D3DXVECTOR3(0.0f, 0.5f, 0.5f),
    D3DXVECTOR3(0.5f, -0.5f, 0.5f),
    D3DXVECTOR3(-0.5f, -0.5f, 0.5f),
};

// Calculate the number of vertices in the array
int numVertices = sizeof(vertices) / sizeof(VertexPosStruct);

D3D10_BUFFER_DESC bufferDescription;
bufferDescription.Usage = D3D10_USAGE_DEFAULT;
bufferDescription.ByteWidth = sizeof(VertexPosStruct) * numVertices;
bufferDescription.BindFlags = D3D10_BIND_VERTEX_BUFFER;
bufferDescription.CPUAccessFlags = 0;
bufferDescription.MiscFlags = 0;

D3D10_SUBRESOURCE_DATA InitData;
InitData.pSysMem = vertices;

// Do the creation of the actual vertex buffer
hr = pD3DDevice->CreateBuffer(&bufferDescription, &InitData, &pVertexBuffer);
if(FAILED(hr))
{
    return false;
}
```

Before drawing can take place, the vertex buffer must be bound to the Direct3D pipeline using the IASetVertexBuffers function. This function allows the vertices in the buffer to be accessed and used for drawing. The IASetVertexBuffers function requires five parameters.

The first parameter is the starting slot. Since this function allows for more than one vertex buffer to be bound at a time, this parameter lets Direct3D know which vertex buffer you want to start with. Multiple vertex buffers can be passed into this function as part of an array.

The second parameter is the number of vertex buffers in the array. Most of the time, only a single buffer is being bound so you'll commonly see 1 being used.

The third parameter is a pointer to the array of vertex buffers. If only one buffer is being used, this will point to the single buffer.

The next parameter is called the stride. The stride is similar to pitch and means the number of bytes that each vertex in the buffer requires. The stride can be determined by using the `sizeof` function on the custom vertex structure. This parameter allows for an array of stride values to be passed in if more than one vertex buffer is being bound.

The final parameter is the offset value. The offset value defines the first vertex in each buffer to be used. If you intend to use all the vertices in a buffer, then this value should be 0.

The following example call shows how to use the `IASetVertexBuffers` function.

```
// Set vertex buffer
UINT stride = sizeof(VertexPosStruct);
UINT offset = 0;
pD3DDevice->IASetVertexBuffers(0, 1, &modelObject->pVertexBuffer, &stride,
&offset);
```

Drawing a Triangle

The order in which the vertices appear in the vertex buffer is important. When Direct3D is drawing, the order the vertices are used is based on their order within the vertex buffer. Ordering the vertices in a haphazard way can cause objects to appear to be missing sides.

The rendering of an object defined by a vertex buffer is easy. Techniques can consist of one or more passes. When drawing, you need to loop through these passes and apply the technique to each pass and then draw the vertices in the vertex buffer. This allows the vertices to be drawn based on the currently active technique. The following code shows a simple drawing call that uses an effect technique.

```
// Bind the vertex buffer and set the input layout before drawing
// Set the input layout
pD3DDevice->IASetInputLayout(modelObject->pVertexLayout);

// Set vertex buffer
UINT stride = sizeof(VertexPosStruct);
UINT offset = 0;
pD3DDevice->IASetVertexBuffers(0,
    1,
    &modelObject->pVertexBuffer,
    &stride,
    &offset);

// Set primitive topology
pD3DDevice->IASetPrimitiveTopology(D3D10_PRIMITIVE_TOPOLOGY_TRIANGLELIST);
```

```
// Render an object
D3D10_TECHNIQUE_DESC techniqueDescription;
pTechnique->GetDesc(&techniqueDescription);

// Loop through the technique passes
for(UINT p=0; p < techniqueDescription.Passes; ++p)
{
    pTechnique->GetPassByIndex(p)->Apply(0);
    pD3DDevice->Draw(numVertices, 0);
}
```

Topology

At this point, Direct3D knows you have a vertex buffer and it knows you want to draw the vertices, but it is still unsure how those vertices should be drawn. Direct3D supports multiple ways of drawing the same set of vertices. Your vertices can be drawn as a series of individual triangles, as a series of lines, or as interconnected triangles with each depending on the one before it. How the vertices are drawn is referred to as *primitive types* or *topology*.

The topology determines how the vertices that make up an object are used. If you draw the vertices as a series of individual triangles, that is called a triangle list. A bunch of interconnected triangles is called a triangle strip. A triangle strip takes three vertices to create the first triangle, but only one vertex is needed to define the second and subsequent triangles. When optimizing your drawing, it is best to send as little information to be drawn as possible. If you need examples of the different primitive types, re-read the last section of Chapter 5.

The topology is set using the IASetPrimitiveTopology function. This function takes only a single parameter and should be used before the vertices in a buffer are sent to be drawn.

```
// Set primitive topology
pD3DDevice->IASetPrimitiveTopology(D3D10_PRIMITIVE_TOPOLOGY_TRIANGLELIST);
```

Some of the acceptable values that can be sent to the IASetPrimitiveTopology function are:

- **D3D10_PRIMITIVE_TOPOLOGY_POINTLIST**—the vertices are a series of unconnected points in space.

- **D3D10_PRIMITIVE_TOPOLOGY_TRIANGLELIST**—a collection of unconnected triangles.

■ **D3D10_PRIMITIVE_TOPOLOGY_TRIANGLESTRIP**—a series of inter-connected triangles.

A few more values can be found in the DirectX SDK help documents.

The Draw Function

The Draw function is the final step needed to get your object on the screen. Draw requires only two parameters.

The first parameter is the number of vertices that are to be drawn. Most of the time, this will reflect the number of vertices within your vertex buffer.

The second parameter is the starting vertex index. You don't have to draw all the vertices within a buffer, so this value allows you to start anywhere.

```
pD3DDevice->Draw(numVertices, 0);
```

A full example of drawing using vertex buffers can be found on the CD-ROM in the Chapter6\example1 directory. Figure 6.1 shows what the triangle will look like when it's drawn.

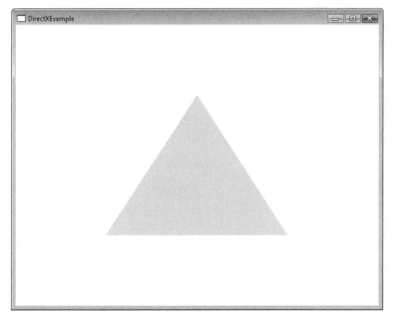

Figure 6.1
The final triangle being drawn.

Collecting the Common Items

When you get to the point where you're drawing more than one object, the number of variables needed for each object starts to get out of hand. I've collected the variables used for each object into a single structure type called ModelObject. All the information Direct3D needs to properly store and draw an object can be stored in ModelObject. Using ModelObject you can create a single object cleanly or even create multiple objects.

```
typedef struct
{
    // Shader variables
    ID3D10Effect* pEffect;
    ID3D10EffectTechnique* pTechnique;

    // Vertex information
    ID3D10Buffer* pVertexBuffer;
    UINT numVertices;
    ID3D10InputLayout* pVertexLayout;
}ModelObject;
```

Optimizing the Drawing Using Index Buffers

Now that you know how to draw an object using a vertex buffer, it's time to take it a step further. You'll notice as you advance to more complicated objects you'll end up using some vertices more than once, sharing them between triangles. For instance, drawing a square consisting of two triangles equates to six vertices. Two of these vertices are used twice, so there's not really a reason that they need to be stored in the vertex buffer more than once. Removing the extra shared vertices and redrawing the object though would give less than desired results. Index buffers give you the power to refer to any vertex in the vertex buffer and use it over and over.

The four unique vertices that make up the square can be stored in the vertex buffer and when the two triangles are created they both just reference the common vertices. While the savings on a small object like a simple square won't be very much, imagine if you're eliminating duplicate vertices from a complicated object containing thousands of triangles.

There are four vertices in the following array declaration. Each of these vertices represents a corner of a square.

```
// Create vertex buffer
VertexPosStruct vertices[] =
```

```
{
    D3DXVECTOR3(-0.5f, 0.5f, 0.5f), // 0
    D3DXVECTOR3(0.5f, 0.5f, 0.5f),  // 1
    D3DXVECTOR3(0.5f, -0.5f, 0.5f),  // 2
    D3DXVECTOR3(-0.5f, -0.5f, 0.5f),   // 3
};
```

Since it would take two triangles to draw the square, there are not enough vertices listed. By introducing an index buffer though, the square can be drawn properly. The following declaration sets up the indices needed for the square.

```
DWORD indices[] =
{
    0,1,3,
    1,2,3
};
```

Note

Triangle strips are not always the answer to solving a problem of too many vertices. Most 3D objects can't be broken down in a single triangle strip but can be optimized using indices.

Creating an Index Buffer

Index buffers and vertex buffers are virtually identical except for the type of data they contain. Being as they are both seen by Direct3D as buffer resources, index buffers are created in a similar fashion to vertex buffers using the CreateBuffer function. The biggest change in the creation process comes in the filling out of the D3D10_BUFFER_DESC structure. Since the buffer being created is an index buffer, the value being passed into the BindFlags variable should be D3D10_BIND-INDEX_BUFFER. This lets Direct3D know the type of buffer to create. An example of how to create an index buffer is shown next.

```
// The indices that will be in the buffer
DWORD indices[] =
{
    0,1,3,
    1,2,3
};

// Get the number of indices based on the size of the index array
numIndices = sizeof(indices) / sizeof(DWORD);
```

```
// The structure describing how the index buffer should be created
D3D10_BUFFER_DESC bd;
bd.Usage = D3D10_USAGE_DEFAULT;
bd.ByteWidth = sizeof(DWORD) * numIndices;
bd.BindFlags = D3D10_BIND_INDEX_BUFFER;
bd.CPUAccessFlags = 0;
bd.MiscFlags = 0;

D3D10_SUBRESOURCE_DATA InitData;
InitData.pSysMem = indices;

// Create the index buffer
HRESULT hr = pD3DDevice->CreateBuffer(&bd, &InitData, &pIndexBuffer);
if (FAILED(hr))
{
    return false;
}
```

Since each object you create will now need to store the index buffer object as well as the number of indices in the buffer, two new variables can be added to the ModelObject structure. The new variables are in bold.

```
typedef struct
{
    ID3D10Effect* pEffect;
    ID3D10EffectTechnique* pTechnique;

    // Vertex information
    ID3D10Buffer* pVertexBuffer;
    UINT numVertices;
    ID3D10InputLayout*        pVertexLayout;

    // Index information
    ID3D10Buffer* pIndexBuffer;
    UINT numIndices;
}ModelObject;
```

DrawIndexed

The Draw function you used previously has a limitation, it can't draw indexed objects. The DrawIndexed function is used to draw objects using an index buffer. DrawIndexed is very similar to the Draw function discussed earlier except it draws based on indices. The DrawIndexed function takes three parameters.

The first parameter is the number of indices to use. This will normally be a value equal to the number of indices in your index buffer.

The second parameter is the starting index offset. You don't have to use all the indices in the index buffer, so this value allows you to begin anywhere in the buffer.

The final parameter is the starting index for the vertices. This value is the same as the vertex index parameter that you pass to the Draw function.

An example DrawIndexed call is shown here:

```
pD3DDevice->DrawIndexed(numIndices, 0, 0);
```

Before DrawIndexed can correctly draw your objects, you need to make sure that your vertex layout and vertex and index buffers have been set correctly. The following code shows the calls that should be made right before you attempt to draw your object.

```
// Set the input layout
pD3DDevice->IASetInputLayout(pVertexLayout);

// Set vertex buffer
UINT stride = sizeof(VertexPosStruct);
UINT offset = 0;
pD3DDevice->IASetVertexBuffers(0, 1, &pVertexBuffer, &stride, &offset);

// Set index buffer
pD3DDevice->IASetIndexBuffer(pIndexBuffer, DXGI_FORMAT_R32_UINT, 0 );

// Set primitive topology
pD3DDevice->IASetPrimitiveTopology(D3D10_PRIMITIVE_TOPOLOGY_TRIANGLELIST);
```

The IASetIndexBuffer function is similar in functionality to IASetVertexBuffers, except the indices are being applied to the hardware.

Although index buffers can definitely benefit you in terms of optimizing your objects, they have one major downside. Because index buffers promote vertex sharing, problems can arise concerning some vertex properties such as colors or texture coordinates. In the case of a cube, a single vertex will affect three different sides. If that single vertex contained blue color data, all three sides will be blending blue. If you then wanted to make each side of the cube a completely separate color, you would need to duplicate the vertices that make up those sides and set them with new vertex color data.

Figure 6.2
A square created using `DrawIndexed`.

A full example of how to use index buffers can be found in the Chapter6\
example2 directory on the CD-ROM.

Figure 6.2 shows a square created by drawing two triangles using the `DrawIndexed`
function.

Adding Complexity

As I mentioned previously, vertices can have any number of properties associated
with them, from texture coordinates and normals to vertex colors. The process of
adding another property to a vertex definition isn't very complicated but does
require a change to the layout of the vertex in memory. To demonstrate the
process, I'm going to walk you through adding vertex colors to the vertex structure.

Vertex Colors

Vertex colors allow each vertex in an object to have a color associated with them.
When drawing an object, the edges are colored based on the color of the vertices.
Sometimes the vertex colors are all the same, but most of the time they're
different, allowing for a shift in the color during rendering.

In the previous examples, you weren't specifically passing around a color for your vertices, but one was defined for you. Within the vertex shader in the simple.fx file you've been using, a default color was being passed along from the vertex shader to the pixel shader causing your objects to appear yellow. You'll see the code for the vertex shader here with the color portion in bold.

```
/////////////////////////////////////////////
// Vertex Shader - Main Function
/////////////////////////////////////////////

PS_INPUT VS(float4 Pos : POSITION)
{
    PS_INPUT psInput;

    psInput.Pos = Pos;
    psInput.Color = float4(1.0f, 1.0f, 0.0f, 1.0f);

    return psInput;
}
```

Instead of the shader implementing this functionality with a default color, you're going to learn how to set the color of each vertex when you create it and then how to pass this value down to the shader to be used.

Updating the Custom Vertex Structure

The first step to adding the support for vertex colors is the updating of the custom vertex structure. Since vertex colors can support any 32-bit RGBA color value, they're going to be stored using a D3DXVECTOR4 type. You can see the updated vertex structure here:

```
struct VertexPosColorStruct
{
    D3DXVECTOR3 Pos;
    D3DXVECTOR4 Color;
};
```

I've updated the name of the structure to reflect the change to the included types. As you build new vertex structures, it helps to make sure the structure name gives a hint to the type of data it contains.

Now that the vertex structure is updated, you can create arrays of vertices using the new format. Each item in the array in the following code contains both a position and vertex color.

```
// Create vertex buffer
// Define both a position and a vertex color
VertexPosColorStruct vertices[] =
{
    { D3DXVECTOR3(0.0f, 0.5f, 0.5f), D3DXVECTOR4(1.0f, 0.0f, 0.0f, 1.0f) },
    { D3DXVECTOR3(0.5f, -0.5f, 0.5f), D3DXVECTOR4(0.0f, 1.0f, 0.0f, 1.0f) },
    { D3DXVECTOR3(-0.5f, -0.5f, 0.5f), D3DXVECTOR4(0.0f, 0.0f, 1.0f, 1.0f) },
};
```

Each vertex being created has a different color associated with it. Any new properties that you add to the vertex structure can be initialized with a default value in this manner.

At this point you can create arrays of vertices using the new properties, but Direct3D still isn't aware of the change; you need to update the vertex layout. The following layout supports both a vertex position and color but can be updated to support any number of new properties.

```
// The vertex input layout
D3D10_INPUT_ELEMENT_DESC layout[] =
{
    { "POSITION", 0, DXGI_FORMAT_R32G32B32_FLOAT, 0, 0,
D3D10_INPUT_PER_VERTEX_DATA, 0 },
    { "COLOR", 0, DXGI_FORMAT_R32G32B32A32_FLOAT, 0, 12,
D3D10_INPUT_PER_VERTEX_DATA, 0 },
};
```

That's all there really is to it. Any new vertices you define using the updated structure will contain the new property. Even though it seems like very little effort, I wanted to walk through the entire process to make sure you knew every piece that was involved. At this point, all the changes are done for the code side of things, but there is a small change to be made to the shader before rendering will work properly.

Shader Changes

Previously, the color of the vertex was determined by a hard coded color value in the shader. Now that the vertex structure allows the color to be defined within the vertex structure, the shader needs to change slightly to handle this.

The vertex shader was only allowing for a vertex position to be passed in before. To support vertex colors properly, the vertex shader needs to allow for the color to be passed in as well as the position. This gives the vertex shader access to the color value defined in the vertex structure. Since the shader is going to allow the color to remain as it was set, it will just pass the color value along to the pixel shader without making any changes. You can see in the following shader code where the psInput.Color is set to the input color value passed into the vertex shader.

The pixel shader doesn't actually have to be changed in any way since the color from the vertex shader was already being passed out as the final color value.

```
// PS_INPUT - input variables to the pixel shader
// This struct is created and filled in by the
// vertex shader
struct PS_INPUT
{
    float4 Pos : SV_POSITION;
    float4 Color : COLOR0;
};


//////////////////////////////////////////////
// Vertex Shader - Main Function
//////////////////////////////////////////////
PS_INPUT VS(float4 Pos : POSITION, float4 Color : COLOR)
{
    PS_INPUT psInput;

    // Pass through both the position and the color
    psInput.Pos = Pos;
    psInput.Color = Color;

    return psInput;
}


//////////////////////////////////////////////
// Pixel Shader
//////////////////////////////////////////////
float4 PS(PS_INPUT psInput) : SV_Target
{
    return psInput.Color;
}
```

Vertex colors were just an example of the types of information that can be added to a vertex definition.

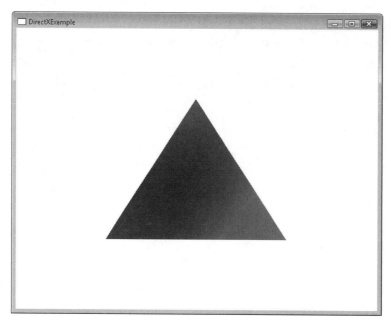

Figure 6.3
A triangle with multiple vertex colors.

Figure 6.3 shows the updated triangle.

A full example of using vertex colors can be found in the Chapter6\example3 directory on the CD-ROM.

Adding a Third Dimension—The Cube

The cube is almost as famous as the triangle when it comes to teaching 3D graphics theories. Because of the cube's simple yet fully 3D shape, it is a great point to start from. The cube is simply an extension of the triangle you've already created. Even though the cube is made up of squares or faces, the faces themselves are made up of triangles.

To create a full cube, four sides, a top, and bottom faces need to be created. These faces are created in such a manner to cause them to touch and form a solid cube. The triangles that make up the cube are defined in the same way the single triangle was defined in the last section. The following `vertices` array defines all the triangles needed to make up the cube.

```
VertexPosColorStruct vertices[] =
{
    // 1st face - first triangle
    { D3DXVECTOR3(-5.0f,  5.0f, 5.0f), D3DXVECTOR4(1.0f,0.0f,0.0f,0.0f)},
    { D3DXVECTOR3(-5.0f, -5.0f, 5.0f), D3DXVECTOR4(1.0f,0.0f,0.0f,0.0f)},
    { D3DXVECTOR3(5.0f,   5.0f, 5.0f), D3DXVECTOR4(1.0f,0.0f,0.0f,0.0f)},
    // 1st face - second triangle
    { D3DXVECTOR3(5.0f,   5.0f, 5.0f), D3DXVECTOR4(1.0f,0.0f,0.0f,0.0f)},
    { D3DXVECTOR3(-5.0f, -5.0f, 5.0f), D3DXVECTOR4(1.0f,0.0f,0.0f,0.0f)},
    { D3DXVECTOR3(5.0f,  -5.0f, 5.0f), D3DXVECTOR4(1.0f,0.0f,0.0f,0.0f)},

    // 2nd face - first triangle
    { D3DXVECTOR3(-5.0f,  5.0f, -5.0f), D3DXVECTOR4(0.0f,1.0f,0.0f,0.0f)},
    { D3DXVECTOR3(5.0f,   5.0f, -5.0f), D3DXVECTOR4(0.0f,1.0f,0.0f,0.0f)},
    { D3DXVECTOR3(-5.0f, -5.0f, -5.0f), D3DXVECTOR4(0.0f,1.0f,0.0f,0.0f)},
    // 2nd face - second triangle
    { D3DXVECTOR3(-5.0f, -5.0f, -5.0f), D3DXVECTOR4(0.0f,1.0f,0.0f,0.0f)},
    { D3DXVECTOR3(5.0f,   5.0f, -5.0f), D3DXVECTOR4(0.0f,1.0f,0.0f,0.0f)},
    { D3DXVECTOR3(5.0f,  -5.0f, -5.0f), D3DXVECTOR4(0.0f,1.0f,0.0f,0.0f)},

    // 3rd face - first triangle
    { D3DXVECTOR3(-5.0f, 5.0f,  5.0f), D3DXVECTOR4(0.0f,0.0f,1.0f,0.0f)},
    { D3DXVECTOR3(5.0f, 5.0f,   5.0f), D3DXVECTOR4(0.0f,0.0f,1.0f,0.0f)},
    { D3DXVECTOR3(-5.0f, 5.0f, -5.0f), D3DXVECTOR4(0.0f,0.0f,1.0f,0.0f)},
    // 3rd face - second triangle
    { D3DXVECTOR3(-5.0f, 5.0f, -5.0f), D3DXVECTOR4(0.0f,0.0f,1.0f,0.0f)},
    { D3DXVECTOR3(5.0f, 5.0f, 5.0f),   D3DXVECTOR4(0.0f,0.0f,1.0f,0.0f)},
    { D3DXVECTOR3(5.0f, 5.0f, -5.0f),  D3DXVECTOR4(0.0f,0.0f,1.0f,0.0f)},

    // 4th face - first triangle
    { D3DXVECTOR3(-5.0f, -5.0f,  5.0f), D3DXVECTOR4(1.0f,0.5f,0.0f,0.0f)},
    { D3DXVECTOR3(-5.0f, -5.0f, -5.0f), D3DXVECTOR4(1.0f,0.5f,0.0f,0.0f)},
    { D3DXVECTOR3(5.0f, -5.0f,  5.0f),  D3DXVECTOR4(1.0f,0.5f,0.0f,0.0f)},
    // 4th face - second triangle
    { D3DXVECTOR3(5.0f, -5.0f,  5.0f),  D3DXVECTOR4(1.0f,0.5f,0.0f,0.0f)},
    { D3DXVECTOR3(-5.0f, -5.0f, -5.0f), D3DXVECTOR4(1.0f,0.5f,0.0f,0.0f)},
    { D3DXVECTOR3(5.0f, -5.0f, -5.0f),  D3DXVECTOR4(1.0f,0.5f,0.0f,0.0f)},

    // 5th face - first triangle
    { D3DXVECTOR3(5.0f,  5.0f, -5.0f),  D3DXVECTOR4(0.0f,1.0f,0.5f,0.0f)},
    { D3DXVECTOR3(5.0f,  5.0f,  5.0f),  D3DXVECTOR4(0.0f,1.0f,0.5f,0.0f)},
    { D3DXVECTOR3(5.0f, -5.0f, -5.0f),  D3DXVECTOR4(0.0f,1.0f,0.5f,0.0f)},
    // 5th face - second triangle
```

```
    { D3DXVECTOR3(5.0f, -5.0f, -5.0f),   D3DXVECTOR4(0.0f,1.0f,0.5f,0.0f)},
    { D3DXVECTOR3(5.0f,  5.0f,  5.0f),   D3DXVECTOR4(0.0f,1.0f,0.5f,0.0f)},
    { D3DXVECTOR3(5.0f, -5.0f,  5.0f),   D3DXVECTOR4(0.0f,1.0f,0.5f,0.0f)},

    // 6th face - first triangle
    {D3DXVECTOR3(-5.0f,  5.0f, -5.0f),   D3DXVECTOR4(0.5f,0.0f,1.0f,0.0f)},
    {D3DXVECTOR3(-5.0f, -5.0f, -5.0f),   D3DXVECTOR4(0.5f,0.0f,1.0f,0.0f)},
    {D3DXVECTOR3(-5.0f,  5.0f,  5.0f),   D3DXVECTOR4(0.5f,0.0f,1.0f,0.0f)},
    // 6th face - second triangle
    {D3DXVECTOR3(-5.0f,  5.0f,  5.0f),   D3DXVECTOR4(0.5f,0.0f,1.0f,0.0f)},
    {D3DXVECTOR3(-5.0f, -5.0f, -5.0f),   D3DXVECTOR4(0.5f,0.0f,1.0f,0.0f)},
    {D3DXVECTOR3(-5.0f, -5.0f,  5.0f),   D3DXVECTOR4(0.5f,0.0f,1.0f,0.0f)},
};
```

You're probably wondering why I declared every triangle in the cube instead of just the six unique vertices that make up the cube. Remember earlier where I said that when you share vertices you have to share colors and texture coordinates? The cube being created above has a different vertex color for each face; sharing the vertices would have caused the colors to blend between vertices.

The triangles were defined as a triangle list to allow the whole cube to be drawn with a single Draw call. Before drawing the newly defined cube, make sure to set the topology to D3D10_PRIMITIVE_TOPOLOGY_TRIANGLELIST.

```
// Set primitive topology
pD3DDevice->IASetPrimitiveTopology(D3D10_PRIMITIVE_TOPOLOGY_TRIANGLELIST);
// draw the cube using all 36 vertices and 12 triangles
pD3DDevice->Draw(36,0);
```

Object Translation and Rotation

If you were to run an example with the cube vertices defined, you'd be disappointed to see just a single colored square sitting in the center of your screen. Because the cube is a 3D object, it exists within a three-dimensional space but is currently oriented in a way where only the front part of the cube is visible. To give you an idea as to what the rest of the cube looks like, you're going to learn how to rotate it. Rotating the cube or any object has a few steps:

1. Translating and rotating the object within world space using the world matrix. This makes sure the object is positioned where you want it.

2. Setting up and positioning of the virtual camera. The virtual camera is set up and positioned using the view matrix.

Figure 6.4
A rotating cube.

3. Creation of the projection matrix. This translates the scene into screen space.

4. The final piece requires these three matrices to be combined and sent to the shader. The shader then makes sure that all the vertices sent through it will be oriented properly.

Each piece of this process is required to put an object through the geometry pipeline described in Chapter 5. The cube shown in Figure 6.4 is what you should see when this process is successful.

The World Space Transformation

This is where the D3DXMatrixRotationY function from the last chapter comes in. Take a look at the following code snippet. A rotation angle is created and applied to the WorldMatrix causing the cube to spin around the Y axis. You'll see the rotationAngle variable update; this constantly gives the rotation a new angle to work with.

```
static float rotationAngle = 0.0f;

// create the rotation matrix using the rotation angle
D3DXMatrixRotationY(&WorldMatrix, rotationAngle);
```

```
// increment the rotationAngle for next time
rotationAngle += (float)D3DX_PI * 0.2125f;
```

Because the rotationAngle and WorldMatrix variables need to be updated constantly, the preceding code should be called once per frame. If you take a look at the code in the Chapter6\example4 directory on the CD-ROM, you'll find an example showing how to rotate the cube where these variables are updated in the PrepareModelObject function.

By updating the world matrix with the cube's rotation, the cube should be positioned correctly.

Setting Up the Virtual Camera

The view matrix positions the virtual camera allowing you to view the scene from any point you want. For this example, the view matrix is initialized and places a virtual camera approximately 20 units back on the Z axis and 10 units up along the Y. This moves the camera far enough back and up to be able to view the rotating cube correctly. By placing the camera slightly above the cube, you'll be able to set the top of the cube as well. The virtual camera will remain stationary, so the view matrix is set only once.

```
D3DXMatrixLookAtLH(&ViewMatrix,
    new D3DXVECTOR3(0.0f, 10.0f, -20.0f),
    new D3DXVECTOR3(0.0f, 0.0f, 0.0f),
    new D3DXVECTOR3(0.0f, 1.0f, 0.0f));
```

The view matrix is initialized using one of Direct3D's functions called D3DXMatrixLookAtLH. This function allows a view matrix to be created by using a vector representing the virtual camera's position, where this camera is looking, and which direction is up.

The Projection Matrix

The projection matrix makes sure that your 3D scene is mapped correctly into the 2D viewport you have available. The matrix is initialized by the D3DXMatrixPerspectiveFovLH function using the width and height of the target window. The projection matrix controls the field of view (FOV) as well. The FOV is the viewing angle for the virtual lens attached to your in-game camera.

For the most part, unless the viewport is constantly resizing or you need to readjust the FOV, the projection matrix can be set once at the start of your application.

```
D3DXMatrixPerspectiveFovLH(&ProjectionMatrix,
    (float)D3DX_PI * 0.5f,
    (float)width/(float)height,
    0.1f,
    100.0f);
```

Combining the Matrices for the Shader

At this point you should have three matrices defined; two of them you won't have to mess with again and the world matrix, which will be constantly updating. Each frame, the shader will need to know what the current transformation matrices are so the objects in the scene can be updated and placed correctly.

Before the matrices are sent into the shader, you'll need to combine them into a single matrix. This reduces the amount of code needed in the shader to apply the transformation.

```
// Combine and send the final matrix to the shader
D3DXMATRIX finalMatrix = (WorldMatrix * ViewMatrix * ProjectionMatrix);
pProjectionMatrixVariable->SetMatrix((float*)&finalMatrix);
```

The shader is the last part I haven't talked about yet. Previously the position of each vertex was just passed along; now each vertex is being multiplied in the shader by the Projection variable. The Projection variable contains the calculation from the variable finalMatrix. This correctly positions the cube based on the rotation values set earlier.

```
///////////////////////////////////////////////
// Vertex Shader - Main Function
///////////////////////////////////////////////
PS_INPUT VS(float4 Pos : POSITION, float4 Color : COLOR)
{
    PS_INPUT psInput;

    // Pass through the color
    psInput.Pos = mul( Pos, Projection );
    psInput.Color = Color;

    return psInput;
}
```

The cube should now be rotating happily on the screen like in Figure 6.4. As it rotates, you'll be able to see the colors are different for each face on the cube. You can update the rotationAngle variable to either speed up or slow down the rotation. You can refer to example four in the Chapter 6 directory on the CD-ROM for a complete example.

Rasterizer State

Looking at the rotating cube from the last section you can see the results of using multiple triangles to create each of the sides, but how do you actually see the triangles? Sure, it's good to know that the triangles were placed correctly, but how can you verify it? Well, Direct3D actually provides a way to look into your objects. You've probably seen 3D modeling software display objects in wireframe mode. This mode displays 3D objects using only their outline. This lets you see how objects are made up, sort of like seeing the frame of a house without the walls getting in the way.

By default, Direct3D operates in solid mode, which causes faces to be drawn opaquely. This can be changed though by altering the rasterizer state.

The rasterizer state tells Direct3D how things in the rasterizer stage should behave, such as what type of culling should take place, whether features like multisampling and scissoring are enabled, and the type of fill mode that should be used.

Rasterizer state objects are inherited from the ID3D10RasterizerState interface and are created using the CreateRasterizerState function.

The CreateRasterizerState function takes two parameters. The first is a pointer to a D3D10_RASTERIZER_DESC structure, which is used to detail the properties the new rasterizer state should have. The second parameter is the ID3D10RasterizerState object to be created.

```
HRESULT CreateRasterizerState(
    const D3D10_RASTERIZER_DESC *pRasterizerDesc,
    ID3D10RasterizerState **ppRasterizerState
);
```

As I mentioned before, the D3D10_RASTERIZER_DESC structure contains the properties the new rasterizer state should have when it is created.

```
typedef struct D3D10_RASTERIZER_DESC {
    D3D10_FILL_MODE FillMode;
    D3D10_CULL_MODE CullMode;
    BOOL FrontCounterClockwise;
    INT DepthBias;
    FLOAT DepthBiasClamp;
```

```
      FLOAT SlopeScaledDepthBias;
      BOOL DepthClipEnable;
      BOOL ScissorEnable;
      BOOL MultisampleEnable;
      BOOL AntialiasedLineEnable;
} D3D10_RASTERIZER_DESC;
```

The two parameters I'm going to talk about here are the D3D10_FILL_MODE and the D3D10_CULL_MODE.

The D3D10_FILL_MODE parameter controls how the geometry is going to be drawn. If you use the value D3D10_FILL_WIREFRAME, the geometry will be drawn in wireframe mode; otherwise, pass the value D3D10_FILL_SOLID to have all geometry drawn solid.

The second parameter is the culling mode parameter named D3D10_CULL_MODE. The culling mode tells the rasterizer which faces to draw and which to ignore. Imagine that you had a sphere made up of triangles. No matter which way you faced the sphere, not all of the triangles that make it up will be visible at any one time; only those triangles directly in front of you could be seen. The triangles on the back of the sphere are said to be back facing. Because of how the vertices that make up the triangles are defined, they have a particular winding order to them. The winding order is the direction in which vertices for a triangle are defined, clockwise or counterclockwise. Because of the nature of 3D objects, even if you defined all your triangles using the same winding order, just the act of rotating the object causes some of the triangles to be reversed from the camera point of view. Going back to the sphere, from the camera's perspective some of the triangles are clockwise and some are counterclockwise. The culling mode tells Direct3D which triangles it can safely ignore and not draw. The D3D10_CULL_MODE has three options:

- D3D10_CULL_NONE—says that no culling should take place, regardless of the winding order.

- D3D10_CULL_FRONT—means that all front facing triangles should be ignored.

- D3D10_CULL_BACK—all back facing triangles will not be drawn.

By specifying a culling mode, this cuts down on the number of triangles that you're asking Direct3D to draw.

If you want the details on all the other parameters in the D3D10_RASTERIZER_DESC structure, please consult the DirectX SDK documentation.

Once you have the structure filled out, it is safe to call the `CreateRasterizerState` function to create the new rasterizer state.

After the new rasterizer state is created, it must be set before its effects take place. You use the function `RSSetState` to change the currently active rasterizer state, which is provided by the `ID3D10Device` interface.

```
void RSSetState(
    ID3D10RasterizerState *pRasterizerState
);
```

The `RSSetState` function takes only a single parameter, a pointer to the new rasterizer state object.

The following code shows how a `D3D10_RASTERIZER_DESC` structure is created and filled out as well as a new rasterizer state created and set. The fill mode is being set to wireframe and the cull mode to front faces. All the other features are being disabled.

```
// The D3D10_RASTERIZER_DESC structure
D3D10_RASTERIZER_DESC rasterDescription;
rasterDescription.FillMode = D3D10_FILL_WIREFRAME;
rasterDescription.CullMode = D3D10_CULL_FRONT;
rasterDescription.FrontCounterClockwise = true;
rasterDescription.DepthBias = false;
rasterDescription.DepthBiasClamp = 0;
rasterDescription.SlopeScaledDepthBias = 0;
rasterDescription.DepthClipEnable = false;
rasterDescription.ScissorEnable = false;
rasterDescription.MultisampleEnable = false;
rasterDescription.AntialiasedLineEnable = false;

// Create a new rasterizer state
ID3D10RasterizerState *g_pRasterizerState;
pD3DDevice->CreateRasterizerState( &rasterDescription, &g_pRasterizerState);

// Set the new rasterizer state
pD3DDevice->RSSetState(g_pRasterizerState);
```

At this point the new rasterizer state will be in effect and all geometry will be drawn using the properties of the new state. Take a look at Figure 6.5, which shows the cube before being drawn in wireframe mode. The example in the Chapter6\example5 folder on the CD-ROM contains the source code for wireframe drawing of the rotating cube.

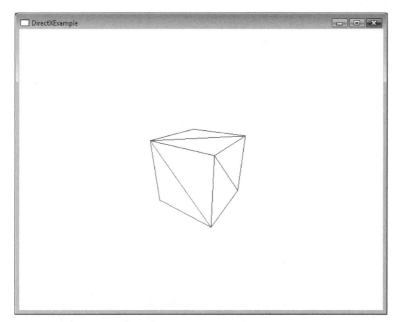

Figure 6.5
The cube drawn using wireframe mode.

Creating a 3D Grid

A cube is a nice start; it shows you how you can create entire 3D objects out of simple triangles. In this section, you're going to take this manual creation a step further with the creation of terrain. If you've ever seen games that take place in an outside area, like a flight simulator, then you've been exposed to terrain rendering. Terrain rendering is the generation of a landscape, normally based on a grid, which includes features like hills, valleys, and mountains. Generating an outdoor environment might seem to be an outlandish leap from a spinning cube, but it really isn't that different.

The entire terrain is going to be based on a two-dimensional grid with a fixed number of columns and rows. The grid is laid out as a series of quads made up of triangles; like I said, it's actually very similar to the cube you just created. Initially, because the grid is flat, your terrain will appear as a large single-colored quad unless you view it in wireframe mode. When viewing the wireframe, you'll be able to see all the triangles that make up the object.

Because it would be difficult and boring to generate every triangle in a huge land-scape by hand, I'm going to show you how to dynamically generate any size terrain.

Because the terrain is going to be based on a grid, the extents of this grid need to be defined first. Just to keep things even, I'm setting up the grid to be sixteen columns and sixteen rows.

```
// Grid Information
#define NUM_COLS 16
#define NUM_ROWS 16
```

The cells that are created by the rows and columns will need to have a bit of space between them so the vertices that will make up the terrain aren't bunched right next to each other. As you can see in the following definitions, each of the cells is going to be 32 × 32 in size.

```
// The width and height of each cell in the grid
#define CELL_WIDTH 32
#define CELL_HEIGHT 32
```

The grid itself will have 16 columns but it takes one more vertex to create the final cell. The following definitions allow for this extra vertex and are used in the generation of the terrain.

```
#define NUM_VERTSX (NUM_COLS + 1)
#define NUM_VERTSY (NUM_ROWS + 1)
```

Generating the Grid

Like the triangle and cube objects you created before, the first step is the filling of a buffer with all the vertices in the object. Instead of hardcoding all the vertices required, they're going to be generated using the extents of the grid. To do this I use a series of nested *for* loops. The outside loop goes through the rows with the inside loop representing the columns. When creating the grid, it is being set up so that the grid will extend away from the viewer in the positive Z direction. This minimizes the amount of movement needed to position the virtual camera.

Each of the vertex positions is created by simply multiplying the current X and Z values by the cell width and heights. You'll notice that the Y value for each vertex is being set to 0. This will be changed later, but for now just understand that this keeps the grid completely flat.

Take a look at the following code. This shows how all the vertices for this grid are generated. The vertices that make up the grid use the VertexPosColorStruct created earlier.

```
// create the vertices array large enough to hold all those needed
VertexPosColorStruct vertices[NUM_VERTSX * NUM_VERTSY];

// Fill the vertices array with the terrain values
for(int z=0; z < NUM_VERTSY; ++z)
{
    for(int x=0; x < NUM_VERTSX; ++x)
    {
        vertices[x + z * NUM_VERTSX].Pos.x = (float)x * CELL_WIDTH;
        vertices[x + z * NUM_VERTSX].Pos.z = (float)z * CELL_HEIGHT;

        // Restrict the height to 0
        vertices[x + z * NUM_VERTSX].Pos.y = 0.0f;

        // Create the default color
        vertices[x + z * NUM_VERTSX].Color = D3DXVECTOR4(1.0, 0.0f, 0.0f, 0.0f);
    }
}
```

After the vertex array is full, you need to create and fill the array of indices for the index buffer. To keep the index array simple, it is going to be filled with a series of triangles to create a triangle list. The first step is the sizing of the indices array. Each cell you create will require two triangles for a total of six vertices. The index array is sized to allow for all six vertices per cell.

Again, the indices are created using a series of nested loops. This keeps you from having to manually define all the indices for the array. Each cell is made up of a quad, so the inside of the loops will need to create two triangles. The triangles themselves are going to be laid out in a counterclockwise manner, making sure that all the triangles have the same winding order. Because the grid is being generated with triangle lists, there are going to be some vertices that are duplicated. Figure 6.6 shows how the triangles in the grid will be laid out.

You'll see that each of the triangles uses vertices from both the surrounding columns and rows. Look at the following code example that uses this layout to define the indices.

```
// Create the indices array, six vertices for each cell
DWORD indices[NUM_VERTSX * NUM_VERTSY * 6];

// The index counter
int curIndex = 0;
```

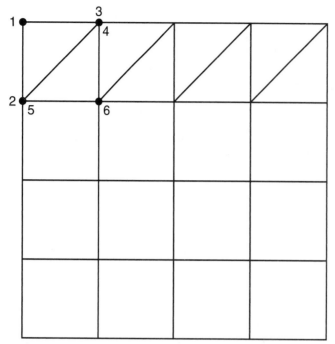

Figure 6.6
The grid layout.

```
// Fill the indices array to create the triangles needed for the terrain
// The triangles are created in a counterclockwise direction
for (int z=0; z < NUM_ROWS; z++)
{
    for (int x=0; x < NUM_COLS; x++)
    {
        // The current vertex to build off of
        int curVertex = x + (z * NUM_VERTSX);

        // Create the indices for the first triangle
        indices[curIndex]   = curVertex;
        indices[curIndex+1] = curVertex + NUM_VERTSX;
        indices[curIndex+2] = curVertex + 1;

        // Create the indices for the second triangle
        indices[curIndex+3] = curVertex + 1;
        indices[curIndex+4] = curVertex + NUM_VERTSX;
        indices[curIndex+5] = curVertex + NUM_VERTSX + 1;
```

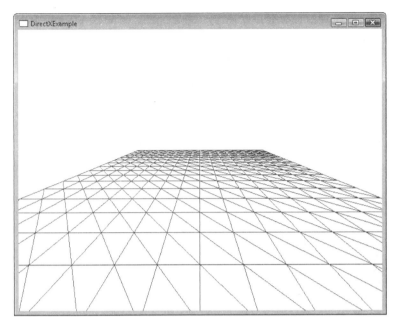

Figure 6.7
A wireframe grid.

```
        // increment curIndex by the number of vertices for the two triangles
        curIndex += 6;
    }
}
```

Once the index array is full, you can use it to create the index buffer you'll need when drawing the grid. Figure 6.7 shows what the grid looks like when rendered in wireframe mode.

Generating Terrain

The only difference between the grid you just created and an outdoor environment is height. As I mentioned before, outdoor environments have hills and valleys, so how do you add these features to the flat grid you have now? The key to adding height is in the code that generates the vertices. Remember how the Y value for all the vertices was being set to 0? By altering the value stored in Y, the height of that cell in the grid is altered as well. This value can be either positive, generating a hill or a negative value, allowing for a dip in the grid.

To allow for more of a dynamic variation, the following code uses the rand function to create the Y value and then uses the modulus (%) operator to restrict the height within the range of `CELL_HEIGHT`. This will keep the heights from being huge numbers.

```
// create the vertices array large enough to hold all those needed
VertexPosColorStruct vertices[NUM_VERTSX * NUM_VERTSY];

// Fill the vertices array with the terrain values
for(int z=0; z < NUM_VERTSY; ++z)
{
    for(int x=0; x < NUM_VERTSX; ++x)
    {
        vertices[x + z * NUM_VERTSX].Pos.x = (float)x * CELL_WIDTH;
        vertices[x + z * NUM_VERTSX].Pos.z = (float)z * CELL_HEIGHT;

        // Allow the height of the cell to be randomly decided
        vertices[x + z * NUM_VERTSX].Pos.y = (float)(rand() % CELL_HEIGHT);

        // Create the default color
        vertices[x + z * NUM_VERTSX].Color = D3DXVECTOR4(1.0, 0.0f, 0.0f, 0.0f);
    }
}
```

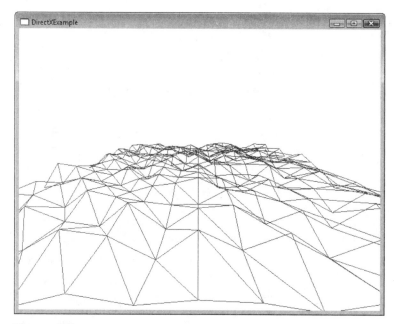

Figure 6.8
A heightmap drawn using wireframe mode.

Note

Terrain height is commonly generated using a heightmap. The heightmap is either an input file with a series of height values for each part of the grid or a grayscale image file where the brightness of each pixel determines the height in the grid.

If you look at Figure 6.8 you'll see the difference that the height makes. A full code example for generating terrain can be found in the Chapter6\example6 directory on the CD-ROM.

Summary

I know this chapter was a lot to take in, but you should now have an introductory understanding of what Direct3D has to offer you. Everything you create from this point will build on the foundations you learned here. In the next chapter, you'll be diving more deeply into the world of shaders.

Review Questions

You can find the answers to Review Questions in Appendix A, "Answers to End-of-Chapter Exercises."

1. What is the difference between a triangle list and a triangle strip?

2. Are index buffers required for all drawing? Why or why not?

3. Which function can be used to create a rotation matrix around the X axis?

4. Why must you be careful about the order in which matrices are combined?

5. What are the two modes the rasterizer can operate in?

On Your Own

1. Change the terrain to use a different color value based on the height.

2. Rotate the cube around more than one axis.

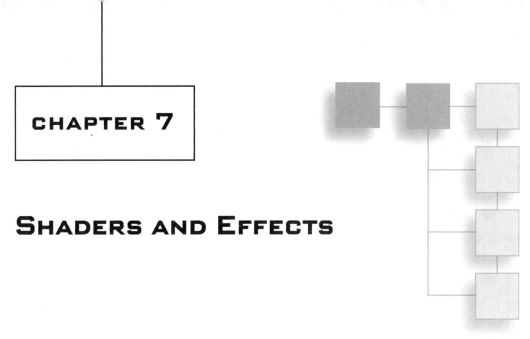

CHAPTER 7

SHADERS AND EFFECTS

Shaders have been a part of Direct3D for a while now. Vertex and pixel shaders have given developers the power to control every detail of how their data is manipulated in multiple stages of the pipeline, giving them an increased realism. Now with Direct3D10, the next iteration of shader technology is being released, shader model 4.0.

The capabilities of both vertex and pixel shaders have been increased. The number of instructions possible has gone up, more textures can be accessed, and shaders can be more complicated. Instead of just limiting the improvements to the previous shader types, shader model 4.0 introduces a third shader type, geometry shaders.

Geometry shaders allow you to work on whole primitive types, increasing the power and control you have over your scene. You'll be introduced to all three shader types in this chapter along with the effects framework.

Here's what you'll learn in this chapter:

- What an effect file is

- How to use the High Level Shading Language

- How to animate using a vertex shader

- How to light and illuminate a 3D scene

- How to use a geometry shader

Effect Files

While using shaders individually is still possible with Direct3D10, you'll find them extremely useful when grouped together into an effect. An effect is a simple way of packaging the needed vertex, pixel, and geometry shaders together to render objects in a particular way. The effect is loaded as a single object and the included shaders are executed when necessary. By changing the effect you're applying to your scene, you easily change the method Direct3D is using to do the rendering. Effects are defined with an effect file: a text format that is loaded in from disk, compiled, and executed.

Effect File Layout

Effect files are a way of containing a particular set of rendering functionality. Each effect, applied when drawing objects in your scene, dictates what the objects look like and how they're drawn. For example, you may create an effect whose job it is to texture objects; or you may create an effect to generate lighting bloom or blur. Effects have an amazing versatility in how they can be used.

Previously, vertex and pixel shaders were loaded and applied separately. Effects combine the shaders into a self-contained unit that encompasses functionality of multiple shader types.

Effects are comprised of a couple of different sections:

- **External variables**—Variables that get their data from the calling program.

- **Input structures**—Structures that define the information being passed between shaders. For example, information output from a vertex shader and passed as input into the pixel shader.

- **Vertex shader**—Portion of the effect file that handles processing of vertices.

- **Pixel shader**—Portion of the effect file that handles pixels.

- **Technique block(s)**—Defines the shaders and passes available within the effect.

There are other sections possible within an effect file, such as a geometry shader and a texture sampler. These will be discussed in other sections.

Below you'll find an example effect that contains all the necessary parts for a valid effect.

```
// constant buffer of external variables
cbuffer Variables
{
    matrix Projection;
};

// PS_INPUT - input variables to the pixel shader
// This struct is created and filled in by the vertex shader
struct PS_INPUT
{
    float4 Pos : SV_POSITION;
    float4 Color : COLOR0;
};

/////////////////////////////////////////////
// Vertex Shader - Main Function
/////////////////////////////////////////////
PS_INPUT VS(float4 Pos : POSITION, float4 Color : COLOR)
{
    PS_INPUT psInput;
    // Pass through both the position and the color
    psInput.Pos = mul(Pos, Projection);
    psInput.Color = Color;

    return psInput;
}


/////////////////////////////////////////////
// Pixel Shader
/////////////////////////////////////////////
float4 PS(PS_INPUT psInput) : SV_Target
{
    return psInput.Color;
}

// Define the technique
technique10 Render
{
```

```
    pass P0
    {
        SetVertexShader( CompileShader(vs_4_0, VS() ));
        SetGeometryShader(NULL);
        SetPixelShader( CompileShader(ps_4_0, PS() ));
    }
}
```

Loading an Effect File

You were introduced to effect file loading in Chapter 6, but I'm going to go over the process in a bit more detail. As I mentioned before, effect files are loaded using the D3DX10CreateEffectFromFile function. When loading most effect files, it is possible to pass this function a series of default parameters causing it to just load the single effect file from the path you specify in the first parameter.

The key parameters to this function are of course the path and file name to the effect file to load, as well as the D3D10_SHADER_ENABLE_STRICTNESS flag. This flag tells the shader compiler to only accept valid syntax and warns you when attempting to use anything that is deprecated. The load function also requires you to pass in a pointer to the current Direct3D device and an object of type ID3D10Effect where it can store the new created effect object.

```
// The effect object
ID3D10Effect* pEffect = NULL;

// Load the effect file and create the effect object
HRESULT hr = D3DX10CreateEffectFromFile (L"..\\simple.fx", // filename
    NULL,
    NULL,
    "fx_4_0", // shader version
    D3D10_SHADER_ENABLE_STRICTNESS,
    0,
    pD3DDevice, // The Direct3D device
    NULL,
    NULL,
    &pEffect,
    NULL,
    NULL);

if (FAILED(hr))
{
    return false;
}
```

If you require more advanced functionality, please review the DirectX SDK documentation for this function.

External Variables and Constant Buffers

Most effects will need additional input past just the list of vertices; this is where external variables are useful. External variables are those variables declared within your effects that are visible from within your application code. Variables that receive information like current frame time, world projection, or light positions can be declared within the effect so they can be updated from the calling program.

With the introduction of Direct3D10, all external variables now reside in constant buffers. Constant buffers are used to group variables visible to the calling program so that they can be optimized for access. Constant buffers are similar in definition to structures and are created using the cbuffer keyword.

```
cbuffer Variables
{
    matrix Projection;
};
```

Constant buffers are commonly declared at the top of an effect file and reside outside of any other section. For ease of use, it can be useful to group together variables based on the amount they are accessed. For instance, variables that get an initial value would be grouped separately from variables that are updated on a frame by frame basis. You have the ability to create multiple constant buffers.

When the effect file is loaded, you can bind the external variables to the effect variables within your application. The following code shows how the external variable "Projection" is bound to the ID3D10EffectMatrixVariable in the application.

```
// declare the effect variable
ID3D10EffectMatrixVariable* pProjectionMatrixVariable = NULL;
// bind the effect variable to the external variable in the effect file
pProjectionMatrixVariable = modelObject->pEffect-
>GetVariableByName ("Projection")->AsMatrix();
// update the effect variable with the correct data
pProjectionMatrixVariable->SetMatrix((float*)&finalMatrix);
```

Input and Output Structures

Effect files consistently need to pass multiple values between shaders; to keep things simple, the variables are passed within a structure. The structure allows for more than one variable to be bundled together into an easy to send package and helps to minimize the work needed when adding a new variable.

For instance, vertex shaders commonly need to pass values like vertex position, color, or normal value along to the pixel shader. Since the vertex shader has the limitation of a single return value, it simply packages the needed variables into the structure and sends it to the pixel shader. The pixel shader then accesses the variables within the structure. An example structure called PS_INPUT is shown next.

```
// PS_INPUT - input variables to the pixel shader
// This struct is created and filled in by the vertex shader
struct PS_INPUT
{
    float4 Pos : SV_POSITION;
    float4 Color : COLOR0;
};
```

Using the structures is simple. First, an instance of the structure is created within the vertex shader. Next, the individual structure variables are filled out and then the structure is returned. The next shader in the pipeline will use the PS_INPUT structure as its input and have access to the variables you set. A simple vertex shader is shown here to demonstrate the definition and usage of a structure.

```
///////////////////////////////////////////////
// Vertex Shader - Main Function
///////////////////////////////////////////////
PS_INPUT VS(float4 Pos : POSITION, float4 Color : COLOR)
{
    PS_INPUT psInput;

    // Pass through both the position and the color
    psInput.Pos = mul( Pos, Projection );
    psInput.Color = Color;

    return psInput;
}
```

Technique Blocks

Effect files combine the functionality of multiple shaders into a single block called a technique. Techniques are a way to define how something should be drawn. For instance, you can define a technique that supports translucency as well as an opaque technique. By switching between techniques, the objects being drawn will go from solid to see through.

Techniques are defined within a shader using the `technique10` keyword followed by the name of the technique being created.

```
technique10 Render
{
    // technique definition
}
```

Because you can create simple or complex rendering techniques, techniques apply their functionality in passes. Each pass updates or changes the render state and shaders being applied to the scene. Because not all the effects you come up with can be applied in a single pass, techniques give you the ability to define more than one. Some post processing effects such as depth of field require more than one pass.

Passes

Each pass is created using the `pass` keyword followed by its pass level. The pass level is a combination of the letter P followed by the number of the pass.

In the following example, there are two passes, P0 and P1, being defined. At least one pass must be defined for the technique to be valid.

```
technique10 Render
{
    pass P0
    {
        // pass shader definitions
    }

    pass P1
    {
        // pass shader definitions
    }
}
```

Setting the Shaders in a Pass

The main job of each pass is the setting of the three types of shaders: the vertex shader, the geometry shader, and the pixel shader. Because the shaders you use can differ for each pass, they must be specifically defined using the functions SetVertexShader, SetGeometryShader, and SetPixelShader.

```
technique10 Render
{
    pass P0
    {
        // Define the vertex shader for this pass
        SetVertexShader( CompileShader(vs_4_0, VS() ));
        // No Geometry shader needed, pass NULL
        SetGeometryShader(NULL);
        // Define the pixel shader for this pass
        SetPixelShader( CompileShader(ps_4_0, PS() ));
    }
}
```

Note

In a pass definition, vertex and pixel shaders are required, while geometry shaders are optional.

As you can see, the shader setting functions include a call to the function CompileShader.

```
CompileShader( shader target, shader function )
```

CompileShader takes the shader you defined within the effect file and converts it into a format usable by Direct3D. CompileShader takes two parameters, the shader target value and the name of the shader function.

The shader target value specifies the shader level to use when compiling. Direct3D10 supports shader model 4.0 so the value vs_4_0 and ps_4_0 are used.

In the previous example, the vertex shader is using the function VS() while the pixel shader is using PS(). The names of these functions can change to suit your needs. Both of the shaders are being set to use shader model 4.0.

High Level Shading Language (HLSL)

The High Level Shading Language (HLSL) is the programming language used to write shaders. Very similar in syntax and structure to C++, HLSL allows you to create small shader programs that are loaded onto the video hardware and executed. In previous versions of Direct3D, shaders were written in a language that was very much like assembler, which really restricted shader programming to those few people with a lot of graphics knowledge. The advent of HLSL opened the world of shaders to a whole new audience and gave them the tools to create some amazing effects.

Because HLSL is all about shaders, the best demonstration of the language is in the form of a simple vertex shader. The small sample below shows a vertex shader as well as a structure created to hold output variables.

```
// PS_INPUT - input variables to the pixel shader
// This struct is created and fill in by the
// vertex shader
struct PS_INPUT
{
    float4 Pos : SV_POSITION;
    float4 Color : COLOR0;
};

/////////////////////////////////////////////
// Vertex Shader - Main Function
/////////////////////////////////////////////
PS_INPUT VS(float4 Pos : POSITION, float4 Color : COLOR)
{
    PS_INPUT psInput;

    // Pass through both the position and the color
    psInput.Pos = mul( Pos, Projection );
    psInput.Color = Color;

    return psInput;
}
```

In the following sections, you'll be given a small introduction to structure and syntax of HLSL.

Note

There are many tools out there that will assist you in writing HLSL shaders such as Nvidia's FX Composer and ATI's RenderMonkey. Both of these tools can be found on their respective websites.

Variable Types

HLSL contains many of the variable types that you'll find in C++ such as `int`, `bool`, and `float`; you'll also find a few new ones like `half`, `int1x4`, and `float4`. Because of the specialized hardware that the shader programs run on, they're afforded the benefit of new variable types that are optimized for the shader architecture.

Common variable types are:

`bool`—Boolean type, holds either true or false.

`int, uint`—32-bit signed and unsigned integer.

`half`—16-bit value.

`float`—32-bit value.

`double`—64-bit value.

`float2, float3, float4`—A packed float type that contains more than one value.

`float2x2, float3x3`—A two- and three-dimensional matrix.

Some variable types can contain multiple components allowing you to pack more than a single value into them. For instance, the variable type float4 allows you to store four float values within it. By storing values using these specialized types, the video hardware can optimize access to the data ensuring quicker access.

```
float4 tempFloat = float4(1.0, 2.0, 3.0, 4.0);
```

Any variable that contains multiple components can have each individual component accessed using swizzling. Swizzling enables you to split, for instance, a `float3` variable into its three components by specifying X, Y, or Z after the variable name. Take a look at the following example; the `singleFloat` variable is filled with the value found in the `newFloat` X component.

```
// Create and fill a float3 variable
float3 newFloat = float3(0.0, 1.0, 2.0);
// Set the variable singleFloat to the value stored in the X component
float singleFloat = newFloat.x;
```

Any variable containing multiple components can be accessed in this way.

Semantics

Semantics are a way of letting the shader know what certain variables will be used for so their access can be optimized. Semantics follow a variable declaration and have types such as COLOR0, TEXCOORD0, and POSITION. As you can see in the following structure, the two variables Pos and Color are followed by semantics specifying their use.

```
// PS_INPUT - input variables to the pixel shader
// This struct is created and filled in by the
// vertex shader
struct PS_INPUT
{
    float4 Pos : SV_POSITION;
    float4 Color : COLOR0;
};
```

Some commonly used semantics are:

- **SV_POSITION**—A float4 value specifying a transformed position.

- **NORMAL0**—Semantic that is used when defining a normal vector.

- **COLOR0**—Semantic used when defining a color value.

There are many more semantics available; take a look at the HLSL documentation in the DirectX SDK for a complete list.

A lot of semantics end in a numerical value because it is possible to define multiples of those types.

Function Declarations

Functions within HLSL are defined in pretty much the same way they are within other languages.

```
ReturnValue FunctionName (parameterName : semantic)
{
    // function code goes here
}
```

The function return value can be any of the defined HLSL types, including packed types and void.

When you're defining a parameter list for a shader function, it is perfectly valid to specify a semantic following the variable. There are a few things you need to be aware of though when defining function parameters. Since HLSL doesn't have a specific way for you to return a value by reference within your parameter list, it defines a few keywords that can be used to achieve the same results.

Using the out keyword before your parameter declaration lets the compiler know that the variable will be used as an output. Additionally, the keyword inout allows the variable to be used both as an input and output.

```
void GetColor(out float3 color)
{
    color = float3(0.0, 1.0, 1.0);
}
```

Vertex Shaders

Vertex shaders are the part of the pipeline where you are given control of every vertex that gets processed by the system. In previous versions of Direct3D, you had the option of using the fixed function pipeline, which had a built-in set of functionality that it used when processing vertices. Now with the latest Direct3D, you must do all the processing yourself. To that end, you'll need to write at least a simple vertex shader.

Vertex shaders are one of three shaders that can exist within an effect file. As objects are sent to be drawn, their vertices are sent to your vertex shader. If you don't want to do any additional processing to the vertices, you can pass them along to the pixel shader to be drawn. In most cases though, you'll at least want to apply a world or projection transform so the vertices are placed in the proper space to be rendered.

In the following example vertex shader, the incoming vertex position is multiplied by the projection matrix before being sent to the pixel shader. You'll also notice that the vertex color is left alone and just passed along.

```
///////////////////////////////////////////////
// Vertex Shader - Main Function
///////////////////////////////////////////////
PS_INPUT VS(float4 Pos : POSITION, float4 Color : COLOR)
{
    PS_INPUT psInput;

    // Pass through both the position and the color
    psInput.Pos = mul( Pos, Projection );
    psInput.Color = Color;
```

```
    return psInput;
}
```

Using vertex shaders, you have a lot of power to manipulate the vertices past just doing a simple transform. The vertex can be translated along any of the axes, its color changed, or any of its other properties manipulated. In the next section you'll be shown how the vertices can be made to animate within a vertex shader.

Grid Animation in the Shader

Just because you want to move around the vertices within an object doesn't mean that you have to do it in your application code. If the movement can be defined into either a set pattern or the movement value can be passed in, all the vertex animation can be done in the shader.

In the following example, the calling program sends in a time value using the TimeStep variable in addition to the vertices. The time value gives the vertex shader knowledge of time passing so that the vertices can be changed each frame.

The object used for this example is the 3D terrain grid created back in Chapter 5. As each vertex from this object is sent through the vertex shader, a new height position is calculated using the TimeStep variable and the built-in sine function. This results in a wave motion being applied to the grid.

```
// constant buffer of external variables
cbuffer Variables
{
    matrix Projection;
    matrix World;
    float TimeStep;
};


///////////////////////////////////////////////
// Vertex Shader - Main Function
///////////////////////////////////////////////
PS_INPUT VS(float4 Pos : POSITION, float4 Color : COLOR)
{
    PS_INPUT psInput;

    float4 newPosition;

    newPosition = Pos;
```

```
// generate a new height value based on the time
newPosition.y = sin((newPosition.x * TimeStep) + (newPosition.z / 3.0f)) *
5.0f;

// Pass through both the position and the color
psInput.Pos = mul(newPosition, Projection);

psInput.Color = Color;

return psInput;
}
```

Timing the Animation

As I mentioned before, the animation in the vertex shader is controlled by an updating time value called TimeStep. TimeStep is created and accessed just like the other variables you've sent to the shader. First an ID3D10EffectScalarVariable is declared to use as a binding between the application and shader code.

```
ID3D10EffectScalarVariable* pTimeVariable = NULL;
```

Next, the pTimeVariable is bound to the TimeStep shader variable.

```
pTimeVariable = modelObject->pEffect->GetVariableByName("TimeStep")->AsScalar();
```

Finally, the pTimeVariable is used to update the time value every frame.

```
// The time is set in the shader using the SetFloat function
pTimeVariable->SetFloat((float)currentTime);
```

The currentTime value is just a float value that contains the amount of time elapsed between frames.

A full example showing how to animate the terrain grid can be found in the Chapter7\example1 directory on the CD-ROM.

Pixel Shaders

Pixel shaders give you access to every pixel being put through the pipeline. Before anything is drawn, you're given the chance to make changes to the color of each pixel. In some cases you'll simply return the pixel color passed in from the vertex or geometry shaders, but in most cases you'll apply lighting or textures that affect the color of the resulting pixel. The code shown next demonstrates the simplest form of pixel shader, which just passes the input color along to be drawn.

```
/////////////////////////////////////////////
// Pixel Shader
/////////////////////////////////////////////
float4 PS(PS_INPUT psInput) : SV_Target
{
    return psInput.Color;
}
```

Changing the Color

Just to give you an idea of one manipulation you can perform on the input color, the following shader divides the color by two. This causes the color to dim as compared to the input color.

```
/////////////////////////////////////////////
// Pixel Shader
/////////////////////////////////////////////
float4 PS(PS_INPUT psInput) : SV_Target
{
    /* psInput.Color / 2 is equivalent to
    psInput.Color.r  = psInput.Color.r / 2;
    psInput.Color.g  = psInput.Color.g / 2;
    psInput.Color.b  = psInput.Color.b / 2;
    psInput.Color.a  = psInput.Color.a / 2;
    */

    return (psInput.Color / 2);
}
```

Lighting

If you look around, chances are there's a light source somewhere in your vicinity. It could be a lamp, the sun, or even just your monitor. Every bit of light, no matter how small, affects how we see the world around us. Some objects are dull and seem to absorb light while others are shiny causing light to be readily reflected. Everything you've done up to this point has assumed that your scene is taking place in a world where there is an all-powerful ambient light source causing everything to be lit from all directions. While it helps to be able to see what you've created, it isn't very realistic.

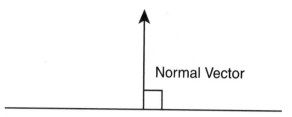

Figure 7.1
A normal vector.

In this section you're going to learn a little about how lights affect a scene and how to get lighting up and running. The first step down the lighting path is the generating of normals.

Generating Normals

A normal is a vector that is perpendicular to the plane of a polygon and is used when adding lighting to a scene. The job of the normal is to help in determining the amount of light a polygon may be receiving. Essentially, what this means is you have to calculate what direction the different pieces of your objects are facing so you know how much to light it.

Normals are calculated by obtaining the cross product of two of the polygon's edges. The vectors representing the edges of the polygon are determined using the polygon's vertices. The normal calculation is shown below. An example of a normal vector is shown in Figure 7.1.

```
NormalVector = CrossProduct( (vertex2 - vertex0), (vertex1 - vertex0) )
```

You can think of the returned value from the normal calculation as the amount of light hitting the object from the three axes directions.

Updating the Code to Support Normals

Like texture coordinates and position, normals are stored in the vertex structure and that means updating the custom vertex structure. Normals have an X, Y, and Z component and can be stored in a D3DXVECTOR3 variable. As you can see in the following structure, a variable called Normal has been added. The name of the structure was also changed to more accurately reflect the type of data it's storing.

```
struct VertexPosColorNormalStruct
{
    D3DXVECTOR3 Pos;
    D3DXVECTOR4 Color;
    D3DXVECTOR3 Normal;
};
```

After the vertex structure is updated, the input layout also needs to be changed. This will enable the application to successfully send the vertices to the shader. In the new layout, the information for the normals is added to the end after position and color. This keeps everything in sync with the order in the vertex structure.

```
// The vertex input layout
D3D10_INPUT_ELEMENT_DESC layout[] = {
  { "POSITION", 0, DXGI_FORMAT_R32G32B32_FLOAT, 0, 0,
D3D10_INPUT_PER_VERTEX_DATA, 0},
  { "COLOR", 0, DXGI_FORMAT_R32G32B32A32_FLOAT, 0, 12,
D3D10_INPUT_PER_VERTEX_DATA, 0},
  { "NORMAL", 0, DXGI_FORMAT_R32G32B32A32_FLOAT, 0, 28,
D3D10_INPUT_PER_VERTEX_DATA, 0},
};
```

The normals themselves are calculated using the array of indices that define all the faces in the object. By looping through the array of indices, the appropriate vertices can be updated for each face. After the normals are calculated, the resulting value is written to the Normal variable for each of the vertices.

```
// compute normals for each face in the model
for (unsigned int i = 0; i < modelObject->numIndices; i+=3)
{
    D3DXVECTOR3 v0 = vertices[indices[i]].Pos;
    D3DXVECTOR3 v1 = vertices[indices[i + 1]].Pos;
    D3DXVECTOR3 v2 = vertices[indices[i + 2]].Pos;

    D3DXVECTOR3 normal;
    D3DXVECTOR3 cross;
    D3DXVec3Cross(&cross, &D3DXVECTOR3(v2 - v0), &D3DXVECTOR3(v1 - v0));
    D3DXVec3Normalize(&normal, &cross);

    // assign the computed normal to each vertex in this face
    vertices[indices[i]].Normal     = normal;
    vertices[indices[i + 1]].Normal = normal;
    vertices[indices[i + 2]].Normal = normal;
}
```

Now that you have normals defined for all the vertices in your object, lighting can be applied within the pixel shader.

Lighting Calculations

In previous versions of Direct3D, the fixed function pipeline included support for a fixed number of built-in lights. With Direct3D10, that support is gone, giving you the freedom to handle as many lights as you care to do the math for. In most situations, this is beneficial as the previous pipeline couldn't take into account the myriad options people really wanted with lighting.

Regardless of the type of lights you choose to employ, they can affect your scene however you want because you have the ability to directly control them in the shader.

Ambient

Ambient light is an all powerful light. It doesn't have a fixed source and seems to come from all around you. Calculating lighting based on ambient light is the simplest of the lighting calculations. Ambient lighting is determined by multiplying the object's material color by the color of the ambient light.

```
outputColor = objectColor * ambientColor
```

Note

An object's material is used to describe how light coming off the object behaves. The material can affect the color of the light being reflected or even the amount of light. For instance, a red ball being lit by a blue light will have its reflected color a combination of the two.

The following function shows how you would determine the output color based on ambient lighting in a shader.

```
/*********************************
* CalculateAmbient -
* inputs -
*     vKa material's reflective color
*     lightColor - the ambient color of the lightsource
* output - ambient color
*********************************/
float3 CalculateAmbient(float3 vKa, float3 lightColor)
{
    float3 vAmbient = vKa * lightColor;

    return vAmbient;
}
```

Diffuse

Diffuse lighting calculates the color of an object based on any directional lights within your scene. Directional lights don't have a fixed position but definitely have a direction. Because directional lights come from a single direction, this means that they will be brighter on one side of your objects and dimmer on the other side. This effect will give your objects that sense of depth.

The `CalculateDiffuse` function shown next demonstrates how this is calculated.

The `CalculateDiffuse` function takes four parameters: the base color of the object, the color of the directional light, the surface normal, and the light vector.

The first step is taking the dot product using the normal and the light vector. This value is then clamped between 0 and 1 using the saturate function. The resulting value is then multiplied by the object's base color and the color of the directional light. As a reminder, this will calculate the angle between the incoming light and the surface of the object.

```
/********************************
* CalculateDiffuse
* inputs -
*      material color
*      The color of the direct light
*      the local normal
*      the vector of the direct light
* output - diffuse color
********************************/
float3 CalculateDiffuse(float3 baseColor, float3 lightColor, float3 normal,
float3 lightVector)
{
    float3 vDiffuse = baseColor * lightColor * saturate(dot(normal,
    lightVector));

    return vDiffuse;
}
```

Specular Highlights

Specular is the shininess of an object. Take a lamp and place it next to a glossy object like a piece of glass. Notice not only how the object is lit, but you'll probably also see what looks like light spots on the object; this is an example of a specular highlight. Specular highlights add that little bit of extra realism to a scene and help show how the light really affects the items in your scene.

Calculating the specular highlight requires a few things from your application. First, you need the view vector. This is a vector that describes the camera's location in relation to the object. Second is the light vector. This is the vector that describes where the light is coming from. Lastly is the surface normal.

The first step is creation of the reflection vector using the `reflect` function. This gives you the direction the light is coming off the surface of the object. Next, the specular value is determined by first taking the dot product of the reflection vector and the view vector. This value is then clamped between 0 and 1 using the saturate function. Finally, the specular value is raised to a power value specified in the `specpower` variable. This value is tunable and can be changed until you obtain the look you like.

```
float specpower = 80.0f;
/********************************
* CalculateSpecular -
* inputs -
*     viewVector
*     the light vector
*     the normal
* output - specular highlight
********************************/
float CalculateSpecular(float3 viewVector, float3 lightVector, float3 normal)
{
    float3 vReflect = reflect(lightVector, normal);

    float fSpecular = saturate(dot(vReflect, viewVector));
    fSpecular = pow(fSpecular, specpower);

    return fSpecular;
}
```

Combining the Lighting

Now that you have the three lighting values, you need to combine them. This will give you an object that takes into account ambient, diffuse, and specular lighting. Be aware that the lighting in this case in not dependent on the camera's point of view. The `LightingCombine` function shown next demonstrates how the lighting methods are brought together.

```
/*********************************
* LightingCombine -
* inputs -
*     ambient component
*     diffuse component
*     specular component
* output - final color
********************************/
float3 LightingCombine(float3 vAmbient, float3 vDiffuse, float fSpecular)
{
    float3 vCombined = vAmbient + vDiffuse + fSpecular.xxx;

    return vCombined;
}
```

All four of these calculations can be placed into a utility shader file and included when needed in your own effect files. These functions contain the generic lighting calculations that you'll be using over and over. These calculations are just one of many ways that lighting can be implemented within your application and are by no means perfect for every instance.

Applying the Light

A shader that uses the lighting functions described in the previous section is shown next. This shader contains a default ambient light and a single directional light.

```
#include "lightfuncs.fxh"

// constant buffer of external variables
cbuffer Variables
{
    matrix Projection;
    matrix World;
    float TimeStep;
};

// hardcoded example camera position
float3   camPos = float3(0.0f, 9.0, -256.0f);

// lighting values
float3   DirectLightColor   = float3(1.0f,1.0f,1.0f);
float3   DirectLightVector  = float3(0.0f,0.602f,0.70f);
float3   AmbientLightColor  = float3(1.0f, 1.0f, 1.0f);
```

```
// PS_INPUT - input variables to the pixel shader
// This struct is created and filled in by the
// vertex shader
struct PS_INPUT
{
    float4 Pos : SV_POSITION;
    float4 Color : COLOR0;
    float3 Normal : TEXCOORD0;
    float3 ViewVector : TEXCOORD1;
};

//////////////////////////////////////////////
// Vertex Shader - Main Function
//////////////////////////////////////////////
PS_INPUT VS(float4 Pos : POSITION, float4 Color : COLOR, float3 Normal : NORMAL)
{
    PS_INPUT psInput;

    // save off the position
    float4 newPosition = Pos;

    // generate a new height value based on the time
    newPosition.y = sin((newPosition.x * TimeStep) + (newPosition.z / 3.0f)) *
5.0f;

    // Pass through both the position and the color
    psInput.Pos = mul(newPosition, Projection);

    // pass the color and normal along to the pixel shader
    psInput.Color = Color;
    psInput.Normal = Normal;

    // Calculate the view vector
    psInput.ViewVector = normalize(camPos - psInput.Pos);

    return psInput;
}

//////////////////////////////////////////////
// Pixel Shader
//////////////////////////////////////////////
float4 PS(PS_INPUT psInput) : SV_Target
{
    float3   normal = -normalize(psInput.Normal);
```

```
    // calculate the color using ambient lighting
    float3 vAmbient = CalculateAmbient(psInput.Color, AmbientLightColor);

    // calculate the diffuse lighting
    vfloat3 vDiffuse = CalculateDiffuse(psInput.Color, DirectLightColor, normal,
    DirectLightVector);

    // calculate specular
    float fSpecular = CalculateSpecular(psInput.ViewVector, DirectLightVector,
    normal);

    // determine the output color using phong shading
    float4 outColor;
    outColor.rgb = LightingCombine(vAmbient, vDiffuse, fSpecular);
    outColor.a = 1.0f;

    return outColor;
}


// Define the technique
technique10 Render
{
    pass P0
    {
        SetVertexShader( CompileShader( vs_4_0, VS() ) );
        SetGeometryShader( NULL );
        SetPixelShader( CompileShader( ps_4_0, PS() ) );
    }
}
```

To demonstrate the usage of this shader, it has been applied to the terrain object from Chapter 6. The result is shown in Figure 7.2 and demonstrates lighting on a per-vertex level.

Check out the Chapter7\example2 directory on the CD-ROM for the source code demonstrating lighting of the terrain.

Figure 7.2
Terrain with lighting applied.

Geometry Shaders

Geometry shaders are a bit more complicated than the shaders you've worked with so far. Unlike vertex and pixel shaders, geometry shaders are able to output more or less than they take in. Vertex shaders must accept a single vertex and output a single vertex; pixel shaders work the same way. Geometry shaders, on the other hand, can be used to remove or add vertices as they pass through this portion of the pipeline. This is useful if you want to clip geometry based on some set criteria or maybe you want to increase the resolution of the object through tessellation.

Geometry shaders exist within an effect file between the vertex and pixel shader stages. Since geometry shaders are optional, you may commonly see them set to a NULL value in effect techniques. When a geometry shader is necessary though, it is set in an identical way as vertex and pixel shaders. The technique shown next defines all three.

```
// Define the technique
technique10 Render
{
    pass P0
    {
        SetVertexShader( CompileShader(vs_4_0, VS()) );
        SetGeometryShader( CompileShader(gs_4_0, GS()) );
        SetPixelShader( CompileShader(ps_4_0, PS()) );
    }
}
```

To give you an example of what geometry shaders can do, take a look at the following code. It contains the full geometry shader function along with the structures and constant buffer to support it. The job of this particular shader is to take as input a single vertex position and generate a full triangle to send along to the pixel shader.

```
// The corners of a triangle, used in the geometry
// shader to create each triangle
cbuffer TriangleVerts
{
    float3 triPositions[3] =
    {
        float3( -0.25, 0.25, 0 ),
        float3( 0.25, 0.25, 0 ),
        float3( -0.25, -0.25, 0 ),
    };
};

// PS_INPUT - input variables to the pixel shader
// This struct is created and filled in by the
// vertex shader
struct PS_INPUT
{
    // Only the pixel shader input uses the fully transformed position
    float4 Pos : SV_POSITION;
    float4 Color : COLOR0;
};

// output structure for the vertex shader
struct VS_OUT
{
    float4 Pos : POSITION;
    float4 Color: COLOR0;
};
```

```
/////////////////////////////////////////////////
// Geometry Shader
/////////////////////////////////////////////////
[maxvertexcount(3)]
void GS(point VS_OUT input[1], inout TriangleStream<PS_INPUT> triangleStream)
{
    PS_INPUT psInput;

    // create the new triangles
    for (int i = 0; i < 3; i++)
    {
        // hold the vertices for the triangle
        float3 position = triPositions[i];

        // move the triangle vertices based on the point position
        position = position + input[0].Pos;

        // Multiply the new vertices by the projection matrix
        psInput.Pos = mul(float4(position, 1.0), Projection);

        // pass the color on through
        psInput.Color = input[0].Color;

        // add this triangle to the triangle stream
        triangleStream.Append(psInput);
    }
}
```

Geometry Shader Function Declaration

Geometry shaders are declared slightly differently than vertex and pixel shaders. Instead of designating the return type for the function, the vertices this shader outputs are done so in the parameter list. The geometry shader itself has a return type of void.

Every geometry shader needs to designate the number of vertices that it will be returning and must be declared above the function using the maxvertexcount keyword. This particular function is meant to return a single triangle so three vertices are required.

```
[maxvertexcount(3)]
void GS(point VS_OUT input[1], inout TriangleStream<PS_INPUT> triangleStream)
```

Geometry shader functions take two parameters.

The first parameter is an array of vertices for the incoming geometry. The type of geometry being passed into this function is based on the topology you used in your application code. Since this example used a point list, the type of geometry coming into the function is a point, and there is only one item in the array. If the application used a triangle list then the type would be set as "triangle" and three vertices would be in the array.

The second parameter is the stream object. The stream object is the list of vertices that are outputted from the geometry shader and passed to the next shader stage. This list of vertices must use the structure format that is used as the input to the pixel shader. Based on the type of geometry you're creating within this shader, there are three stream object types available:

- `PointStream`—The shader should expect to output a series of points.

- `TriangleStream`—The shader will output a triangle strip.

- `LineStream`—A series of lines.

When adding vertices to a stream object, it will be occasionally necessary to end the strip being created. In that instance, you should make a call to the `restartstrip` function. This is useful when generating a series of inter-connected triangles.

The Geometry Shader Explained

The geometry shader in the previous example generates three vertices for every vertex passed to it. The vertices are created by taking the initial position vertex and merging it with the vertex positions found in the `triPositions` variable. This variable holds a list of three vertices that are used to create a triangle at any position.

Because each triangle the shader is trying to create requires three vertices, a `for` loop within the shader loops three times generating a new vertex for each point of the triangle.

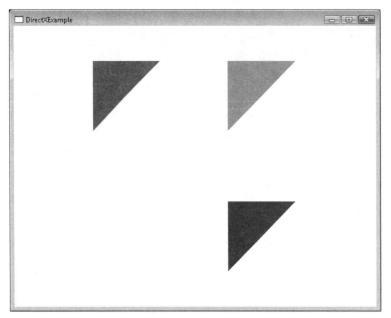

Figure 7.3
Three geometry shader generated triangles.

The final triangle points are then multiplied by the projection matrix to create the final positions. Each point in the triangle is added to the triangle stream after its creation. Figure 7.3 shows what the generated triangles look like.

A full source example demonstrating the use of geometry shaders can be found in the chapter7\example3 directory on the CD-ROM.

Summary

You should now be familiar with at least the basics of shader programming and what benefits they provide you. The best way to continue to learn shader programming is to play around with the shader code you've already written and see what effects you can come up with. A small change can have profound effects.

What You Have Learned

In this chapter, you learned the following:

- How to write vertex, pixel, and geometry shaders

- How to use HLSL

- How to provide lighting in your scene

Review Questions

You can find the answers to Review Questions in Appendix A, "Answers to End-of-Chapter Exercises."

1. Effect files are loaded using which function?

2. What is HLSL?

3. What is the purpose of the vertex and pixel shaders?

4. What two variables are required to calculate ambient lighting?

5. What is the purpose of semantics?

On Your Own

1. Update example1 to change the grid animation values and see what kinds of effects you can create.

2. Using a geometry shader, generate a star from a single point.

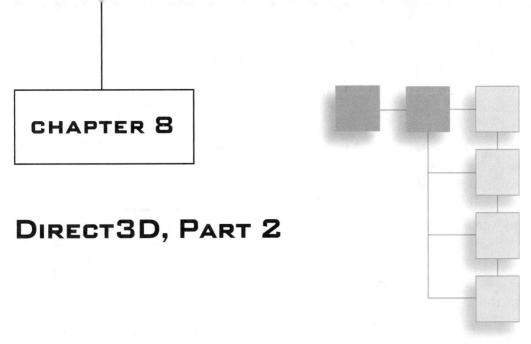

CHAPTER 8

DIRECT3D, PART 2

Until now, your 3D world has been fairly boring. While lighting gave the scenes some depth, it didn't add realism—that's where textures come in. Early generation 3D applications represented their objects using only flat-shaded polygons, giving their scenes a very dated look. Just in the last few years, computing power has increased dramatically enabling scenes that can be created in so much more detail using more polygons and high resolution textures.

Here's what you'll learn in this chapter:

- How textures can be applied to 3D objects

- How texture blending is accomplished

- How alpha blending works

- What a mesh is and why they're useful

Textures and Details

If you've seen any 3D game in the past ten years then you've seen texturing in action. Texture mapping is simply the process of applying an image to a surface to add realism. Mapping a texture isn't difficult and in fact, you've already done it; the sprites you created in Chapter 3 were actually quads with a texture applied to the surface.

When exploring virtual worlds, the more realistic the environment the more it draws you in; textures are a big part of that experience. Simple spheres become living worlds ready to explore or a single rectangle becomes a road ready for racing, all thanks to textures. Because of the details that textures can add to your scene, it helps to minimize the amount of geometry you have to create. Take, for instance, a brick wall. You could create all the geometry to model each brick in the wall or you could take a single quad and apply a brick texture to it. You get the result you want either way, but the textured version is computationally cheaper, takes less time to create, and tends to look better. Game programming is all about making things look the best you can and getting away with it using the cheapest possible method.

In most games, textures take up a majority of the memory and asset budget. As video RAM has been increasing so has the want to fill it with larger and more complex textures. Video cards have grown from 32 megabytes of memory for first-generation 3D cards to most cards on the market now having upwards of 256 megabytes available, and game developers are having no problem taking advantage of it.

Texture Coordinates

Textures are mapped to objects using texture coordinates. Very much like vertex coordinates detail where a vertex should be positioned in world space, texture coordinates describe where a texture should be positioned on an object.

Texture coordinates have two components designated U and V. The U component maps horizontally while V maps vertically. Together, these two components can describe any area within the texture being mapped. Figure 8.1 shows how texture coordinates are laid out.

Texture coordinates are clamped to a fixed set of values ranging from 0.0f to 1.0f, regardless of the size of the texture, allowing all textures to be represented in the same way. Since texture coordinates range from 0.0f to 1.0f, it may help to think of them in percentages of a texture. Mapping a texture to a square using (0.0f, 0.0f) for the upper-left corner and (1.0f, 1.0f) in the bottom-right will use 100% of the texture in both the U and V directions.

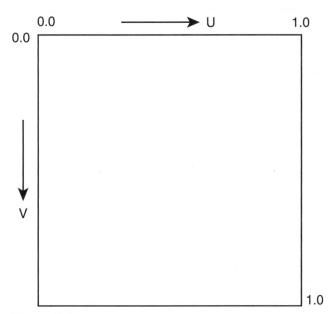

Figure 8.1
How texture coordinates are mapped.

Adding Support for Texture Mapping

Supporting texture mapping in your application isn't difficult but does require a few changes:

- The vertex format needs to be updated to support storing texture coordinates.

- The texture needs to be loaded and sent to the shader.

- The shader needs to be changed to allow the texture map to be used.

The Vertex Format

Texture coordinates are designated on the vertex level within your scene. To support texture mapping, you need to change the vertex structure and input layout and update the vertices for each object. Previously you were working with a vertex format that included only position and a color. To support texture mapping, you'll need to add texture coordinates to the structure.

```
// Vertex Structure
struct VertexPosUVStruct
{
    D3DXVECTOR3 Pos;     // Position
    D3DXVECTOR2 Tex;     // Texture Coordinates
};
```

The new structure contains a position and D3DXVECTOR2 to hold the texture coordinates. The vertex color was removed to keep the example simple since it won't be needed.

Besides updating the vertex structure, the input layout also needs to be altered.

```
// The vertex input layout now including texture coordinates
D3D10_INPUT_ELEMENT_DESC layout[] = {
    { "POSITION", 0, DXGI_FORMAT_R32G32B32_FLOAT, 0, 0,
    D3D10_INPUT_PER_VERTEX_DATA, 0 },
    { "TEXCOORD", 0, DXGI_FORMAT_R32G32_FLOAT, 0, 12,
    D3D10_INPUT_PER_VERTEX_ DATA, 0 },
};
```

The last step required to allow support for texture coordinates is the updating of the vertices themselves. Following the format defined in the vertex structure, the position is placed first with the vertex coordinates following.

```
// Create vertex buffer for the quad
VertexPosUVStruct vertices[] =
{
    { D3DXVECTOR3(-0.5f, -0.5f, 0.0f), D3DXVECTOR2(0.0f, 1.0f)},
    { D3DXVECTOR3(-0.5f, 0.5f, 0.0f), D3DXVECTOR2(0.0f, 0.0f)},
    { D3DXVECTOR3(0.5f, -0.5f, 0.0f), D3DXVECTOR2(1.0f, 1.0f)},
    { D3DXVECTOR3(0.5f, 0.5f, 0.0f), D3DXVECTOR2(1.0f, 0.0f)},
};
```

An updated InitModel function is shown next with new added support for texture mapping.

```
/***************************************************************
* InitModel
* Initializes a ModelObject struct with the data to draw a single
* quad
* Inputs - ModelObject *modelObject - the modelObject struct to fill
* Outputs - bool - true if successful
```

```
*****************************************************************/
bool InitModel(ModelObject *modelObject)
{
    // Create the effect
    HRESULT hr = D3DX10CreateEffectFromFile(L"./texturing.fx",
        NULL,
        NULL,
        "fx_4_0",
        D3D10_SHADER_ENABLE_STRICTNESS,
        0,
        pD3DDevice,
        NULL,
        NULL,
        &modelObject->pEffect,
        NULL);

    if (FAILED(hr))
    {
        return false;
    }

    // Obtain the technique
    modelObject->pTechnique = modelObject->pEffect-
>GetTechniqueByName("Render");

    // Bind the texture variable
    pBaseTextureVariable = modelObject->pEffect-
>GetVariableByName("baseTexture")
        ->AsShaderResource();

    // The vertex input layout
    D3D10_INPUT_ELEMENT_DESC layout[] = {
    { "POSITION", 0, DXGI_FORMAT_R32G32B32_FLOAT, 0, 0,
    D3D10_INPUT_PER_VERTEX_DATA, 0 },
    { "TEXCOORD", 0, DXGI_FORMAT_R32G32_FLOAT, 0, 12,
    D3D10_INPUT_PER_VERTEX_DATA, 0 },
    };

    // Calculate the number of elements in the layout array
    UINT numElements = (sizeof(layout) / sizeof(layout[0]));

    // Create the vertex input layout
    D3D10_PASS_DESC PassDesc;
    modelObject->pTechnique->GetPassByIndex(0)->GetDesc(&PassDesc);
```

```
hr = pD3DDevice->CreateInputLayout(layout,
    numElements,
    PassDesc.pIAInputSignature,
    PassDesc.IAInputSignatureSize,
    &modelObject->pVertexLayout);


if(FAILED(hr))
{
    return false;
}

// Create vertex buffer for the quad
VertexPosUVStruct vertices[] =
{
    { D3DXVECTOR3(-0.5f, -0.5f, 0.0f), D3DXVECTOR2(0.0f, 1.0f)},
    { D3DXVECTOR3(-0.5f, 0.5f, 0.0f), D3DXVECTOR2(0.0f, 0.0f)},
    { D3DXVECTOR3(0.5f, -0.5f, 0.0f), D3DXVECTOR2(1.0f, 1.0f)},
    { D3DXVECTOR3(0.5f, 0.5f, 0.0f), D3DXVECTOR2(1.0f, 0.0f)},
};

// Calculate the number of vertices in the array
modelObject->numVertices = sizeof(vertices) / sizeof(VertexPosUVStruct);

D3D10_BUFFER_DESC bd;
bd.Usage = D3D10_USAGE_DEFAULT;
bd.ByteWidth = sizeof(VertexPosUVStruct) * modelObject->numVertices;
bd.BindFlags = D3D10_BIND_VERTEX_BUFFER;
bd.CPUAccessFlags = 0;
bd.MiscFlags = 0;


D3D10_SUBRESOURCE_DATA InitData;
InitData.pSysMem = vertices;


// Do the creation of the actual vertex buffer
hr = pD3DDevice->CreateBuffer(&bd, &InitData, &modelObject->pVertexBuffer);
if(FAILED(hr))
{
    return false;
}
```

```
      return true;
}
```

Texture Loading and Shaders

When texturing a 3D object, the texture and the method used to load it is very similar to the way textures were loaded for sprites. First the texture itself needs to be loaded into an ID3D10Texture2D object and a resource view created from it. The helper functions created in the sprite chapter, GetTexture2DFromFile and GetResourceViewFromTexture, can be used to perform these tasks.

Secondly, the shader needs to know how to gain access to the texture you just loaded in. Letting the shader know to expect a texture is simply a matter of creating a named variable that is set as external using the extern keyword.

```
// Set up a named variable within the shader to hold the texture.
extern Texture2D baseTexture;
```

The variable is then accessible to the runtime portion of your code through binding.

```
// Bind the texture variable
ID3D10EffectShaderResourceVariable* pBaseTextureVariable = NULL;
pBaseTextureVariable = modelObject->pEffect->
    GetVariableByName("baseTexture")->AsShaderResource();
```

The pBaseTextureVariable is now bound to the baseTexture variable declared in the shader. Similar to the matrix and float variables you've bound before, this gives you access to change and update the values used by the shader.

The texture can be updated using the SetResource method available through the pBaseTextureVariable.

```
// Set the texture resource view
pBaseTextureVariable->SetResource(pTextureRV);
```

Note

Shaders make use of the texture resource view, not the actual texture object.

Texturing Coordinates and Sampling

Since the texture coordinates were added to the vertex format previously, the shader now needs to be updated to handle them as well. Since all the vertices pass through the vertex shader portion first, the input parameters need to be changed.

Additionally, the PS_INPUT structure must support the inclusion of texture coordinates to pass on to the pixel shader.

The new versions of the PS_INPUT structure and vertex shader are shown next.

```
////// This structure is created and filled in by the
// vertex shader
struct PS_INPUT
{
    float4 Pos : SV_POSITION;
    float4 Color : COLOR0;
    float2 Tex : TEXCOORD0;
};


///////////////////////////////////////////////
// Vertex Shader - Main Function
///////////////////////////////////////////////
PS_INPUT VS(float4 Pos : POSITION, float2 Tex: TEXCOORD)
{
    PS_INPUT psInput;
    psInput.Pos = Pos;
    psInput.Color = float4(1.0f, 1.0f, 1.0f, 1.0f);
    psInput.Tex = Tex;

    return psInput;
}
```

The vertex shader isn't responsible for doing anything to the texture coordinates other than just setting them and passing them along to the pixel shader.

Texturing is performed in the pixel shader portion of an effect. Instead of the pixel shader returning a preset color as its output, the shader returns a color based on the texture coordinate location in the texture file; this process is called sampling.

Sampling uses the texture coordinates to determine which area of the texture is going to be used as the output color. How the texture is sampled is controlled by the SamplerState. The SamplerState is a named section within the shader file that

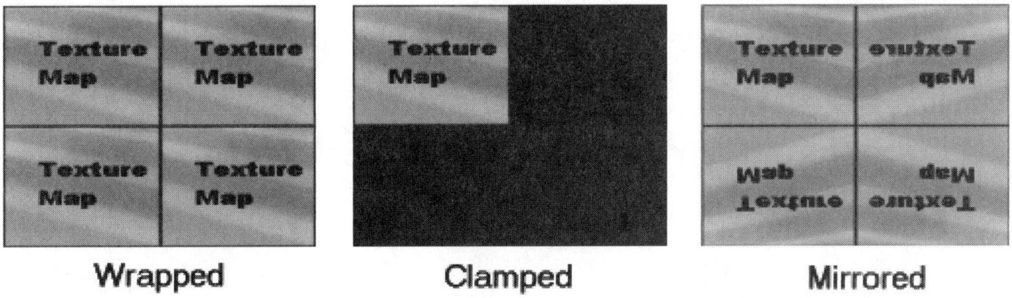

Figure 8.2
A wrapped, clamped, and mirrored texture.

contains information as to how the texture is to be filtered as well as how the texture should be mapped. There are three ways the texture can be mapped:

- **Wrap**—The texture repeats across the surface.

- **Clamp**—If the texture does not completely map to the area, the edge color will be repeated causing the texture to look streaked.

- **Mirror**—The texture is repeated but reversed each time it is drawn.

Figure 8.2 shows an example of each type of mapping.

An example `SamplerState` is shown next. It uses linear filtering and wraps the texture during sampling.

```
SamplerState samLinear
{
    Filter = MIN_MAG_MIP_LINEAR;
    AddressU = Wrap;
    AddressV = Wrap;
};
```

The `SamplerState` is needed within the pixel shader during the actual sampling process. The ability to sample a texture is built-in to Direct3D and uses the shader function `Sample`.

`Sample` is one of the functions made available through the `Texture2D` object and takes two parameters. The first parameter is a `SamplerState` object. The second parameter is the pair of texture coordinates to be sampled. The `Sample` function uses the input texture coordinates to do a lookup in a texture and then uses the `SamplerState` to determine the color to be mapped.

```
//////////////////////////////////////////////
// Pixel Shader
//////////////////////////////////////////////
float4 PS(PS_INPUT psInput) : SV_Target
{
    return baseTexture.Sample(samLinear, psInput.Tex) * psInput.Color;
}
```

Note

Previous versions of HLSL used the `tex2D` function for sampling from 2D textures. The `Sample` function was introduced in Shader Model 4.0 and has the advantage of supporting 2D and 3D textures based on the texture object.

Drawing the Textured Object

It might seem like a lot of work just to map a single texture to a 3D object, but once you have the changes made to the shader, that code can be reused, simplifying your job in the future.

At this point the vertex format has been changed to support texture coordinates, the texture is loaded, and the shader knows how to map that texture to the object; finally, you can see what it looks like.

The `Render` function that makes use of the changes you've already made is shown next, with the additional `SetResource` call made to update the texture with the shader.

```
/*****************************************************************
* Render
* All drawing happens in the Render function
* Inputs - void
* Outputs - void
*****************************************************************/
void Render()
{
    if (pD3DDevice != NULL)
    {
        // clear the target buffer
        pD3DDevice->ClearRenderTargetView(pRenderTargetView, D3DXCOLOR(0.0f,
        1.0f, 1.0f, 0.0f));
```

```
// Set the input layout
pD3DDevice->IASetInputLayout(gModelObject.pVertexLayout);

// Set vertex buffer
UINT stride = sizeof(VertexPosUVStruct);
UINT offset = 0;
pD3DDevice->IASetVertexBuffers(0, 1, &gModelObject.pVertexBuffer,
&stride, &offset);

// Set primitive topology
pD3DDevice-
>IASetPrimitiveTopology(D3D10_PRIMITIVE_TOPOLOGY_TRIANGLESTRIP);

// Set the texture resource view
pBaseTextureVariable->SetResource(pTextureRV);

// Render a model object
D3D10_TECHNIQUE_DESC techniqueDescription;
gModelObject.pTechnique->GetDesc(&techniqueDescription);

// Loop through the technique passes
for(UINT p=0; p < techniqueDescription.Passes; ++p)
{
    gModelObject.pTechnique->GetPassByIndex(p)->Apply(0);
    pD3DDevice->Draw(gModelObject.numVertices, 0);
}

// display the next item in the swap chain
pSwapChain->Present(0, 0);
    }
}
```

Figure 8.3 shows what the texture-mapped quad should look like.

The full source code to texture map a quad is available in the Chapter8\example1 directory on the CD-ROM.

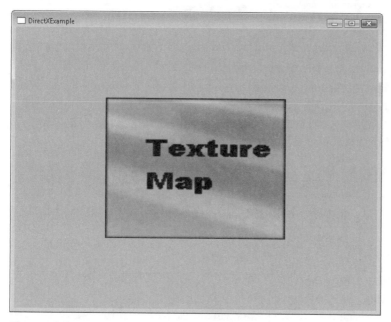

Figure 8.3
The texture-mapped quad.

Multi-texturing

Multi-texturing is the process of applying more than one texture to the face of an object. You're probably wondering where this would ever be needed, but surprisingly it comes up a lot. For instance, if you're creating a baseball field, the lines have to pass over the dirt area as well as the grassy area. Instead of adding the lines to each of the other textures, the lines can be added in the shader, blending just as well with the grass as with the dirt.

Because multi-texturing requires more than one texture, your application will need to be changed to support this.

To keep things from being too confusing, the two textures will be called `baseTexture` and `topTexture`. Previously, only one texture was being used so the code supported the loading of only one texture. The second texture can be loaded using the same methods. After the new texture is loaded, it needs to be sent to the shader as well.

The `baseTexture` will be the first texture applied to the quad, with the `topTexture` applied afterwards. The following code shows how both texture variables are bound to their respective shader variables.

```
// Bind the texture variable
pTextureVariable = modelObject->pEffect->GetVariableByName("baseTexture")-
>AsShaderResource();
pTexture2Variable = modelObject->pEffect->GetVariableByName("topTexture")-
>AsShaderResource();
```

The new texture will be sent to the shader in the exact same manner as the texture in the above section through the SetResource function. An updated Render function is shown next that sets both textures.

```
/********************************************************************
* Render
* All drawing happens in the Render function
* Inputs - void
* Outputs - void
********************************************************************/
void Render()
{
    if (pD3DDevice != NULL)
    {
        // clear the target buffer
        pD3DDevice->ClearRenderTargetView(pRenderTargetView,
        D3DXCOLOR(0.0f, 1.0f, 1.0f, 0.0f));

        // Set the input layout
        pD3DDevice->IASetInputLayout(gModelObject.pVertexLayout);

        // Set vertex buffer
        UINT stride = sizeof(VertexPosUVStruct);
        UINT offset = 0;
        pD3DDevice->IASetVertexBuffers(0, 1, &gModelObject.pVertexBuffer,
        &stride, &offset);

        // Set primitive topology
        pD3DDevice-
        >IASetPrimitiveTopology(D3D10_PRIMITIVE_TOPOLOGY_TRIANGLESTRIP);

        // Set the texture resource view
        pTextureVariable->SetResource(pTextureRV);
        pTexture2Variable->SetResource(pTextureRV2);

        // Render a model object
        D3D10_TECHNIQUE_DESC techniqueDescription;
        gModelObject.pTechnique->GetDesc(&techniqueDescription);
```

```
// Loop through the technique passes
for(UINT p=0; p < techniqueDescription.Passes; ++p)
{
    gModelObject.pTechnique->GetPassByIndex(p)->Apply(0);
    pD3DDevice->Draw(gModelObject.numVertices, 0);
}

// display the next item in the swap chain
pSwapChain->Present(0, 0);
    }
}
```

The next section shows how the two textures are used in the shader to create a blending effect.

Texture Blending

Blending takes place when the color components from two or more textures are combined to create a new output color. This allows you to mix colors from multiple textures, causing the textures to appear blended together when displayed.

The following pixel shader combines the two textures by multiplying their colors.

```
/////////////////////////////////////////////
// Pixel Shader
/////////////////////////////////////////////
float4 PS(PS_INPUT psInput) : SV_Target
{
    float4 baseColor = baseTexture.Sample(samLinear, psInput.Tex);
    float4 topColor = topTexture.Sample(samLinear, psInput.Tex);

    // merge the two textures together
    float4 mergedColor = baseColor * topColor;

    return mergedColor;
}
```

Change the multiply to use addition or subtraction to see what other kinds of ways you can combine the textures. Figure 8.4 shows the output of two blended textures. The source code demonstrating this technique can be found in the Chapter8\example2 directory on the CD-ROM.

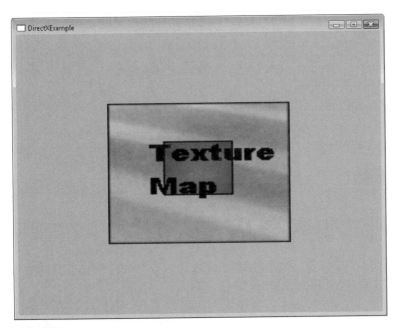

Figure 8.4
Two textures blended together.

Texture Blending Using Alpha

In the last example you saw how two textures can be blended together using each of their respective colors. Because of the way that the textures were blended, the alpha component wasn't really taken into account.

As you learn when dealing with sprites, the alpha component allows you to create translucency effects which give you the ability to see through certain areas. To demonstrate texture blending that takes the alpha component into account, a new texture needs to be created that contains data in the alpha channel.

I created a small texture using Paint Shop Pro that contains a circle in the center with an alpha value of 1.0. When blended together with the base texture in the pixel shader, this circular area should become transparent. Figure 8.5 shows what the new texture looks like.

Previously, the textures were blended together by just doing a multiply. This effectively combined the component values from each texture without really caring what those values contained. To take advantage of the alpha component, you're now going to use one of the built-in functions called `lerp`. `lerp` is shorthand for linear interpolation, and allows for the textures to be multiplied based on a third value.

Figure 8.5
The new texture with an alpha circle.

```
float4 outValue = lerp(a, b, c);
```

The `lerp` function takes three parameters. The first parameter, a, is the color component of the first texture. The second parameter, b, is the color component of the second texture. The final parameter is the percentage by which the first two will be combined. Passing in values such as 0.5 will cause the two textures to be combined equally. Increasing or decreasing this value will cause the textures to be combined using more or less of each texture.

Because you won't know for sure how much of each texture you'll want, you can't really put a fixed value in the third parameter. Instead, you'll be using the alpha component value from the top texture. This causes the `lerp` calculation to use the alpha value from the second texture when the blend is occurring.

Take a look at the following pixel shader to see how `lerp` works.

```
//////////////////////////////////////////////////
// Pixel Shader
//////////////////////////////////////////////////
float4 PS(PS_INPUT psInput) : SV_Target
{
    float4 outColor;

    float4 baseColor = baseTexture.Sample( samLinear, psInput.Tex );
    float4 topColor = topTexture.Sample(samLinear, psInput.Tex);

    // blend the two textures together based on the alpha channel
    // in the second texture
    outColor = lerp(baseColor, topColor, topColor.a);
```

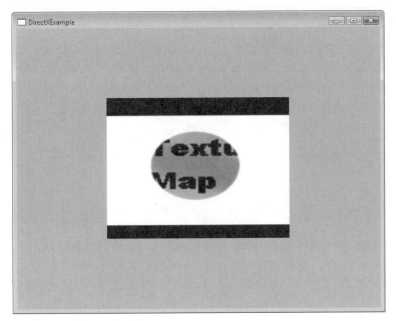

Figure 8.6
Textures alpha blended using the `lerp` function.

```
    return outColor;
}
```

Figure 8.6 shows the result of blending the two textures. The full source code that demonstrates alpha blending textures can be found in the Chapter8\example3 directory on the CD-ROM.

A Couple of Texture Tricks

Occasionally it's necessary to alter a texture in some way. For instance, you may be writing an application that does image manipulation, or perhaps the main character in your game has been poisoned, affecting their vision, or any number of reasons. Because you have direct access to the textures as they're applied, you control whether the pixels get mapped out using their original colors or are altered.

To show just a few of the things that are possible, I'm going to demonstrate how to alter a pixel shader to perform both color inversion and color shifting.

Texture Color Inversion

Color inversion is the reversing of a texture color, giving it the appearance of a film negative. Inverting a color is actually a simple procedure. Since all color components range from 0.0 to 1.0, an opposite color can be calculated by subtracting the current color from 1.0.

```
newColor = 1.0 - oldColor
```

An updated pixel shader that demonstrates this effect is shown here:

```
/////////////////////////////////////////////
// Pixel Shader
/////////////////////////////////////////////
float4 PS(PS_INPUT psInput) : SV_Target
{
    float4 baseColor = baseTexture.Sample(samLinear, psInput.Tex);

    // Invert the texture color
    float4 outColor = (1 - baseColor);
    outColor.a = 1.0;

    return outColor;
}
```

Figure 8.7 shows the output of this effect.

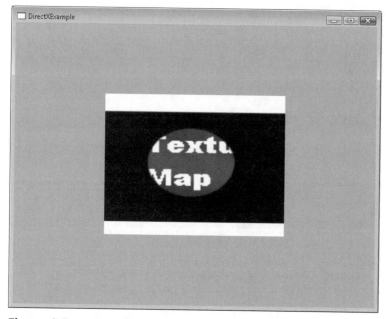

Figure 8.7
The colors of a texture inverted.

Color Shifting

Color shifting is exactly what it sounds like, shifting the color in a texture toward a certain color. This can either shift the colors toward a single color component, such as red, or shift all equally toward white or black, allowing you to create a fade effect.

The following pixel shader utilizes a simple version of this effect by multiplying the current texture color value by a full red value.

```
/////////////////////////////////////////////
// Pixel Shader
/////////////////////////////////////////////
float4 PS(PS_INPUT psInput) : SV_Target
{
    float4 baseColor = baseTexture.Sample(samLinear, psInput.Tex);
    float4 redColor = float4(1.0, 0.0, 0.0, 1.0);

    // shift the texture color towards red
    float4 outColor = baseColor * redColor;

    return outColor;
}
```

Figure 8.8 shows the output of this effect.

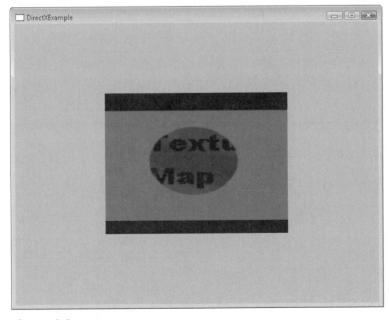

Figure 8.8
The colors of a texture shifted towards red.

There are a bunch of effects you can perform using just the color values available to you in the pixel shader. Experiment using some of the built-in shader functions to see what kind of effects you can come up with.

Meshes

Direct3D contains an interface called `ID3DX10Mesh` specifically for creating and manipulating 3D meshes. A 3D mesh contains all the vertices and indices as well as materials needed to draw an object.

In Chapter 6 you were shown how to create 3D objects by defining their vertices and placing them into vertex buffers. To encapsulate everything that makes up a single 3D object, the buffers and other data have been placed into a `ModelObject` structure. The structure helped to keep things organized when handling more than one object. With Direct3D, the `ID3DX10Mesh` object performs this task.

Although the `ID3DX10Mesh` object may contain all the necessary data for drawing an object, it doesn't contain all the data you may need to make it a game object. It's useful to keep the `ModelObject` structure around and allow the `ID3DX10Mesh` object to become a member of this structure. As you can see in the following updated structure, `ModelObject` can still be used to store information regarding the shader effects necessary for drawing.

```
typedef struct
{
    ID3D10Effect* pEffect;
    ID3D10EffectTechnique* pTechnique;

    // Vertex information
    ID3DX10Mesh* mesh;
    ID3D10InputLayout* pVertexLayout;
}ModelObject;
```

The Mesh Creation Process

Creating a mesh is accomplished using the following steps:

1. Create the list of vertices and indices your mesh will need.

2. Create the `ID3DX10Mesh` object.

3. Fill the `ID3DX10Mesh` object with the vertices and indices you defined.

Generating the Vertex and Index Data

Generating the array of vertices and indices is identical to how you did it in Chapter 6. Simply define an array using a vertex format and fill the array with the vertices. The following code snippet is shown as a reminder of how to generate an array of vertices for a terrain environment. The terrain is going to be used as the test data for creating a mesh.

```
// create the vertices array large enough to hold all those needed
VertexPosColorStruct vertices[NUM_VERTSX * NUM_VERTSY];

// Fill the vertices array with the terrain values
for(int z=0; z < NUM_VERTSY; ++z)
{
    for(int x=0; x < NUM_VERTSX; ++x)
    {
        vertices[x + z * NUM_VERTSX].Pos.x = (float)x * CELL_WIDTH;
        vertices[x + z * NUM_VERTSX].Pos.z = (float)z * CELL_HEIGHT;

        // Allow the height of the cell to be randomly decided
        vertices[x + z * NUM_VERTSX].Pos.y = (float)(rand() % CELL_HEIGHT);

        // Create the default color
        vertices[x + z * NUM_VERTSX].Color = D3DXVECTOR4(1.0, 0.0f, 0.0f, 0.0f);
    }
}

// Calculate the number of vertices in the array
UINT numVertices = sizeof(vertices) / sizeof(VertexPosColorStruct);
```

Previously, right after you created the array of vertices, they were dropped in a vertex buffer. This time, since the buffer they use will be contained within the mesh object, that part of the process will have to wait.

Next up is the creation of the index array. Again, the indices used for the terrain environment are shown.

```
// Create the indices array
DWORD indices[NUM_VERTSX * NUM_VERTSY * 6];

// The index counter
int curIndex = 0;
```

```
// Fill the indices array to create the triangles needed for the terrain
// The triangles are created in a counterclockwise direction
for (int z=0; z < NUM_ROWS; z++)
{
    for (int x=0; x < NUM_COLS; x++)
    {
        // The current vertex to build off of
        int curVertex = x + (z * NUM_VERTSX);

        // Create the indices for the first triangle
        indices[curIndex]   = curVertex;
        indices[curIndex+1] = curVertex + NUM_VERTSX;
        indices[curIndex+2] = curVertex + 1;

        // Create the indices for the second triangle
        indices[curIndex+3] = curVertex + 1;
        indices[curIndex+4] = curVertex + NUM_VERTSX;
        indices[curIndex+5] = curVertex + NUM_VERTSX + 1;

        // increment curIndex by the number of vertices for the two triangles
        curIndex += 6;
    }
}

// determine the number of indices
UINT numIndices = sizeof(indices) / sizeof(DWORD);
```

Creating the ID3DX10Mesh Object

Now that you have the needed vertex and index data, you can create the mesh object. Meshes can be created using the D3DX10CreateMesh function. This is one of the more complicated functions, requiring eight parameters.

The first parameter is simply a pointer to the Direct3D object.

The second parameter is the number of items in the vertex layout. For example, if your vertex layout includes only position and color, then this value will be two. It can be calculated like so:

```
// The vertex input layout
D3D10_INPUT_ELEMENT_DESC layout[] =
{
    {"POSITION", 0, DXGI_FORMAT_R32G32B32_FLOAT, 0, 0,
```

```
    D3D10_INPUT_PER_VERTEX_DATA, 0 },
    {"COLOR", 0, DXGI_FORMAT_R32G32B32A32_FLOAT, 0, 12,
    D3D10_INPUT_PER_VERTEX_DATA, 0 },
};

// Calculate the number of elements in the layout array
UINT numElements = (sizeof(layout) / sizeof(layout[0]));
```

The third parameter is the name of the element that stores the position information for the vertex. In most cases this will be the text "POSITION".

Fourth is the number of vertices. This is the number of vertices that you stored in the vertex array earlier.

The next parameter is the number of faces, or polygons, the mesh will contain. Since you generated only a list of vertices and indices, you may be wondering where the number of faces will come from. Since it takes three vertices to create a single face, the number of faces can be calculated by dividing the number of indices by 3.

The sixth parameter is a flag that tells Direct3D whether to generate a mesh whose vertices are stored in 16- or 32-bit values. Since we want the most available precision, the flag D3DX10_MESH_32_BIT should be passed in. If you know the range of values required for your mesh will be within the 16-bit range, it will save you memory to use D3DX10_MESH_16_BIT.

The final parameter is a pointer to the ID3DX10Mesh object to be created.

```
// create the mesh object
HRESULT hr = D3DX10CreateMesh(pD3DDevice,
    layout,
    numElements,
    "POSITION",
    numVertices,
    (numIndices/3),
    D3DX10_MESH_32_BIT,
    &modelObject->mesh);
```

If everything went correctly you should now have a valid ID3DX10Mesh object to play with. In the next section I'll show you how to fill that object with the data you generated earlier.

Filling the Mesh Object with Data

The ID3DX10Mesh object provides a collection of methods that are very helpful for filling and accessing the embedded data.

When setting vertices to the vertex buffers within the mesh, the function SetVertexData can be used. This function takes an index to the buffer to fill and then the array of vertices. Meshes can actually contain more than one vertex buffer so an index into the buffer is required. Passing a value of 0 will place the vertices into the first buffer. In instances where your object may contain more than one distinct piece, creating more than one vertex buffer would be beneficial.

```
// set the vertex buffer data
modelObject->mesh->SetVertexData(0, vertices);
```

Setting the indices is an almost identical procedure. The SetIndexData function also takes two parameters, but in this case the array of indices is passed as the first parameter, with the second parameter being just an index count.

```
// set the index buffer data
modelObject->mesh->SetIndexData(indices, numIndices);
```

These two functions allow you to perform quick updates to the data contained within the mesh. Before the mesh can take advantage of this new data though, you must call the CommitToDevice function. This function lets the mesh know that new data is available and ready to be used. If you don't call this function, the mesh will continue to use the values it contained previously.

```
// save the changes to the mesh object
modelObject->mesh->CommitToDevice();
```

Drawing the Mesh

Drawing the mesh is actually the simplest part. By using the DrawSubset method provided by the mesh object, the data contained within the mesh is drawn. Meshes allow for multiple subsets of vertices and indices to be declared so mesh drawing can be split up into different portions. This is necessary when your mesh needs to use a different set of textures or shaders for each piece of the mesh. The simplest mesh example contains only a single portion and can be drawn by calling DrawSubset with a parameter of 0. More details on creating meshes with multiple portions can be found in the DirectX SDK documentation.

```
/*****************************************************************
* DrawModelObject
* Draws a single model object
* Inputs - const ModelObject *modelObject
* Outputs - void
*****************************************************************/
void DrawModelObject(const ModelObject *modelObject)
{
    // make sure modelObject is valid
    if (modelObject == NULL)
    {
        return;
    }

    // Render a model object
    D3D10_TECHNIQUE_DESC techniqueDescription;
    modelObject->pTechnique->GetDesc(&techniqueDescription);

    // Loop through the technique passes
    for(UINT p=0; p < techniqueDescription.Passes; ++p)
    {
        modelObject->pTechnique->GetPassByIndex(p)->Apply(0);

        modelObject->mesh->DrawSubset(0);
    }
}
```

Summary

As you can see, this is just the beginning of what Direct3D offers you. I encourage you to take the information you've learned and experiment, trying different parameters or data and just see what it does. You can only gain so much by reading and then you have to get in there yourself. In the next chapter you'll be introduced to another aspect of DirectX, user input.

What You Have Learned

In this chapter, you should have learned the following:

- How to properly texture an object

- What texture coordinates are and how they are applied

- How to use a shader for alpha blending

- How to generate a mesh object from a list of vertices

Review Questions

Answers to Review Questions can be found in Appendix A, "Answers to End-of-Chapter Exercises."

1. What must be added to the vertex format to allow support for texture mapping?

2. What is multi-texturing?

3. Which shader function is used to interpolate between textures?

4. Which interface is the Direct3D mesh object based on?

5. Which function is used to create the mesh object?

On Your Own

1. Take advantage of the min and max shader functions to see how they affect texture blending.

2. Use the `ID3DX10Mesh` utility functions to find the number of vertices and faces contained within a mesh.

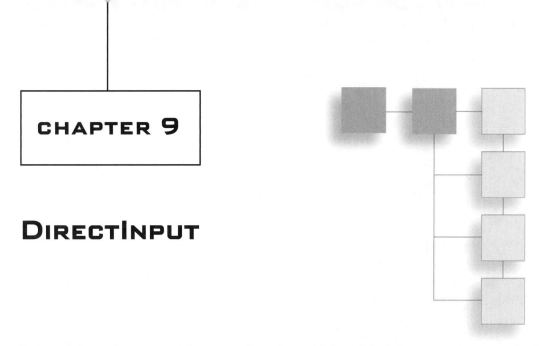

CHAPTER 9

DIRECTINPUT

Being able to interact with your virtual world is critical in any game—be it through the keyboard, mouse, or any number of other devices. In this chapter, I'll be explaining the benefits of DirectInput and how to use it.

Here's what you'll learn in this chapter:

- How DirectInput can make your life easier

- The types of devices DirectInput can support

- How to detect the input devices currently installed

- How to use keyboards, mice, and joysticks

- How to use analog or digital controls

- How to support more than one input device

- How to use force feedback

I Need Input

Every game needs the ability to interact with its user. Be it through a keyboard, mouse, dance pad, or other device, your game needs a way of getting direction from the person playing. The input device can be used to drive a car around a track, move your character around its world, or anything else that you can imagine.

Back in the days of DOS, game developers had very little choice but to poll hardware interrupts if they wanted to get keystrokes from the keyboard. Standard C functions of the time, like getchar, were too slow to be useful for games. Developers needed a better way; enter the Basic Input Output System (BIOS). The *BIOS* is the lowest level of software in a computer.

Stored normally in a flash ROM on the motherboard, the BIOS tells the system how to initialize and prepares the hardware for the operating system. The BIOS itself used to be directly accessible to programmers through assembly language while under DOS. Since the BIOS knew everything that the hardware was doing, developers were able to ask it for certain information. One of the important bits of the system that the BIOS was always watching was the keyboard. Every stroke of a key triggered a hardware interrupt, informing the system that a key had been pressed. Since this happened almost instantaneously, a very quick and efficient method for getting keystrokes from the keyboard was available.

When Windows NT came along, the ability to read the keyboard directly from the hardware was eliminated. Windows became an absolute boundary between applications and the hardware. Any information needed about the system had to be gained from the operating system since applications were no longer allowed direct access to the hardware. Windows had its own way of getting user input and that was through the message queue. You saw the message queue earlier in the book:

```
MSG msg = {0};
while (WM_QUIT != msg.message)
{
    // check for messages
    while( PeekMessage( &msg, NULL, OU, OU, PM_REMOVE ) == TRUE )
    {
        TranslateMessage( &msg );
        DispatchMessage( &msg );
    }
}
```

The message queue collects events, such as mouse movement and keyboard input, from the system. While this method is normally sufficient for Windows applications, it isn't fast enough for games. Most developers at this point turned to another Windows function, `GetAsyncKeyState`, to get the information they needed.

This function allowed for very quick checking of the keys on the keyboard and even allowed for checking of multiple keys and the state of the mouse buttons. This method of collecting user input became common among game developers, but it had one major issue; it didn't allow for input to be collected from other devices like game pads and joysticks. Game makers were stuck specifically supporting only certain devices because each device had a different way of collecting and transmitting the input data to the system.

A standard way of getting fast input from the user was needed regardless of the method or the device used. DirectInput provided the common layer needed to solve this problem.

Which Devices Does DirectInput Support?

DirectInput allows your game to support myriad of input devices without forcing you to know the exact details of each device. A small sample of the devices supported by DirectInput is shown here.

- Keyboard

- Mouse

- Game pads

- Joysticks

- Steering wheels

Using DirectInput

DirectInput is initialized in a very similar manner to other DirectX components, requiring the creation of both a DirectInput object as well as an input device.

The DirectInput object provides the interface needed to access DirectInput devices. Through this interface, you are able to create an instance of a device, enumerate the devices on a system, or check the status of a particular device.

Once you have the DirectInput object created, you have to create the device. The DirectInput device that you create will enable you to gain specific access to an input device, be it a keyboard, joystick, or other gaming device.

After creating the device, you need to gain access to its input. This is done through a process called *acquiring a device*. When you acquire a device, you are provided with access to initialize the device, get a list of its capabilities, or read its input.

It may seem like a lot of trouble to go through just to get a couple of keystrokes from a keyboard or game pad, but having direct access to your input device will make your life simpler later on.

Now that you have access to the device, you're able to read input from it each frame. For example, if you are using a game pad as your input device, you can check to see if the user has pressed the direction buttons or if one of the predefined action buttons has been pressed. If so, you can then act on this information.

At this point, you should have a clear understanding of the process needed to get DirectInput up and running and getting data from an input device. I'm now going to step you through the code needed to do just that.

Creating the DirectInput Object

As I mentioned before, the first step to using DirectInput is the creation of the DirectInput object. The function `DirectInput8Create` is used to create the DirectInput object.

The `DirectInput8Create` function is defined as:

```
HRESULT WINAPI DirectInput8Create(
    HINSTANCE hinst,
    DWORD dwVersion,
    REFIID riidltf,
    LPVOID *ppvOut,
    LPUNKNOWN punkOuter
);
```

There are five parameters that need to be passed to the `DirectInput8Create` function.

- **hInst.** An instance to the application that is creating the DirectInput object.

- **dwVersion.** This is the version number of DirectInput that this application requires. The standard value for this parameter is `DIRECTINPUT_VERSION`.

- **riidltf.** The identifier of the required interface. Using the default value of IID_IDirectInput8 is acceptable for this parameter.

- **ppvOut.** The pointer to the variable that will hold the created DirectInput object.

- **punkOuter.** This parameter is normally set to NULL.

Below is a small snippet of code that will create a DirectInput object.

```
LPDIRECTINPUT8          directInputObject;    // the direct input object

// Create the DirectInput object.
HRESULT hr = DirectInput8Create( hInst,
                    DIRECTINPUT_VERSION,
                        IID_IDirectInput8,
            ( void** )&directInputObject,
            NULL );

// check the return code for DirectInput8Create
if FAILED( hr )
{
    return false;
}
```

Note

As a reminder, make sure to check the return value when creating DirectX objects. This will let you know when an object creation has failed as well as help you track down bugs in your code.

The preceding code first creates two variables: hr and directInputObject. The first variable, hr, is defined as a standard HRESULT. This variable is used to check the return code of a function call. The second variable, directInputObject, is used to hold the soon to be created DirectInput object.

The code then continues by making the call to DirectInput8Create. A quick check of the return code in the variable hr is done to make sure that the function returned successfully.

Creating the DirectInput Device

Now that you have a valid DirectInput object, you are free to create the device. The device is created using the function CreateDevice.

```
HRESULT CreateDevice(
    REFGUID rguid,
    LPDIRECTINPUTDEVICE *lplpDirectInputDevice,
    LPUNKNOWN pUnkOuter
);
```

The CreateDevice function requires three parameters.

- **rguid**. The variable holds a reference to the GUID of the desired input device. This value can either be a GUID returned from the function EnumDevices or one of the two default values:

  - GUID_SysKeyboard
  - GUID_SysMouse

- **lplpDirectInputDevice**. The variable that will hold the returned Direct-Input device upon its creation.

- **pUnkOuter**. Address of the controlling object's interface. This value will normally be NULL.

The following code assumes that you want to create a DirectInput device for an installed system keyboard.

```
LPDIRECTINPUTDEVICE8  directInputDevice;   // the DirectInput device for the
keyboard

// Retrieve a pointer to an IDirectInputDevice8 interface
HRESULT hr = directInputObject ->CreateDevice( GUID_SysKeyboard,
&directInputDevice, NULL );

// check the return code from CreateDevice
if FAILED(hr)
{
    return false;
}
```

The preceding code first creates the variable directInputDevice. This variable of type LPDIRECTINPUTDEVICE8 is used to hold the created DirectInput device.

The call to CreateDevice, which is a method available to you through the DirectInput object, is made by passing in the value GUID_SysKeyboard as the first parameter. This tells CreateDevice that you want a device object created based on the system keyboard. The second parameter is the directInputDevice variable that was created earlier, and the third parameter is NULL.

After this function call is complete, the directInputDevice variable will hold a valid DirectInput device. Be sure that the return code for this function is checked to confirm that the device is valid.

Setting the Data Format

After a valid DirectInput device has been created, you need to set up the data format that DirectInput will use to read input from the device. The SetDataFormat function defined next requires a DIDATAFORMAT structure as its only parameter.

```
HRESULT SetDataFormat (
    LPCDIDATAFORMAT lpdf
);
```

The DIDATAFORMAT structure describes various elements of the device for DirectInput. The DIDATAFORMAT structure is defined here:

```
typedef struct DIDATAFORMAT {
    DWORD dwSize;
    DWORD dwObjSize;
    DWORD dwFlags;
    DWORD dwDataSize;
    DWORD dwNumObjs;
    LPDIOBJECTDATAFORMAT rgodf;
} DIDATAFORMAT, *LPDIDATAFORMAT;
```

Table 9.1 DIDATAFORMAT Structure

Member	Description
dwSize	Size of this structure in bytes.
dwObjSize	Size of the DIOBJECTDATAFORMAT in bytes.
dwFlags	A DWORD value that specifies attributes of this data format. Valid values are DIDF_ABSAXIS, meaning the axes are absolute values, or DIDF_RELAXIS, meaning the axes of this device are relative.
dwDataSize	This value holds the size of the data packet returned from the input device in bytes.
dwNumObjs	The number of objects with the rgodf array.
rgodf	Address to an array of DIOBJECTDATAFORMAT structures.

It is necessary to create and use your own DIDATAFORMAT structure if the input device you want to use is not a standard device. There are a number of predefined DIDATAFORMAT structures for common input devices.

- **c_dfDIKeyboard.** This is the data format structure that represents a system keyboard object.

- **c_dfDIMouse.** This data format structure is used when the input device being used is a mouse with up to four buttons.

- **c_dfDIMouse2.** This data format structure is used when the input device being used is a mouse or similar device with up to eight available buttons.

- **c_dfDIJoystick.** The data format structure for a joystick.

- **c_dfDIJoystick2.** The data format structure for a joystick with extended capabilities.

If the input device you want to use is not included as one of the predefined types, you will need to specifically create a DIDATAFORMAT structure. Most of the common input devices will not require this.

The following code sample calls the SetDataFormat function using the predefined DIDATAFORMAT structure for a keyboard device.

```
// set the data format for the device by calling the SetDataFormat function
HRESULT hr = directInputDevice ->SetDataFormat(&c_dfDIKeyboard);

// check the SetDataFormat return code
if FAILED(hr)
{
    return false;
}
```

Setting the Cooperative Level

The cooperative level is needed to tell the system how the input device that you are creating will work with the system. Input devices can be set to use either exclusive or non-exclusive access. Exclusive access means that only your application has the ability to use a particular device and does not need to share it with other applications that Windows may be running. This is most useful when your game is a full-screen application. When a device, such as the mouse or keyboard, is being used exclusively by a game, any attempt for another application to use this device will fail.

If your game doesn't mind sharing the device, then this is called non-exclusive access. When a game creates the device with non-exclusive access, other applications running will be able to use that same device. This is most useful when your game is running in windowed mode on the Windows desktop. Using the mouse as a non-exclusive input device will not restrict the use of the mouse in other application windows.

Each game that uses a DirectInput device must set the cooperative level for its use. This is done through the function SetCooperativeLevel, defined here:

```
HRESULT SetCooperativeLevel(
    HWND hwnd,
    DWORD dwFlags
);
```

The SetCooperativeLevel function requires only two parameters.

- **hwnd.** A handle to the window that is requesting access to the device.

- **dwFlags.** A series of flags that describe the type of access that you are requesting. The available flags are:

  - **DISCL_BACKGROUND.** The application is requiring background access to the device. This means that the input device can be used even when the game window is not the currently active window.
  - **DISCL_EXCLUSIVE.** The game is requesting total and complete control over the input device, restricting its use from other applications.
  - **DISCL_FOREGROUND.** The game only requires input when the window is the current active window on the desktop. If the game window loses focus, input to this window is halted.
  - **DISCL_NONEXCLUSIVE.** Exclusive access is not needed for this application. Defining this flag allows the device to continue to be used by other running applications.
  - **DISCL_NOWINKEY.** This tells DirectInput to disable the Windows key on the keyboard. Normally by pressing this key the Start Bar on the desktop is activated and focus is removed from the currently active window. When this flag is set, the Windows key is deactivated, allowing your game to retain focus.

Note

Each application must specify whether it needs foreground or background access to the device by setting either the DISCL_BACKGROUND or DISCL_FOREGROUND flags. The application is also required to set either the DISCL_EXCLUSIVE or DISCL_NONEXCLUSIVE flags. The DISCL_NOWINKEY flag is completely optional.

The following code sample sets the device to use non-exclusive access and only be active when the application window has focus.

```
// Set the cooperative level
hr = directInputDevice ->SetCooperativeLevel( wndHandle,
                          DISCL_FOREGROUND | DISCL_NONEXCLUSIVE );
// check the return code for SetCooperativeLevel
if FAILED(hr)
{
    return false;
}
```

You'll notice that the SetCooperativeLevel function is a method callable through the DirectInput device interface. The directInputDevice variable above represents the current DirectInput device created by the call to CreateDevice.

The parameters being passed in the example SetCooperativeLevel function above consist of wndHandle, which represents the handle to the window requesting access to the input device, and the flags DISCL_FOREGROUND and DISCL_NONEXCLUSIVE, telling DirectInput the access you are requesting for the device.

Acquiring Access

The final step required before you are able to read input from a particular device is called "acquiring the device." When you acquire access to an input device, you are telling the system that you are ready to use and read from this device. The function Acquire, another method of the DirectInput device, performs this action. The Acquire function, defined next, takes no parameters and returns only whether it was successful or not.

```
HRESULT Acquire(VOID);
```

The following small code example shows how the Acquire function is called.

```
// Get access to the input device.
HRESULT hr = directInputDevice ->Acquire();
if FAILED(hr)
```

```
{
    return false;
}
```

You'll notice again that the return code for this function is checked to make sure it was completed successfully. Since this is the last step needed before reading input from a device, it's best to check the return code to make sure the device is ready and available.

Getting Input

Now that we've completed the required steps to initialize an input device through DirectInput, it's time to actually use it. All devices use the function GetDeviceState when reading input. Whether the input device is a keyboard, mouse, or game pad, the GetDeviceState function is used.

```
HRESULT GetDeviceState(
    DWORD cbData,
    LPVOID lpvData
);
```

The first parameter required is a DWORD value that holds the size of the buffer being passed as the second parameter. The second parameter is a pointer to the buffer that will hold the data read from the device. As a reminder, the format of the data from the input device was defined earlier using the SetDataFormat function.

The next few sections will show how to enumerate the input devices available to your application through DirectInput.

Enumerating Input Devices

Most games available for the PC allow for use of input devices other than a keyboard or a mouse, such as a game pad or joystick. Many computers do not have these non-standard devices by default so DirectInput cannot just assume their presence. Also, since Windows allows for multiple game pads or joysticks to be installed simultaneously, DirectInput needs a way of determining how many and of what type these devices are. The method DirectInput uses to get the needed information on the input devices is called enumeration.

Like Direct3D can enumerate through the video adapters installed in a system and get the capabilities of each, DirectInput can do the same for input devices.

Using functions available through the DirectInput object, DirectInput is able to retrieve the number of input devices available in a system as well as each one's type and functionality. For instance, if your game requires the use of a game pad with an analog control stick, you can enumerate the installed devices and see if any of them meet your criteria.

The process of enumerating the installed devices on a system requires first gathering a list of the devices that meet your input needs and secondly, gathering the specific capabilities of these devices.

DirectInput uses the function EnumDevices to gather the list of installed input devices. Since there are different types of devices possibly installed on a machine and you probably wouldn't be interested in getting a list of them all, EnumDevices allows you to specify the type of devices you are searching for. For instance, if you're not interested in the mouse and keyboard devices and are searching specifically for joystick devices, EnumDevices provides a way of eliminating the unwanted devices from the list.

First, I'm going to explain how EnumDevices is used. The function EnumDevices is defined as:

```
HRESULT EnumDevices(
    DWORD dwDevType,
    LPDIENUMDEVICESCALLBACK lpCallback,
    LPVOID pvRef,
    DWORD dwFlags
);
```

This function requires four parameters.

- **dwDevType.** This parameter sets the filter for the device search. As I mentioned above, you can tell EnumDevices to only search the system for a particular type of device. This parameter can use any of the following values.

  - **DI8DEVCLASS_ALL.** This value will cause EnumDevices to return a list of all input devices installed in a system.
  - **DI8DEVCLASS_DEVICE.** This value will cause a search for devices that do not fall into another class of device, such as keyboard, mice, or game controllers.
  - **DI8DEVCLASS_GAMECTRL.** This causes EnumDevices to search for all game controller types of devices, such as game pads or joysticks.

- **DI8DEVCLASS_KEYBOARD.** `EnumDevices` will search the system for all keyboard devices.
- **DI8DEVCLASS_POINTER.** This value tells `EnumDevices` to search for pointer devices, such as mice.

- **lpCallback.** `EnumDevices` utilizes a callback mechanism when searching the system for input devices. This parameter is the address of the function you define to work as the callback.

- **pvRef.** This parameter is used to pass data to the callback function defined in the `lpCallback` parameter. Any 32-bit value can be used here. If no information is needed to be sent to the callback function, then you can pass `NULL`.

- **dwFlags.** The final parameter is a `DWORD` value consisting of a set of flags letting `EnumDevices` know the scope of the enumeration. For instance, if you want `EnumDevices` to search the system for only installed devices or those with force feedback, then you would specify one of the following values.

  - **DIEDFL_ALLDEVICES.** This is the default value. All devices in the system will be enumerated.
  - **DIEDFL_ATTACHEDONLY.** Only devices currently attached to the system are returned.
  - **DIEDFL_FORCEFEEDBACK.** Only the devices supporting force feedback will be returned.
  - **DIEDFL_INCLUDEALIASES.** Windows allows aliases to be created for devices. These aliases appear to the system as input devices but they represent another device in the system.
  - **DIEDFL_INCLUDEHIDDEN.** This causes `EnumDevices` to only return hidden devices.
  - **DIEDFL_INCLUDEPHANTOMS.** Phantom devices are placeholder devices.

The following code sample utilizes the `EnumDevices` function call to gather a list of game controllers that are currently attached to the system.

```
HRESULT hr;          // variable used to hold the return code

// Call the EnumDevices function
hr = directInputObject->EnumDevices( DI8DEVCLASS_GAMECTRL,
                                     EnumDevicesCallback,
                                     NULL,
                     DIEDFL_ATTACHEDONLY ) ;
```

```
// check the return value of the EnumDevices function
If FAILED( hr )
        return false;
```

The call to EnumDevices used the values DI8DEVCLASS_GAMECTRL to search for game controllers. The value DIEDFL_ATTACHEDONLY was used to only look for those devices attached to the system.

The second parameter value of EnumDevicesCallback represents the name of the callback function that will receive the devices found.

The third parameter is NULL because no additional information needs to be sent to the callback function.

The EnumDevices Callback

The callback function provided to EnumDevices is called every time a device matching the search criteria is found. For instance, if you are searching the system for game pads and there are currently four plugged in, the callback function will be called a total of four times.

The purpose of the callback function is to give your application the chance to create a DirectInput device for each piece of hardware, allowing you to then scan the device for its capabilities.

The callback function must be defined in your code utilizing a specific format, DIEnumDevicesCallback.

```
BOOL CALLBACK DIEnumDevicesCallback(
    LPCDIDEVICEINSTANCE lpddi,
    LPVOID pvRef
);
```

The DIEnumDevicesCallback function requires two parameters, the first being a pointer to a DIDEVICEINSTANCE structure and the second parameter being the value passed to the pvRef parameter of EnumDevices.

The DIDEVICEINSTANCE structure (described in Table 9.2) holds the details concerning an input device, such as its GUID and its product name. The information within this structure is useful when displaying a choice of devices to the user because it enables them to recognize a device based on its name.

Table 9.2 DIDEVICEINSTANCE Structure

Member Name	Description
dwSize	The size of this structure in bytes.
guidInstance	GUID for the specific device. This value can be saved and used later with CreateDevice to gain access to the device.
guidProduct	The unique identifier for the input device. This is basically the device's product ID.
dwDevType	This value is the device-type specifier. This can be any value specified in the DirectX documentation for this structure.
tszInstanceName	The friendly name for the device, such as "Joystick 1", "AxisPad".
tszProductName	The full product name for this device.
guidFFDriver	If this device supports force feedback, this value will represent the GUID of the driver being used.
wUsagePage	This value holds the Human Interface Device (HID) usage page code.
wUsage	The usage code for a HID.

```
typedef struct DIDEVICEINSTANCE {
    DWORD dwSize;
    GUID  guidInstance;
    GUID  guidProduct;
    DWORD dwDevType;
    TCHAR tszInstanceName[MAX_PATH];
    TCHAR tszProductName[MAX_PATH];
    GUID  guidFFDriver;
    WORD  wUsagePage;
    WORD  wUsage;
} DIDEVICEINSTANCE, *LPDIDEVICEINSTANCE;
```

The DIEnumDevicesCallback function requires a Boolean value to be returned. DirectInput has defined two values that should be used instead of the standard true or false.

- **DIENUM_CONTINUE.** Returning this value tells the enumeration to continue.

- **DIENUM_STOP.** This value forces the device enumeration to stop.

These values are used to control the device enumeration process. If you are searching the system for only one joystick device, it's useless to enumerate through all the installed joysticks. Returning `DIENUM_STOP` after finding the first suitable device would be all that was needed.

Commonly, you will want to collect a list of all the suitable devices so the user can select which specific device they want to use. Using the callback mechanism, you can create DirectInput devices for each piece of hardware and place them in a list. The user would then be able to select the device they want to use.

The following code example shows the callback function that will return upon finding the first joystick device that meets the `EnumDevices` criteria.

```
BOOL CALLBACK EnumDevicesCallback ( const DIDEVICEINSTANCE* pdidInstance,
                                              VOID* pContext )
{
    // variable to hold the return code
    HRESULT hr;

    // Use create device
    hr = directInputObject ->CreateDevice( pdidInstance->guidInstance,
    &directInputDevice, NULL );

    // the call to CreateDevice failed, keep looking for another
    if FAILED(hr)
    {
        return DIENUM_CONTINUE;
    }

    // the device was found and is valid, stop the enumeration
    return DIENUM_STOP;
}
```

The code first attempts to use the `CreateDevice` function to gain access to the device passed into the callback function. If the call to `CreateDevice` fails, the callback function returns `DIENUM_CONTINUE` telling the enumeration of input devices to continue. Otherwise, if the call to `CreateDevice` was successful, then the callback returns the value `DIENUM_STOP`.

An example demonstrating how to enumerate the devices in your system and display their device names can be found in the Chapter9\example3 directory on the CD-ROM. Figure 9.1 shows the dialog created from this example.

Figure 9.1
Listing of installed input devices.

Getting the Device Capabilities

After you have a valid device returned from EnumDevices, you may need to check for specific functionality. For instance, you may need to find the type of force feedback the device can support.

Enumerating the capabilities of a device is very similar to enumerating for the devices themselves. To get the specific details for a device, you call a function called EnumObjects. Like the call to EnumDevices, this function works along with a callback method.

```
HRESULT EnumObjects(
    LPDIENUMDEVICEOBJECTSCALLBACK lpCallback,
    LPVOID pvRef,
    DWORD dwFlags
);
```

The EnumObjects function requires three parameters.

- **lpCallback**. The name of the callback function.

- **pvRef**. Extra data that will be sent to the callback function when it is called.

- **dwFlags**. The flags are a DWORD value that specifies the types of objects on the input device that you are interested in enumerating.

The EnumObjects Callback

The purpose of the EnumObjects callback function is to gather information regarding a particular input device. The information collected for each device is passed to the callback as a DIDEVICEOBJECTINSTANCE structure.

Table 9.3 EnumObjects Flags

Flag Name	Description
DIDFT_ABSAXIS	Absolute Axis.
DIDFT_ALIAS	Looks for controls identified by a HID usage alias.
DIDFT_ALL	Looks for all types of objects on the device.
DIDFT_AXIS	Looks for an axis, relative or absolute.
DIDFT_BUTTON	Checks for push or toggle buttons.
DIDFT_COLLECTION	HID link collections.
DIDFT_ENUMCOLLECTION	An object that belongs to a link collection.
DIDFT_FFACTUATOR	Object that contains a force feedback actuator.
DIDFT_FFEFFECTTRIGGER	Object that contains a force feedback trigger.
DIDFT_NOCOLLECTION	Looks for objects that do not belong to a link collection.
DIDFT_NODATA	Object that does not generate data.
DIDFT_OUTPUT	Object that supports output.
DIDFT_POV	Looks for a POV controller.
DIDFT_PSHBUTTON	Looks for a push button.
DIDFT_RELAXIS	Relative Axis.
DIDFT_TGLBUTTON	Looks for a toggle button.
DIDFT_VENDORDEFINED	Object of a type defined by the manufacturer.

The callback function defined in the call to EnumObjects must follow the function signature of DIEnumDeviceObjectsCallback.

```
BOOL CALLBACK DIEnumDeviceObjectsCallback (
    LPCDIDEVICEOBJECTINSTANCE lpddoi,
    LPVOID pvRef
);
```

The DIEnumDeviceObjectsCallback function takes two parameters. The first parameter is the structure of type DIDEVICEOBJECTINSTANCE, which holds the returned information regarding the device. The second parameter is any value that was passed into the EnumObjects function in its pvRef parameter.

The DIDEVICEOBJECTINSTANCE structure contains a wealth of valuable information about the device. It's useful for setting the limits for force feedback as well as helping to determine the specific types and number of controls on the device.

A full explanation of the DIDEVICEOBJECTINSTANCE structure can be found in the DirectInput documentation.

Getting Input from a Keyboard

Getting input from the keyboard is rather simple because it is a default device. The keyboard requires a buffer consisting of a 256-element character array.

```
char      buffer[256];
```

The character array holds the state of each key on the keyboard. The state of one or multiple keys can be held in this array each time the keyboard device is read from. Most games will require that the input device be read from each frame from within the main game loop.

Before you can read from the keyboard though, you need an easy way of determining which key on the keyboard was pressed. The macro KEYDOWN, provided next, simply returns TRUE or FALSE based on whether the key you are checking for is pressed.

```
#define KEYDOWN(name, key) (name[key] & 0x80)
```

An example of reading from the keyboard is found here:

```
// Define the macro needed to check the state of the keys on the keyboard
#define KEYDOWN(name, key) (name[key] & 0x80)

// this is the required keyboard buffer
char      buffer[256];

// this is the main game loop, read from the input device each frame
while ( 1 )
{

        // check the keyboard and see if any keys are currently
        // being pressed

        directInputDevice->GetDeviceState( sizeof( buffer ),
                                LPVOID )&buffer );

        // Do something with the input

        // Here the KEYDOWN macro is used to check whether the left arrow key was
        pressed.
        if (KEYDOWN(buffer, DIK_LEFT))
        {
                // Do Something with the left arrow
        }
```

```
        // KEYDOWN is used again to check whether the up arrow key was pressed.
        if (KEYDOWN(buffer, DIK_UP))
        {
                // Do Something with the up arrow
        }
}
```

As you can see, the main game loop calls GetDeviceState each frame and places the current state of the keyboard into the input buffer. The KEYDOWN macro is then used to check for the state of certain keys.

Figure 9.2 shows a small demonstration of using keyboard input to display which directional arrow was pressed.

An example showing how to read from the keyboard using DirectInput can be found in the chapter9\example1 directory on the CD-ROM.

Getting Input from a Mouse

Reading input from the mouse is very similar to reading it from the keyboard. The main difference is the GUID passed to the CreateDevice function and the DIDATAFORMAT structure used to hold the input for this device.

In the previous example, the call to CreateDevice used GUID_SysKeyboard as the first parameter. When using the mouse, the GUID for CreateDevice must be set to GUID_SysMouse.

Note

Setting the cooperative level to exclusive mode for mouse input keeps the Windows cursor from being displayed. In exclusive mode, you are responsible for drawing the mouse cursor yourself.

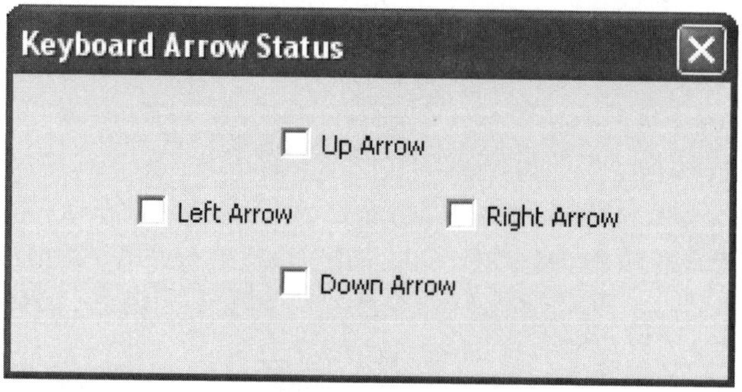

Figure 9.2
Keyboard demonstration sample.

```
// call the CreateDevice function using the GUID_SysMouse parameter
hr = directInputObject->CreateDevice(GUID_SysMouse, &directInputDevice, NULL);

// check the return code for the CreateDevice function
if FAILED(hr)
{
    return FALSE;
}
```

Also, the call to SetDataFormat used the predefined data format c_dfDIKeyboard. This value must be changed to c_dfDIMouse when using the mouse as the input device.

```
// set the Data Format for the mouse
hr = directInputDevice->SetDataFormat( &c_dfDIMouse );

// check the return code for the SetDataFormat function
if FAILED(hr)
{
    return FALSE;
}
```

The final change that needs to be made before you can read from the mouse is the addition of the DIDATAFORMAT buffer. The keyboard needs a character buffer consisting of 256 elements, whereas the mouse needs a buffer of type DIMOUSESTATE.

The DIMOUSESTATE structure consists of three variables holding the X, Y and Z position of the mouse as well as a BYTE array of four elements for holding the state of the mouse buttons. The DIMOUSESTATE structure is defined as:

```
typedef struct DIMOUSESTATE {
    LONG lX;      // holds the distance the mouse has traveled in the X direction
    LONG lY;      // holds the distance the mouse has traveled in the Y direction
    LONG lZ;      // holds the distance the mouse has traveled in the Z direction
    BYTE rgbButtons[4];    // the current state of the mouse buttons
} DIMOUSESTATE, *LPDIMOUSESTATE;
```

Previously, a macro was used to help determine if specific keys on the keyboard had been pressed. A similar macro can be used to check the state of the mouse buttons.

```
#define BUTTONDOWN( name, key ) ( name.rgbButtons[ key ] & 0x80 )
```

This macro will return TRUE or FALSE for each button on the mouse.

Note

The X, Y, and Z values in the DIMOUSESTATE structure do not hold the current position of the mouse but rather the relative position to where the mouse previously was. For example, if you moved the mouse slightly to the left about 5 pixels, the X value would be −5. If you moved the mouse down 10 pixels, the Y value would be 10.

When reading from a mouse, you must keep track of the values read from the mouse on the previous frame to be able to correctly interpret the mouse movement.

The following code fragment demonstrates the code needed to read from the mouse device. This code handles checking both the movement of the mouse as well as the state of the mouse buttons.

```
// Define the macro needed to check the state of the keys on the keyboard
#define BUTTONDOWN (name, key) (name.rgbButtons[key] & 0x80)

// this is required to hold the state of the mouse
DIMOUSESTATE   mouseState; // This variable will hold the current state of the
                mouse device
LONG            currentXpos; // This variable will hold the current X position of
                the mouse
LONG            currentYpos; // This variable will hold the current Y position of
                the mouse

// set the default position for the sprite
curX = 320;
curY = 240;

// this is the main game loop, read from the input device each frame
while ( 1 )
{
    // check the mouse and get the current state of the device
    // being pressed
    directInputDevice->GetDeviceState (sizeof ( mouseState ),
                        LPVOID) &mouseState);

    // Do something with the input

    // Here the BUTTONDOWN macro checks if the first mouse button is pressed
    if (BUTTONDOWN( mouseState, 0 ) )
```

```
    {
        // Do something with the first mouse button
    }

    // BUTTONDOWN is used again to check whether the second mouse button is
    pressed
    if ( BUTTONDOWN( mouseState, 1 ) )
    {
        // Do Something with the up arrow
    }

    // Next check the movement of the mouse

    // See how far in the X direction the mouse has been moved
    curX += mouseState.lX;
    // See how far in the Y direction the mouse has been moved
    curY   += mouseState.lY;

    // Do something with the mouse movement
}
```

A full code example can be found in the chapter9\example2 directory on the CD-ROM. Figure 9.3 shows this sample in action.

Figure 9.3
Showing mouse movement.

The structure `DIMOUSESTATE2` provides variables to hold the current state of up to eight mouse buttons.

Using a Game Pad or Joystick

Game pads and joysticks have been common game input devices for a while now. Whereas most joystick controllers used to be plugged into the game port on sound cards, most devices sold now utilize a USB connection. The USB connection gives devices an advantage over the previous devices. USB devices are easily detectable by the system and are handled through the common HID interface. Because of this, reading from game pads and joysticks has become easier.

The main difference in the use of a joystick is the absolute need to enumerate the input devices. Since multiple joysticks can be plugged into a system, DirectInput does not have a `GUID` predefined for these devices. Before you can call `CreateDevice` to prepare a joystick for use, you must enumerate the input devices installed on the system.

Joystick Enumeration

Enumerating the devices causes DirectInput to query each device against the search criteria you have set. For instance, if you called `EnumDevices` like this:

```
hr = directInputObject->EnumDevices( DI8DEVCLASS_GAMECTRL,
                                      EnumDevicesCallback,
                             NULL,
                    DIEDFL_ATTACHEDONLY );
```

the devices returned to the `EnumDevicesCallback` function would only be of type `DI8DEVCLASS_GAMECTRL`, which is exactly what you need when searching for joysticks.

Polling a Joystick

Another change is the need to poll the device. Keyboards and mice generate hardware interrupts when they're used, informing the system that there is new input data available. Most joysticks require that they be "polled" occasionally. The term polling refers to the checking of the device for new input. After a device has been polled, the new valid input can be retrieved from it.

Note

Joysticks and game pads use the predefined DIDATAFORMAT structures, DIJOYSTATE and DIJOYSTATE2.

Joysticks are not completely digital devices; they consist of an analog piece as well. Commonly, joysticks will utilize digital input for buttons, meaning they are either up or down, and analog input for the stick itself. Analog input allows you to detect the distance the joystick was moved.

A slight movement of the joystick towards the right will send a small value to the controlling program, whereas pulling the joystick completely to the right will send a much higher value. The amount of this value is determined by the range property of the device.

The range property is normally set for the analog portions of a joystick and consists of the minimum value that the device will generate along with the maximum value. For instance, setting the minimum portion of the range to –1000 and the maximum range to 1000 will provide your game with only values that fall into this range. Moving the joystick to the left completely will send the value of –1000, while moving it to the right will send up to a value of 1000. The range of the device can be set to any values that will make sense to your application.

Setting the Range of a Joystick

In order to set the range property for the analog portion of the joystick, you must use the EnumObjects function. As you recall, the EnumObjects function works similarly to EnumDevices but instead sends its callback function details on the different pieces of the device itself. An example callback function is shown here:

```
/*****************************************************************
* EnumObjectsCallback
*****************************************************************/

BOOL CALLBACK EnumObjectsCallback( const DIDEVICEOBJECTINSTANCE*
deviceObjectInstance,
VOID* pContext )
{
    // If this object is an axis type object, then attempt to set its range
    if (deviceObjectInstance->dwType & DIDFT_AXIS )
    {
```

```
// Create a DIPROPRANGE structure
DIPROPRANGE diproRange;

// Create a structure to hold the analog range
diproRange.diph.dwSize       = sizeof(DIPROPRANGE);
diproRange.diph.dwHeaderSize = sizeof(DIPROPHEADER);
diproRange.diph.dwHow        = DIPH_BYID;
diproRange.diph.dwObj        = deviceObjectInstance->dwType;

// The Minimum and Maximum portions of the range are being set here
diproRange.lMin  = -1;
diproRange.lMax = 1;

// Set the range for the axis
HRESULT hr = directInputDevice->SetProperty( DIPROP_RANGE,
&diproRange.diph ) ;
// Check to see if setting the range property was successful
if FAILED(hr)
{
    return DIENUM_STOP;
}

// Tell EnumObjects to continue to the next object in this device
return DIENUM_CONTINUE;
}
```

This example first checks to see if the object being passed to the callback is an axis type. An axis object is a type representing the analog stick portions of a joystick controller. If a valid axis device is used, then the code attempts to set its range.

First, a DIPROPRANGE structure is created, which will hold the information regarding the range. A DIPROPRANGE structure is defined like this.

```
typedef struct DIPROPRANGE {
    DIPROPHEADER diph;
    LONG        lMin;
    LONG        lMax;
} DIPROPRANGE, *LPDIPROPRANGE;
```

The second and third variables within this structure, lMin and lMax, actually represent the minimum and maximum range values. These two values can be set to anything your game requires as long as the lMin variable is less than the value stored in lMax.

The first variable within the DIPROPRANGE structure is actually another structure, DIPROPHEADER. The DIPROPHEADER structure is required for all property structures.

```
typedef struct DIPROPHEADER {
    DWORD     dwSize;
    DWORD     dwHeaderSize;
    DWORD     dwObj;
    DWORD     dwHow;
} DIPROPHEADER, *LPDIPROPHEADER;
```

The DIPROPHEADER structure requires only four variables to be set. The first variable dwSize, represents the size of the enclosing structure in bytes. In this instance, it's the DIPROPRANGE structure.

The second variable, dwHeaderSize, is the size of the DIPROPHEADER structure.

The third and fourth variables work together. The contents of the dwHow variable describe the type of data within the dwObj variable. dwHow can be any of the following values.

- **DIPH_DEVICE**. dwObj must be set to 0.

- **DIPH_BYOFFSET**. dwObj is the offset into the current data format.

- **DIPH_BYUSAGE**. dwObj must be set to the HID usage page and usage values.

- **DIPH_BYID**. dwObj is set to the object identifier. This can be found in the DIDEVICEOBJECTINSTANCE structure passed to the callback function.

Finally, after these structures are filled in, you can call the SetProperty function. The SetProperty function accepts the GUID of the property to be set as its first parameter and an address to the structure containing the new property information.

Note

Some devices do not allow the range to be changed. The range property is read-only.

Other properties of a device can be changed using the same method as was used with the range property. Properties exist for other settings, like DIPROP_DEADZONE, a range value that specifies which portion of the joystick movement to ignore; DIPROP_FFGAIN, which sets the gain for force feedback; and DIPROP_AUTOCENTER, which tells the device whether it should auto-center itself when the user releases the device.

Reading from a Joystick

Joysticks, like other input devices, require the use of the `GetDeviceState` function. In the instance of joysticks and game pads though, the buffer needed to hold the input data is either of type `DIJOYSTATE` or `DIJOYSTATE2`. The main difference between the two structures is the number of objects on a joystick device that can be read. The `DIJOYSTATE` structure allows for only two analog devices, whereas the `DIJOYSTATE2` structure can handle more.

Since the input from the joystick is not an absolute position, you must keep track of any previous movement by your game. For instance, if you were using joystick input to control the movement of an object around the screen, you would need to keep separate variables, the object's current X and Y positions. When new input is read from the joystick, the new input is then added to the current X and Y positions. The following code sample demonstrates this.

```
// These are the two variables that will hold the current position of an object
LONG curX = 320;
LONG curY = 240;

while (1)
{
    // Use the DIJOYSTATE2 structure to hold the data from the joystick
    DIJOYSTATE2 js;

    // First, poll the joystick
    directInputDevice->Poll();

    // Get the current input from the device
    directInputDevice->GetDeviceState( sizeof(DIJOYSTATE2), &js ) );

    // add the new values to the current X and Y positions
    curX += js.lX;
    curY += js.lY;

    // Draw the object in its updated position
}
```

The small bit of code first polls the joystick device for new input. Then the new input is placed into the `DIJOYSTATE2` structure. Finally, the `lX` and `lY` values are added to the current X and Y position of the sprite. The `lX` and `lY` variables represent the returned input from the first analog stick.

A full source example of reading from the joystick can be found in the chapter9\example4 directory on the CD-ROM.

Supporting Multiple Input Devices

Most console games support more than one player. PCs should be no different. With the ability to plug in many USB game pads or joysticks, games on the PC are limited to only what you can think of. In this section, I'm going to explain the process to support multiple devices.

As you recall, each input device requires its own DirectInput device. Because of this, your code needs to be able to hold multiple DirectInput devices. Creating either an array or vector of IDirectInputDevice8 objects enables you to do this.

The next step is the enumeration of the installed devices. For instance, if your game needs to support four game pads, you call EnumDevices and gather the information returned through its callback function for each game pad device. Once you have stored the data for each device, you then call CreateDevice. You use the Create-Device function for each device that your callback saved. After you have created all the devices, you then have access to do whatever you want with them.

The following code shows an elementary example of this process.

```
#define NUM_DEVICES 4

// The 4 DirectInput Devices
LPDIRECTINPUTDEVICE8  devices[ NUM_DEVICES ];

// The DirectInput Object
LPDIRECTINPUT8          directInputObject  =  NULL;


Int curCount = 0;          // holds the number of devices we currently have
int APIENTRY WinMain( HINSTANCE hInst, HINSTANCE, LPSTR, int )
{
    // Create the DirectInput Object
    HRESULT hr = DirectInput8Create(hInstance,
        DIRECTINPUT_VERSION,
        IID_IDirectInput8,
                    ( void** ) &directInputDevice,
                    NULL );

    // Call the EnumDevices function
    hr = directInputObject->EnumDevices( DI8DEVCLASS_GAMECTRL,
```

```
                        EnumDevicesCallback,
                        NULL,
                        DIEDFL_ATTACHEDONLY ) ;

    // check the return value of the EnumDevices function
    If FAILED(hr)
    {
        return false;
    }

    // Do something interesting with the devices here
}


/***********************************************************************
 * EnumDevicesCallback
 ***********************************************************************/
BOOL CALLBACK EnumDevicesCallback( const DIDEVICEINSTANCE* pdidInstance, VOID*
pContext )
{
    // call CreateDevice for this returned device
    HRESULT hr = directInputObject->CreateDevice( pdidInstance->guidInstance,
            &devices[curCount]
            NULL );

    // If the call to CreateDevice failed, then stop enumerating more devices
    if FAILED(hr)
    {
        return DIENUM_STOP;
    }

    // else, increase the curCount variable by one and try to grab another device
    else
    {
        curCount++;
    }
    // continue the enumeration
    return DIENUM_CONTINUE;
}
```

The callback function doesn't actually do very much. It attempts to call
CreateDevice on each input device that is passed to it. If a device is able to be
created, it increments the counter variable and keeps looking for more. The code
will currently support up to four devices. If more than four game pads are needed,

then the size of the array holding the DirectInput devices will have to change. If you don't know how many devices you have or want to keep things dynamic, then it's useful to use a vector of IDIRECTINPUTDEVICE8 objects.

Reacquiring an Input Device

Sometimes during the course of a game the input device may be lost. If your game set the cooperative level for the device to non-exclusive, the possibility exists for another application to start and restrict your access to the device. In this case, you need to attempt to reacquire the device before you can continue to read from it and use its input.

When access to a device is lost, the return code from the GetDeviceState function is DIERR_INPUTLOST. When this happens, you need to call the Acquire function in a loop until access to the device is restored.

The following code demonstrates how to reacquire a device once access to it has been lost.

```
// this is the main game loop, read from the input device each frame
while ( 1 )
{
    // Call the GetDeviceState function and save the return code
    HRESULT hr = directInputDevice->GetDeviceState(sizeof(DIMOUSESTATE),
        (LPVOID)&mouseState);

    // check the return state to see if the device is still accessible
    if FAILED(hr)
    {
        // try and reacquire the input device
        hr = directInputDevice->Acquire( );
        // do a continuous loop until the device is reacquired
        while (hr == DIERR_INPUTLOST)
        {
            hr = directInputDevice ->Acquire( );
        }

        // just return and do nothing this frame
        continue;
    }

    // Check input and do something with it
}
```

Note

Most games require more than one input device for multiple people to play. By creating multiple DirectInput devices, you can support a number of separate devices.

Cleaning Up DirectInput

DirectInput, like Direct3D, requires that you release the objects that you've defined upon completion of your application. In addition to the DirectInput objects, you must also unacquire any devices that you have gained control over. If you forget to unacquire the input devices you've been using, when your game ends those devices may still be locked by the system and not able to be used. While a joystick or game pad wouldn't be too big a deal, forgetting to release the mouse or keyboard could make you have to restart your machine to get them back.

The function Unacquire is used to release a device that had been previously acquired through DirectInput.

```
HRESULT Unacquire( VOID );
```

Unacquire is a method provided by the DirectInput device interface.

The following example code will correctly unacquire the input devices and release both the DirectInput device and object.

```
// Check if you have a valid DirectInput Object
if (directInputObject)
{
    // Check to see if you have a valid DirectInput Device
    if (directInputDevice)
    {
        // Unacquire the input device
        directInputDevice->Unacquire( );

        // Release the DirectInput Device
        directInputDevice->Release( );

        // Set the DirectInput device variable to NULL
        directInputDevice = NULL;
    }

    // release the DirectInput Object
    directInputObject->Release( );
```

```
    // Set the DirectInput object variable to NULL
    directInputObject = NULL;
}
```

At this point you should have a clear understanding of initializing and reading from standard input devices through DirectInput. In the next section you will learn how to use force feedback to help immerse the player in your world.

Force Feedback

Since the release of the current generation of video game consoles onto the market, gamers have become familiar with the concept of force feedback. It's the ability to send different levels of vibration to an input device.

Force Feedback Effects

Force feedback devices perform their vibrations based on effects. A force feedback effect is made up of one or more forces acting on the controller. Forces within DirectInput are the push or resistance felt on a controller during the playing of an effect. Effects come in a couple of different flavors:

- **Constant Force.** A steady continual force in a single direction.

- **Ramp Force.** A force that will increase or decrease in intensity steadily over time.

- **Periodic Effect.** A pulsating force.

- **Conditional.** An effect that is triggered as a reaction to a particular motion.

Each force has a magnitude, or intensity, and a duration, or length of time. Changing the magnitude allows you to increase or decrease the amount of vibration or resistance the user feels while playing your game.

Tip

Overusing force feedback or using it at the wrong times within your game may cause player annoyance. Use force feedback sparingly.

To use a force feedback device, like a game pad, in your game, you need to do the following.

1. Create the DirectInput object.

2. Enumerate the installed game controller devices that support force feedback.

3. Create a device based on the game pad.

4. Create the force feedback effect you want to use.

5. Start the effect.

Enumerating the Input Devices for Force Feedback

Since force feedback is still not widespread in game controllers, you need to specifically look for this feature when enumerating the input devices. Previously, the only flag that you sent to EnumDevices was DIEDL_ATTACHEDONLY, which specified that this function should only return installed and attached devices to the callback. If this is left as the only flag, the callback will receive both force feedback and non-feedback devices. Since you know from the start that you want to look for only force feedback devices, you should add the flag DIEDFL_FORCEFEEDBACK to the EnumDevices call. This informs EnumDevices to only report back with force feedback enabled devices.

The following code shows the updated call to EnumDevices.

```
// The variable used to hold the input device
LPDIRECTINPUTDEVICE8 FFDevice   = NULL;

// Enumerate through the installed devices looking for a game controller or
   joystick

// that supports force feedback
HRESULT hr;
hr = directInputObject->EnumDevices( DI8DEVCLASS_GAMECTRL,
                                                  FFDeviceCallback,
                            NULL,
                            DIEDFL_ATTACHEDONLY | DIEDFL_FORCEFEEDBACK ) );
```

The EnumDevices function call above has been updated with the DIEDFL_ FORCEFEEDBACK flag.

The following code shows the callback function needed to find the force feedback device.

```
/*********************************************************************
*******************
* FFDeviceCallback
*********************************************************************
*****************/
BOOL CALLBACK FFDeviceCallback ( const DIDEVICEINSTANCE* pInst,
                                              VOID* pContext )
{
    // Create the device
    HRESULT hr = directInputObject->CreateDevice( pInst->guidInstance, &
    FFDevice, NULL );

    // this device could not be created, so keep looking for another one.
    if FAILED(hr))
    {
        return DIENUM_CONTINUE;
    }

    // We found a device, stop the enumeration
    return DIENUM_STOP;
}
```

At this point, only valid force feedback devices are being reported to the callback function. The callback attempts to create a device based on the first one it comes across. If the callback succeeds in creating the device, it stops the enumeration; otherwise, the enumeration continues to look for a suitable device.

Creating a Force Feedback Effect

After you've found the controller you're going to use and have a DirectInput device created for it, you need to create an effect object. DirectInput force feedback effect objects are based on the IDirectInputEffect interface. Each IDirectInputEffect object details the effect to the system.

The effect is created first by filling in a DIEFFECT structure. This structure describes the different aspects of the effect such as the duration, which axes are affected, and its force.

The DIEFFECT structure, once complete, is passed as a parameter to the CreateEffect function. The CreateEffect function registers the effect with DirectInput and the effect is downloaded to the device. Once the effect has been downloaded to the force feedback device, it's ready to be played.

Note

In order for an effect to be downloaded to a force feedback device, the device object must have a cooperative level of exclusive set. Force feedback devices are not able to share their feedback functionality among different applications.

To describe the process in a bit more detail, I'm going to take you through a quick rundown of the DIEFFECT structure using CreateEffect.

The DIEFFECT structure must be declared for each effect object that you want to create. The DIEFFECT structure is defined here:

```
typedef struct DIEFFECT {
    DWORD   dwSize;
    DWORD   dwFlags;
    DWORD   dwDuration;
    DWORD   dwSamplePeriod;
    DWORD   dwGain;
    DWORD   dwTriggerButton;
    DWORD   dwTriggerRepeatInterval;
    DWORD   cAxes;
    LPDWORD rgdwAxes;
    LPLONG  rglDirection;
    LPDIENVELOPE lpEnvelope;
    DWORD   cbTypeSpecificParams;
    LPVOID  lpvTypeSpecificParams;
    DWORD   dwStartDelay;
} DIEFFECT, *LPDIEFFECT;
```

The DIEFFECT structure consists of the following variables:

- **dwSize**. The size of the DIEFFECT structure in bytes.

- **dwFlags**. The flags that describe how some of the variables are to be used.

  - **DIEFF_CARTESIAN**. The values within the rglDirection variable are considered Cartesian coordinates.
  - **DIEFF_OBJECTIDS**. The values within the dwTriggerButton and rgdwAxes variables are object identifiers.
  - **DIEFF_OBJECTOFFSETS**. The values within the dwTriggerButton and rgdwAxes variables are data format offsets.
  - **DIEFF_POLAR**. The values within the rglDirection variable are considered to be Polar coordinates.
  - **DIEFF_SPHERICAL**. The values within the rglDirection variable are considered to be spherical coordinates.

- **dwDuration.** The duration of the effect in microseconds. If the duration of the effect should be continuous, then the value of INFINITE should be used.

- **dwSamplePeriod.** The sample rate of the effect playback. 0 indicates the default sample rate is to be used.

- **dwGain.** The gain of the effect.

- **dwTriggerButton.** The identifier of the button to be used to trigger the effect. This variable is dependent on the value within the dwFlags variable.

- **dwTriggerRepeatInterval.** The delay time between repeating the effect. This value is in microseconds.

- **cAxes.** The number of axes used by the effect.

- **rgdwAxes.** A pointer to a DWORD array that contains the IDs or offsets to the axes that the effect will use.

- **rglDirection.** An array of coordinates corresponding to the types of coordinates selected in the dwFlags variable.

- **lpEnvelope.** An optional pointer to a DIENVELOPE structure. This structure defines the envelope to be applied to this effect. Since no effects require this, NULL can be used.

- **cbTypeSpecificParams.** The number of bytes of additional parameters for the type of effect.

- **lpvTypeSpecificParams.** This variable holds the parameters discussed in the preceding variable. This variable can hold any of these defined structures:

    - **DIEFT_CUSTOMFORCE.** A structure of type DICUSTOMFORCE is passed.
    - **DIEFT_PERIODIC.** A structure of type DIPERIODIC is used.
    - **DIEFT_CONSTANTFORCE.** A constant force structure, DICONSTANTFORCE, is used.
    - **DIEFT_RAMPFORCE.** A ramp force structure of DIRAMPFORCE is used.
    - **DIEFT_CONDITION.** A structure of type DICONDITION must be passed.

- **dwStartDelay.** The time in microseconds that the device should wait before playing an effect.

The complete DIEFFECT structure is then passed to the CreateEffect function. The CreateEffect function requires four parameters and is defined like this:

```
HRESULT CreateEffect(
    REFGUID rguid,
    LPCDIEFFECT lpeff,
    LPDIRECTINPUTEFFECT *ppdeff,
    LPUNKNOWN punkOuter
);
```

The first parameter refers to the GUID of the type of force to be created. For instance, if you are trying to create a constant force effect, you would use the predefined GUID of GUID_ConstantForce. The second parameter is the passed-in DIEFFECT structure defined earlier. The third parameter is the address of the variable that will hold the newly created effect. This variable must be of type IDirectInputEffect. The final parameter to CreateEffect is normally NULL.

After you have your effect created and ready to go, the next step is playing it.

Starting an Effect

Before the user can feel your effect in action, it has to be played. The playback of a force feedback effect is handled through the function Start, which is a member function of IDirectInputEffect.

The Start function requires two parameters. The first is the number of times the effect should be played. The second parameter is a set of flags that relates to how the effect should be played on the device.

There are only two valid flags for the second parameter, and both can be applied. If no flags are required, then this parameter can be set to 0.

- **DIES_SOLO**. Any other effects currently playing will stop when this effect is played.

- **DIES_NODOWNLOAD**. The effect will not be downloaded automatically to the device.

Note

If an effect is currently playing and the Start function is called, this effect is started over from the beginning.

This example call to the Start function tells DirectInput to play the effect once and that no flags should be applied.

```
g_pEffect->Start( 1, 0 );
```

After calling the Start function, the effect will begin to play on the device. If the effect has duration, the effect will end when the duration is reached. If the duration of the effect is infinite, then you must stop the effect yourself.

Stopping an Effect

If an effect has duration, it will end when the duration is reached. But what about an effect whose duration is infinite or if the user has hit the pause button? Both of these instances require that an effect be stopped manually. This is accomplished through the function Stop. The Stop function requires no parameters and returns only whether the call was successful or not. The Stop function is declared next.

```
HRESULT Stop(VOID);
```

A return code of DI_OK means that the call to the Stop function was successful.

Summary

Input is such an integral part of any game and should be paid attention to during the development cycle. When games are reviewed, how well the input performs can make or break it. Always paying proper attention to the input system during development will only enhance the gamer's experience.

What You Have Learned

In this chapter you've learned how to use input devices and should now understand the following:

- How to use the mouse and keyboard devices

- The difference between analog and digital controls

- How to support more than one input device

- How to create and play force feedback effects through a game controller

- The proper way to release and shut down DirectInput

In the next chapter, you'll be introduced to DirectSound and how to use music and sound to enhance your game.

Review Questions

You can find the answers to Review Questions in Appendix A, "Answers to End-of-Chapter Exercises."

1. DirectInput allows for what type of input devices?

2. Which function creates the IDirectInput8 interface?

3. What is the detecting of input devices on a system called?

4. Reading from the keyboard requires what kind of buffer?

5. What is the data format type for mouse input?

On Your Own

1. Change the mouse input example to remove the Windows cursor.

2. Modify the game pad example to read from the controller buttons.

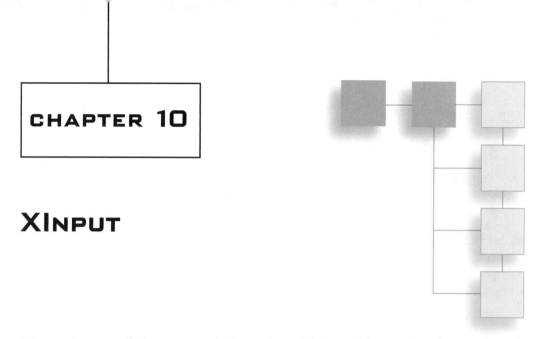

CHAPTER 10

XINPUT

XInput is one of the newest APIs to be added to DirectX. To keep up with constantly changing needs in game development, Microsoft updates DirectX with new functionality on an as-needed basis. Sometimes pieces will be deprecated, such as DirectDraw, while others like XInput will be added. XInput allows you to use the new Xbox 360 controller with your applications.

Here's what you'll learn in this chapter:

- How to quickly get XInput up and running

- How to read input from the user

- The types of controls available

- When and how to use the different methods of input

The XInput API

Instead of making developers rely on DirectInput when using the Xbox 360 controller, a more simple and straightforward API was created, XInput. This new API greatly reduces the amount of code needed to handle input from multiple users or vibrate the controller.

With the release of the Xbox 360, Microsoft has designated the Xbox 360 controller to be their cross-platform input solution. Instead of relying on third-party

Figure 10.1
The Xbox 360 controller.

controllers with different input methods, they chose to support the Xbox 360 controller under Windows XP and Vista. Games created with the Xbox 360 controller in mind can more easily be ported to the Xbox 360 console. Because of the specific scope of the XInput API, keyboards and mice are not supported.

The Xbox 360 controller can be seen in Figure 10.1.

Getting User Input

Gathering input from the user with XInput is very simple. A single call to the function XInputGetState is all that is needed to get the current state of a controller. The XInputGetState function takes only two parameters. The first parameter is the index of the controller to poll. The second parameter is a pointer to an XINPUT_STATE structure.

Since there can be multiple controllers attached to the system, more than one call to XInputGetState will be needed. The following code sample loops through a possible four controllers gathering the current input state from each one. The XInputGetState function stores the current input in the XINPUT_STATE structure.

```
// Set up the number of controllers to check
#define MAX_CONTROLLERS 4

// An Array of MAX_CONTROLLERS XINPUT_STATE structures
XINPUT_STATE inputState[MAX_CONTROLLERS];
```

```
// loop through the number of controllers
for (DWORD i=0; i < MAX_CONTROLLERS; i++)
{
    // Get the current state of the controller
    DWORD dwResult = XInputGetState(i, &inputState[ i ]);
}
```

Note

The Xbox 360 controller can be used with DirectInput, but not all functionality will be available.

Controller State

The XINPUT_STATE structure contains very few variables. The most important is the embedded XINPUT_GAMEPAD structure. This is the structure that is tasked with storing the user input. While XINPUT_STATE is the structure passed to the XInputGetState function, the actual user input gets stored in the embedded XINPUT_GAMEPAD structure. This structure will be discussed in more detail in a bit.

```
typedef struct _XINPUT_STATE
{
    DWORD dwPacketNumber;
    XINPUT_GAMEPAD Gamepad;
} XINPUT_STATE;
```

The other variable contained in the XINPUT_STATE structure is dwPacketNumber. This variable keeps track as to whether the state of the controller has changed from the last time it was read. If the user is holding down the exact same keys as the last time the controller was checked, this value will remain constant. If the controller state has changed, this value will be incremented. It's a good way to determine quickly if anything has changed without specifically checking each of the controls.

Each controller will normally have more than just the current input state associated with it. For instance, you may need to keep track of the user's previous input. This is useful when you need to detect whether the user is holding down a particular button or if it was quickly pressed and released. You may also want to keep a timestamp for the last input. Because of the multiple bits of information that can be associated with each controller, it's beneficial to create a container structure like CONTROLLER_INFO.

```
struct CONTROLLER_INFO
{
    XINPUT_STATE     curState;
};
```

Note

The Xbox Live button is used when connected to the Xbox 360 only.

Enabling User Input

Even though your ability to read from input devices is on by default, XInput provides a function for enabling or disabling input from the controllers. In some cases where the application may not be active or has been minimized, any input coming from the user should be ignored. Instead of setting up flags everywhere telling your game to ignore the controller input, you can use the `XInputEnable` function.

The `XInputEnable` function takes one parameter, a Boolean that tells XInput whether to listen for input. If you pass false to `XInputEnable`, any activity from the controller is ignored and your application will receive nothing but zeros in response to the `XInputGetState` function.

Re-enabling input is as simple as passing in true to the `XInputEnable` function.

Detecting Controller Insertion

One of the most important things you need to track about user input during your game is whether the player's controller is still connected. Controllers may be removed at any time either on purpose or accidentally. Your game should track the current state of the controllers, pause the game, and notify the player to re-insert their controller. Because you're constantly polling the controller for new input, you should be aware of the controller being removed almost immediately.

The function `XInputGetState`, while returning an `XINPUT_STATE` structure, also has a return value. This return value will either be `ERROR_SUCCESS`, if the controller was able to be read properly or an error value indicating that there was a problem. When reading the controller, always check the return value of the `XInputGetState`. If the function returns any value other than `ERROR_SUCCESS`, you can assume the controller has been removed.

You should track the current status of the controller in your `CONTROLLER_INFO` structure. In the following structure, the `isConnected` Boolean variable is used to track the controller state.

```
struct CONTROLLER_INFO
{
    XINPUT_STATE curState;
    BOOL isConnected;      // variable to hold controller status
};
```

The isConnected variable should be set each time you call the XInputGetState function.

```
for (DWORD i = 0; i < MAX_CONTROLLERS; i++)
{
    // Get the current state of the controller
    DWORD dwResult = XInputGetState(i, &controllers[i].curState);

    // Set whether this controller is connected by checking the dwResult
    controllers[i].isConnected = (dwResult == ERROR_SUCCESS);
}
```

By adding the isConnected variable to the CONTROLLER_INFO structure, each controller can be tracked individually.

Reading the Digital Controls

The Xbox 360 controller contains two sets of controls, a series of digital buttons, and two sets of analog controls. The digital buttons have only two states, on or off. Because of the simple states, they can be easily checked.

The XINPUT_STATE structure contains an embedded structure called XINPUT_GAMEPAD. The XINPUT_GAMEPAD structure holds the current state of each of the controls in the Xbox 360 controller. The ones we're interested in at the moment are the fourteen digital buttons.

```
typedef struct _XINPUT_GAMEPAD {
    WORD wButtons; // holds the current state of all the digital buttons
    BYTE bLeftTrigger; // the current value for the left trigger
    BYTE bRightTrigger; // the current value for the right trigger
    SHORT sThumbLX; // the left thumb stick, X Axis
    SHORT sThumbLY; // the left thumb stick, Y Axis
    SHORT sThumbRX; // the right thumb stick, X Axis
    SHORT sThumbRY; // the right thumb stick, Y Axis
} XINPUT_GAMEPAD;
```

The state of all the digital buttons is tracked with a single WORD variable called wButtons. Because the buttons can either be on or off, they can be tracked using only a single bit. Each of the buttons has a position in the wButtons variable and can be checked separately by using a bitwise AND.

```
// Loop through all the controllers
for (DWORD i = 0; i < MAX_CONTROLLERS; i++ )
{
    // check the current controller for the Y Button
    if (controllers[i].curState.Gamepad.wButtons & XINPUT_GAMEPAD_Y))
    {
        // handle the Y button pressed
    }
}
```

The wButtons variable is compared against the button constants found in the XInput.h header file. These constants are listed in Table 10.1.

Note

If you're ever unsure of a value for any of the digital buttons, you can check the values in the XInput.h header file.

Table 10.1 Digital Button Controller Constants

Button	Code Constant
D-Pad Up	XINPUT_GAMEPAD_DPAD_UP
D-Pad Down	XINPUT_GAMEPAD_DPAD_DOWN
D-Pad Left	XINPUT_GAMEPAD_DPAD_LEFT
D-Pad Right	XINPUT_GAMEPAD_DPAD_RIGHT
Start	XINPUT_GAMEPAD_START
Back	XINPUT_GAMEPAD_BACK
Left Thumb	XINPUT_GAMEPAD_LEFT_THUMB
Right Thumb	XINPUT_GAMEPAD_RIGHT_THUMB
Left Shoulder	XINPUT_GAMEPAD_LEFT_SHOULDER
Right Shoulder	XINPUT_GAMEPAD_RIGHT_-SHOULDER
A Button	XINPUT_GAMEPAD_A
B Button	XINPUT_GAMEPAD_B
X Button	XINPUT_GAMEPAD_X
Y Button	XINPUT_GAMEPAD_Y

Example 1 in the Chapter 10 directory on the CD-ROM provides an example of reading from the digital controls.

Analog Controls

The second type of control is called analog. Where digital allows for only an on or off state, analog allows for an entire range of input. The Xbox 360 controller contains two types of analog controls, the triggers and the two thumb sticks. Because of the extent of the input range, analog controls are used wherever more detailed input is needed.

The left thumb stick is commonly used for main character movement and the right thumb stick for camera control. The triggers are used for anything from an actual gun trigger to gas and brake for a racing game.

Reading the input from one of the analog controls requires a little more work on the game side. Each of the thumb sticks contains both an X and a Y axis, each one with a range from −32768 to 32767. If your game is using the thumb sticks to control character movement, you will need to take both the X and Y values into account. The following code shows an example of how the X and Y values could be used.

```
// loop through the controllers
for (DWORD I = 0; I < MAX_CONTROLLERS; i++ )
{
    // get the current X and Y values
    int currentX = controllers[i].curState.Gamepad.sThumbLX;
    int currentY = controllers[i].curState.Gamepad.sThumbLY;

    // handle player movement using the thumb stick values
    HandlePlayerMovement(currentX, currentY);
}
```

The triggers are a bit easier to deal with, providing a simpler range from 0 to 255. The current values for the left and right triggers are held in the bLeftTrigger and bRightTrigger variables, respectively, in the XINPUT_GAMEPAD structure.

The following code shows an example of how the values from the triggers might be used in a racing game scenario.

```
// loop through the controllers
for (DWORD I = 0; I < MAX_CONTROLLERS; i++ )
{
    // Use the value from the left trigger
    ApplyAccelerationAmount(controllers[i].curState.Gamepad.bLeftTrigger);
```

```
    // Use the value from the right trigger
    ApplyBrakeAmount(controllers[i].curState.Gamepad.bRightTrigger);
}
```

The code above used the values from the controls directly; it is usually best to store these variables off somewhere before applying them.

Dead Zones

Since analog controls allow for such a wide range of values, they can be very temperamental. Barely touching the control will register as input or occasionally the controls will not fully reset themselves to their default positions, causing random input values to be sent to your game code.

Dead zones restrict a certain percentage of the input range, giving the analog control a bit of leeway before registering as input. XInput provides a default dead zone value for each of the analog controls. These values are not automatically taken into account when you read from the control; you have the option of using the defaults or specifying your own values. Table 10.2 shows the dead zone constants defined in XInput.h for each of the analog controls.

When you get the input data from the XInputGetState function, each of the values from the analog controls should be normalized using the dead zone constants. Any value from the controls that falls within the dead zone should be ignored and considered zero. The following code shows an example of how the dead zones can be utilized.

```
// Loop through the controllers
for (DWORD i = 0; i < MAX_CONTROLLERS; i++)
{
    // Get the current state of the controller
    DWORD dwResult = XInputGetState(i, &controllers[i].curState);
```

Table 10.2 Default Dead Zone Constants

Analog Control	Dead Zone Constant
Left Thumb Stick	XINPUT_GAMEPAD_LEFT_THUMB_DEADZONE
Right Thumb Stick	XINPUT_GAMEPAD_RIGHT_THUMB_DEADZONE
Triggers	XINPUT_GAMEPAD_TRIGGER_THRESHOLD

```
    // normalize the data from the thumb sticks with the dead zone
    if ( (controllers[i].curState.Gamepad.sThumbLX <
XINPUT_GAMEPAD_LEFT_THUMB_DEADZONE) &&

        (controllers[i].curState.Gamepad.sThumbLX > -
XINPUT_GAMEPAD_LEFT_THUMB_DEADZONE) )
    {
        controllers[i].curState.Gamepad.sThumbLX = 0;
    }

    if ( (controllers[i].curState.Gamepad.sThumbLY <
XINPUT_GAMEPAD_LEFT_THUMB_DEADZONE) &&

                    (controllers[i].curState.Gamepad.sThumbLY > -
XINPUT_GAMEPAD_LEFT_THUMB_DEADZONE) )
    {
        controllers[i].curState.Gamepad.sThumbLY = 0;
    }
}
```

Example 2 in the Chapter 10 directory on the CD-ROM provides an example of reading from the analog controls.

Controller Vibration

The ability for a controller to vibrate has been a staple of gaming since the PlayStation Dual Shock became popular. Since then, every gaming console system has supported a vibration feature and it's had many different names; vibration, rumble, and force feedback to name a few. The PlayStation 3 is the first next-generation console to remove this feature.

Vibration or rumble is commonly used to give the player additional feedback to what they are experiencing on the screen. Seeing your race car hit the wall just isn't the same unless the controller in your hands jumps when the crash happens. Many people find that their immersion in a game world is heightened when more than just their sense of sight and sound are used.

Controller vibration doesn't always add to the user experience. Occasionally you come across a game where vibration was used just for the sake of using it. Like every piece of technology you put into your game, it should serve a purpose and add to the user experience. Before you start vibrating the controller, ask yourself, will this reinforce the situation the player finds himself in? If the answer is no, or you think the user will only be annoyed, don't use it. If you find you must use vibration on a constant basis, for example, the feel of a car engine, make sure to provide the player with a way to disable it.

Motors

The Xbox 360 controller contains two motors that are used to create vibration. The first motor, which resides in the left side of the controller, is a low frequency motor. This motor can generate strong, slow pulses.

The right side contains a high frequency motor. This motor allows for a faster spin and gives the impression of a high pitched hum. Ideally, both motors are used at the same time to create the vibration effect you want.

Starting and Stopping the Motors

Vibration in the Xbox 360 controller is handled using an XINPUT_VIBRATION structure. This structure includes two variables, wLeftMotorSpeed and wRightMotor-Speed, each one used to control the speed of its respective motors.

```
typedef struct _XINPUT_VIBRATION
{
    WORD wLeftMotorSpeed;
    WORD wRightMotorSpeed;
} XINPUT_VIBRATION;
```

The motors are never just on or off; like the analog controls, the motors have a wide range of values that they use to vary their speed. Each motor allows for an input value between 0 and 65,535. As the value is increased, the speed at which the motors spin also increases.

Since you need to be able to turn on vibration on a per controller basis, the XINPUT_VIBRATION structure should be added to the CONTROLLER_INFO structure from earlier.

```
struct CONTROLLER_INFO
{
    XINPUT_STATE    curState;
    BOOL            isConnected;

    // vibration
    XINPUT_VIBRATION curVibration;
};
```

Now that you have a valid XINPUT_VIBRATION structure filled out, there's one more step: setting the vibration to the controller. The function XInputSetState is a function used to send vibration data to a controller. This function takes two parameters, the first being the index of the controller to set the vibration data for. The second parameter is a pointer to an XINPUT_VIBRATION structure. By placing different values in the structure, the speed of each motor can be adjusted. Stopping the motors is just as easy. Simply set the motor speeds to zero and call XInputSetState.

The following code snippet shows an example of how the motors can be controlled using the values from the trigger controls. Each of the trigger values is multiplied by a hard coded value of 256 because of the limited range of the trigger controls.

```
// Loop through the controllers
for (DWORD i = 0; i < MAX_CONTROLLERS; i++ )
{
    // set the speed of the motors based on the input from the triggers

    controllers[i].curVibration.wLeftMotorSpeed =
(controllers[i].curState.Gamepad.bLeftTrigger * 256);

    controllers[i].curVibration.wRightMotorSpeed =
(controllers[i].curState.Gamepad.bRightTrigger * 256);

    // Set the vibration for the controller
    XInputSetState( i, &controllers[i].curVibration );
}
```

As you can see, the vibration values are set on a per controller basis, allowing each controller to have different vibration effects. An example of using vibration with the Xbox 360 controller can be found in the chapter 10\example3 directory on the CD-ROM.

Device Capabilities

Since you're not always sure of the devices connected to the system, XInput gives you a way of gathering information about the available controllers. This information, called the device capabilities, provides your game with details such as the type of controller connected and the range of controls it contains. By collecting the device capabilities, you can tailor the user experience to the controller connected.

XInput contains a function called XInputGetCapabilities just for this reason.

The XInputGetCapabilities function requires just three parameters. The first parameter is the index of the current controller.

The second parameter is used to tell the XInputGetCapabilities function which types of controllers you're gathering information for. Passing in a value of XINPUT_FLAG_GAMEPAD will return information for Xbox 360 controllers.

The third parameter is the most important, a pointer to an XINPUT_CAPABILITIES structure. This structure is used to store all the information regarding the controller.

```
typedef struct _XINPUT_CAPABILITIES {
    BYTE Type;
    BYTE SubType;
    WORD Flags;
    XINPUT_GAMEPAD Gamepad;
    XINPUT_VIBRATION Vibration;
} XINPUT_CAPABILITIES;
```

The Type variable will contain the type of controller the information in the structure pertains to. Since only Xbox 360 controllers are supported, the only value that will be in the Type variable will be XINPUT_DEVTYPE_GAMEPAD.

The SubType variable contains more information about the type of controller attached. Since the Xbox 360 can support more than one type of controller, SubType is used to give a more detailed description of the device.

SubType can be one of three values:

- **XINPUT_DEVSUBTYPE_GAMEPAD**—The standard Xbox 360 controller.

- **XINPUT_DEVSUBTYPE_ARCADE_STICK**—An arcade joystick.

- **XINPUT_DEVSUBTYPE_WHEEL**—A racing wheel type controller.

SubType can be used to make sure the proper type of controller is connected for your game.

The Flags variable is a bitmask, designating controller features. Currently, XInput supports only one feature, XINPUT_CAPS_VOICE_SUPPORTED.

The next two variables are embedded structures, XINPUT_GAMEPAD and XINPUT_VIBRATION. These two structures contain the input and vibration ranges of the controller. For each control in the input device, the XINPUT_GAMEPAD structure will contain a variable giving is maximum input range. For instance, the left and right trigger variables, bLeftTrigger and bRightTrigger, should each contain 255, the maximum range of the trigger controls. By utilizing the values returned in these structures, you can allow your game to dynamically support different types of controllers.

The following code shows how easy it is to collect the capabilities of the controllers.

```
// The structure to hold the device information
XINPUT_CAPABILITIES xinputCapabilities;

// Return code
HRESULT hr;

// Loop through the controllers
for (int i = 0; i < MAX_CONTROLLERS; i++)
{
    // Get the capabilities of the device
    hr = XInputGetCapabilities( i, 0, &xinputCapabilities );

    // If the controller is not connected, hr will
    // equal ERROR_DEVICE_NOT_CONNECTED
    if (hr != ERROR_DEVICE_NOT_CONNECTED)
    {
        // Do something with the device capabilities
    }
}
```

The xinputCapabilities structure should now contain the current capabilities of the controller. The following code sample shows how to get a subset of the information from the structure.

```
/****************************************************************
* GetCapabilitiesString
* Inputs - XINPUT_CAPABILITIES structure
    TCHAR *buffer
* Returns - None
****************************************************************/
void GetCapabilitiesString(XINPUT_CAPABILITIES xinputCapabilities, TCHAR*
buffer)
{
    if (buffer != NULL)
    {
        wcscpy(buffer, TEXT("Controller capabilities\n"));

        // add the subtype
        switch (xinputCapabilities.SubType)
```

```
        {
            case XINPUT_DEVSUBTYPE_ARCADE_STICK:
                wcscat(buffer, TEXT("Device SubType: Arcade Joystick\n"));
            break;

            case XINPUT_DEVSUBTYPE_GAMEPAD:
                wcscat(buffer, TEXT("Device SubType: Game Pad\n"));
            break;

            case XINPUT_DEVSUBTYPE_WHEEL:
                wcscat(buffer, TEXT("Device SubType: Steering Wheel\n"));
            break;
        }

        // Does the controller have voice support
        if (xinputCapabilities.Flags == XINPUT_CAPS_VOICE_SUPPORTED)
        {
            wcscat(buffer, TEXT("Voice Supported: True\n"));
        }
        else
        {
            wcscat(buffer, TEXT("Voice Supported: False\n"));
        }
    }
}
```

Note

Only four Xbox 360 controllers can be connected at any one time. This keeps the user experience consistent between Windows and the Xbox 360.

Best Practices

When people play your game, you want to ensure that not only is your game enjoyable, but the way the user interacts with it is as well. There is nothing more frustrating than finding a game you know you'll love but not being able to get into it because the controls just aren't intuitive.

Here are a few guidelines to follow to make the user experience more enjoyable.

- Follow the generally accepted common functionality of the Xbox 360 controller. What this means is making sure your game uses the controls in a way that the user expects. For instance, the A button is used to accept a prompt while the B button is used to cancel or go back. Don't come up with your own methods just to be different.

- Just because you have fourteen means of input on one controller doesn't mean you have to use them all. Don't confuse the user with too many hotkeys; sometimes simpler is better.

- Track the current plugged in status of in-use controllers. If a controller all of a sudden is removed in the middle of a game, your game should handle this gracefully; pausing the game is an acceptable practice. Checking the return value from the `XInputGetState` function will give you this information.

- When reading from the controllers, there is no need to read from controllers that are not currently active. If your game is for a single player, keep track of the index of the controller being used and only read data from that one.

- Never scan for a hard-coded controller index. Never assume that index 0 is always valid. Just because there is one controller plugged in doesn't mean that it will be assigned index 0.

Summary

As you can see, XInput is one of the easier DirectX libraries to work with. Quick and concise user input is vital to any gaming application. By applying the XInput functions properly you'll enhance the user's experience with your game.

What You Have Learned

In this chapter you've learned how to use XInput to read from the Xbox 360 controller and should now understand:

- How to get user input from the Xbox 360 controller.

- Why you should detect if the user has removed his controller.

- How to read both analog and digital controls.

- How and when to use vibration.

In the next chapter, you'll be introduced to the DirectSound library and how to add an audio dimension to enhance your game.

Review Questions

You can find the answers to Review Questions in Appendix A, "Answers to End-of-Chapter Exercises."

1. Which function is used to get the current data from a controller?

2. How many controllers can be used at a time?

3. How is controller removal detected?

4. How is user input from a controller disabled?

5. Which structure is used to gather user input?

On Your Own

1. Change the analog example to remove the dead zone check. See how the lack of a dead zone affects the input.

2. Change the motor speed values in the vibration example to see how different types of vibration affect the controller.

CHAPTER 11

DIRECTSOUND

DirectSound helps your game come to life. When you take advantage of background music and sound effects, the world you create takes on a whole new depth. In this chapter, you'll learn how you can use sound effectively in your game.

Here's what you'll learn in this chapter:

- What DirectSound is
- How to use DirectSound
- What sound buffers are
- How to play a sound file
- How to cause a sound file to loop
- How to set and change a sound's volume

Sound

Sound is important in every game. It is used to set the mood, build tension, or celebrate the end of a level. Sound helps create your environment, from the engines of cars racing around a track to the gunfire you hear as bullets zoom over your head. DirectX provides the DirectSound API, allowing you to easily add an audio element to your game.

DirectSound

DirectSound provides a single API for the playback of sounds and music. Previously, developers had to make due with support for only certain sound cards because they were tasked with writing software for each one. With the birth of DirectX and hardware abstraction, developers only need to write to one common set of functions, which can support a wide array of sound cards.

How Does DirectSound Work?

DirectSound manages the sound data through the use of *buffers*. Buffers are areas of memory that hold data—in this case sound data. DirectSound works by mixing the sounds contained in multiple buffers into a single buffer, which is then sent to the speakers as the final audio the user hears.

Note

Sound buffers can reside either on sound card memory or in system memory.

You can access buffers that are contained in memory on the sound card more quickly than those buffers in system memory. You should use the latter type of buffers sparingly because they are limited by the amount of memory on the sound card.

For example, if you wanted to play the audio contained in a WAV file, the sound data would need to be loaded into a sound buffer and mixed by DirectSound for output.

DirectSound has the following types of buffers available:

■ **Primary buffer.** All sounds played are mixed into the primary buffer. The sound card uses the resulting mixed sound in the primary buffer to create the actual sound that you hear.

■ **Secondary buffer.** These are the buffers that hold all the sound data that your game needs. DirectSound lets you play multiple sounds by accessing more than one secondary buffer simultaneously.

■ **Static buffer.** When sound data is of limited size, you can create a static or fixed size buffer; these normally reside in memory on the audio card. This buffer allows for the complete loading of a particular sound into memory.

■ **Streaming buffer.** Sometimes, sounds that you want to play might be too large to fit into memory at one time. In this instance, you need a streaming buffer. The streaming buffer allows for only a portion of a sound to be loaded before being sent off to be played. As the sound within the streaming buffer is played, new sound data is loaded into it. Streaming buffers are sometimes referred to as circular buffers.

Using DirectSound

Before you can use DirectSound, you need to know the steps involved. Like other DirectX components, DirectSound must be initialized before you can use it. The first step to using DirectSound is creating the DirectSound device. The Direct-Sound device is represented by the IDirectSound8 interface. This interface provides methods for gaining control of the sound card, creating sound buffers, and gathering sound hardware capabilities.

The DirectSound Device

The DirectSound device represents an interface to a specific piece of sound hardware within your machine. For DirectSound to work, you must select an available sound card and create a DirectSound device to represent it. Because most machines contain only a single sound card, DirectSound allows you to create a DirectSound device based on a default sound card. If a machine has more than one sound card, you will need to enumerate through them to find the one that best meets your application's needs.

You create the DirectSound device by using the DirectSoundCreate8 function.

```
HRESULT WINAPI DirectSoundCreate8(
  LPCGUID  lpcGuidDevice,
  LPDIRECTSOUND8 * ppDS8,
  LPUNKNOWN  pUnkOuter
);
```

The DirectSoundCreate8 function requires three parameters:

- **lpcGuidDevice**. The GUID that represents the sound device to use. This can either be DSDEVID_DefaultPlayback or NULL if you want to use the default sound device.

- **ppDS8**. The address to the variable that will hold the newly created DirectSound device.

- **pUnkOuter**. The controlling object's IUnknown interface. This value should be NULL.

A standard call to DirectSoundCreate8 that uses the default sound device is shown next:

```
// variable that will hold the created DirectSound device
LPDIRECTSOUND8 directSoundDevice;

// Attempt to create the DirectSound device
// Passing NULL will use the default sound device
HRESULT hr = DirectSoundCreate8( NULL, &directSoundDevice, NULL ) ;

// Check the return value to confirm that a valid device was created
if FAILED (hr)
{
    return false;
}
```

If the code fails to create a valid DirectSound device, then the function returns FALSE.

Enumerating the Sound Devices

Occasionally, you might need to enumerate the sound hardware within a system. If, for instance, the default sound device does not have all the functions that your game might need, you can search for another device in the system.

If you're not going to use the default sound device, you need to enumerate through the available devices looking for the one suited to your purpose. When the device is found, pass its GUID to the DirectSoundCreate8 function instead of NULL.

The process of enumeration is handled through the function DirectSound-Enumerate. Enumerating sound devices requires a callback function. The DirectSoundEnumerate function triggers the callback every time a new sound device is detected. Within the callback function, you can determine the capabilities of the device and choose whether you want to use it.

The DirectSoundEnumerate function is defined as follows:

```
HRESULT WINAPI DirectSoundEnumerate(
  LPDSENUMCALLBACK  lpDSEnumCallback,
  LPVOID  lpContext
);
```

The `DirectSoundEnumerate` function requires just two parameters:

- **`lpDSEnumCallback`**. The address of the callback function.

- **`lpContext`**. Any data that you want sent to the callback function.

The following code shows a sample `DirectSoundEnumerate` function call:

```
// Call DirectSoundEnumerate to look for sound devices
HRESULT hr = DirectSoundEnumerate( (LPDSENUMCALLBACK) EnumCallback, 0);

// Check the return code to make sure that the call was successful
if FAILED ( hr)
{
    return false;
}
```

The code creates a callback function called `EnumCallback`. The second parameter is 0 because no information needs to be sent to the callback function.

The DirectSoundEnumerate Callback Function

The callback function provided to `DirectSoundEnumerate` is called every time the enumeration finds a new sound device. If multiple sound devices are installed in the system, the callback function is called once for each of them.

The main purpose of the callback function is to give your code a chance to create a DirectSound device and to use it to gather information about the device. If you were searching for a sound device that allowed for sound capture, you would check the capabilities of each device passed to the callback function to see if this functionality existed.

The `DirectSoundEnumerate` function requires the callback function to be in the `DSEnumCallback` format.

```
BOOL CALLBACK DSEnumCallback(
  LPGUID   lpGuid,
  LPCSTR   lpcstrDescription,
  LPCSTR   lpcstrModule,
  LPVOID   lpContext
);
```

You must declare the callback function using the DSEnumCallback signature. The callback function requires four parameters:

- **lpGuid.** The address to the GUID that identifies the current sound device. If this value is NULL, then the current device being enumerated is the primary device.

- **lpcstrDescription.** A NULL-terminated string that provides a text description of the current device.

- **lpcstrModule.** A NULL-terminated string that provides the module name of the DirectSound driver for this device.

- **lpContext.** The extra data that was passed to the callback function through the lpContext variable in DirectSoundEnumerate.

The DSEnumCallback function returns a Boolean value. If the return value is TRUE, then the DirectSoundEnumerate function continues to enumerate additional devices. If the return value is FALSE, then the enumeration of additional devices stops.

Note

The primary device is always enumerated twice: once with a value of NULL being passed to the lpGuid parameter and a second time with its proper GUID.

The sample callback function that follows creates a message box that displays the name of the current sound device and its driver.

```
/*****************************************************************-
******
* DirectSoundEnumerate callback function
*****************************************************************-
*****/
BOOL CALLBACK DSCallback( GUID* pGUID, LPSTR strDesc,
                          LPSTR strDrvName,   VOID* pContext )
{
    TCHAR buffer[256] = {0};

    // Create the output string to display to the user
    wsprintf(buffer, TEXT("Device name = %s\nDriver Name = %s"), strDesc,
    strDrvName);
```

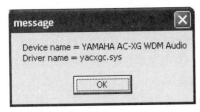

Figure 11.1
Message box showing the sound device name and driver.

```
// Display the device description and driver name
MessageBox(NULL, buffer, TEXT("message"), MB_OK);

    return TRUE;
}
```

A temporary character array is created to hold the information. The function returns a value of TRUE, so it will enumerate all the sound devices in the system. The full source listing for this example is located in the chapter11\example1 directory on the CD-ROM. Figure 11.1 shows what the message box will look like when displaying the sound device information.

Setting the Cooperative Level

Because DirectSound gives you access to a hardware device, it needs to have a cooperative level set. Similar to DirectInput, DirectSound attempts to gain primary access to a device. In DirectInput, you can gain exclusive access to an input device, restricting its use to only your application. In DirectSound, you cannot gain exclusive access to the sound device, but you can let the operating system know that you want your application to have the highest priority when it comes to using the sound hardware. Because you cannot gain exclusive access to the sound card, other applications—including the operating system—can still trigger sounds to be played.

The three DirectSound cooperative levels are shown next:

- **DSSCL_NORMAL.** This level works best with other applications that still allow other events. Because your application must share the device, though, you cannot change the format of the primary buffer.

- **DSSCL_PRIORITY.** If you want to be able to have more control over the primary buffer and your sounds, you should use this cooperative level. Most games should use this level.

- **DSSCL_WRITEPRIMARY.** This level allows your application to have write access to the primary buffer. This is used when you want to perform the sound mixing yourself.

The cooperative level is set using the SetCooperativeLevel function. The IDirectSound8 interface provides this function. The SetCooperativeLevel function is defined as follows:

```
HRESULT SetCooperativeLevel(
  HWND hwnd,
  DWORD dwLevel
);
```

This function requires two parameters:

- **hwnd.** The handle of the application window requesting the change in cooperative level.

- **dwLevel.** One of the three cooperative levels shown earlier.

Here is a sample call to SetCooperativeLevel:

```
// variable that contains a valid DirectSound device
LPDIRECTSOUND8 directSoundDevice = NULL;

// First, create the DirectSound device
HRESULT hr = DirectSoundCreate8( NULL, &directSoundDevice, NULL );

// Set DirectSound cooperative level
If (directSoundDevice != NULL)
{
    hr = directSoundDevice ->SetCooperativeLevel( hwnd, DSSCL_PRIORITY );

    // Check the return code
    if FAILED (hr)
    {
        return false;
    }
}
```

In this code sample, the cooperative level is being set to the value of DSSCL_PRIORITY. Before you can call the SetCooperativeLevel function, you must have a valid pointer to a DirectSound device.

Now that the cooperative level is set, you can create buffers and load sound data.

Sound Files

Sound data must be loaded into a buffer before being played. As we've discussed, sound data is loaded into secondary buffers. You have the option of using either a static or streaming buffer.

A *static buffer* is a fixed-length buffer that has full sound loaded into it. A *streaming buffer* is needed when the sound being loaded is larger than what the buffer can accommodate. In this case, a small buffer is used and parts of the sound data are continuously loaded and played. The next section discusses how buffers are used in DirectSound.

The Secondary Buffer

All sound data that DirectSound works with must originate in a secondary buffer. From every little sound effect to the constant background music, all this sound data is loaded into a secondary buffer before being played. Now, creating a secondary buffer isn't difficult and DirectSound allows you to create as many as you have the memory for.

Before you can create a secondary buffer, you need to know the format of the sound that will reside in it. DirectSound requires that the buffers you create be of the same format as the sound within them. For example, if you are loading a 16-bit WAV file that needs two channels of sound, then the secondary buffer you create must be of this format.

Most of the time, the sounds you use for your game will share a common format, allowing you to know beforehand what format your buffers require. If you are tasked with writing a generic audio player, though, you cannot be guaranteed that all the sound files you load will be the same format.

The formats of the buffers in DirectSound are described using the WAVEFORMATEX structure. The WAVEFORMATEX structure is defined next:

```
typedef struct {
  WORD  wFormatTag;
  WORD  nChannels;
  DWORD nSamplesPerSec;
  DWORD nAvgBytesPerSec;
  WORD  nBlockAlign;
  WORD  wBitsPerSample;
  WORD  cbSize;
} WAVEFORMATEX;
```

This structure consists of seven variables.

- **wFormatTag.** The type of waveform audio. For one or two-channel PCM data, this value should be WAVE_FORMAT_PCM.

- **nChannels.** The number of channels needed.

- **nSamplesPerSec.** The sample rate.

- **nAvgBytesPerSec.** The average data-transfer rate in bytes per second.

- **nBlockAlign.** The alignment in bytes. You determine the value needed here by multiplying the number of channels by the bits per sample and then dividing by 8.

- **wBitsPerSample.** The number of bits per sample. This value will be either 8 or 16.

- **cbSize.** The extra number of bytes to append to this structure.

You can create a standard WAVEFORMATEX structure if you know the format of the WAV file data that you will be using. If you aren't sure, then you can create this structure and fill it in after opening the audio file.

The WAVEFORMATEX structure is only part of the information you need when creating a secondary buffer. Besides specifying the format of the buffer, you need to know additional information, such as the size of the audio contained in the sound file.

You need a second structure to finish describing the secondary buffer to DirectSound: DSBUFFERDESC. The DSBUFFERDESC structure is defined here:

```
typedef struct {
    DWORD          dwSize;
    DWORD          dwFlags;
    DWORD          dwBufferBytes;
    DWORD          dwReserved;
    LPWAVEFORMATEX lpwfxFormat;
    GUID           guid3DAlgorithm;
} DSBUFFERDESC;
```

The DSBUFFERDESC structure contains six variable components:

- **dwSize.** The size of the DSBUFFERDESC structure in bytes.

- **dwFlags.** A `DWORD` set of flags that specify the capabilities of the buffer.

- **dwBufferBytes.** The size of the new buffer. This is the number of bytes of sound data that this buffer can hold.

- **dwReserved.** A reserved value that must be 0.

- **lpwfxFormat.** An address to a `WAVEFORMATEX` structure.

- **guid3DAlgorithm.** A `GUID` identifier to the two-speaker virtualization algorithm to use.

Buffers, besides having a format associated with them, also have controls. The controls of a buffer allow you to manipulate the volume, frequency, and movement. You must specify the types of controls you want in the `DSBUFFERDESC` structure shown earlier.

Table 11.1 DSBUFFERDESC Flags

Value	Description
DSBCAPS_CTRL3D	The buffer has 3D control.
DSBCAPS_CTRLFREQUENCY	The buffer can control the frequency of the sound.
DSBCAPS_CTRLFX	The buffer supports effects processing.
DSBCAPS_CTRLPAN	The buffer can pan the sound.
DSBCAPS_CTRLPOSITIONNOTIFY	This is the position notification buffer.
DSBCAPS_CTRLVOLUME	You can control the volume of this buffer.
DSBCAPS_GLOBALFOCUS	If this flag is set and the user switches focus to another application, the sounds in the current application continue to play.
DSBCAPS_LOCDEFER	You can place the buffer in software or hardware memory at runtime.
DSBCAPS_LOCHARDWARE	The buffer is to use hardware mixing. If this flag is specified and not enough memory is available, the call to create the buffer fails.
DSBCAPS_LOCSOFTWARE	The buffer is to be placed in software memory, and software mixing is to be used.
DSBCAPS_MUTE3DATMAXDISTANCE	The sound in this buffer is reduced as its virtual position gets farther away.
DSBCAPS_PRIMARYBUFFER	This is the primary buffer.
DSBCAPS_STATIC	The buffer is to be placed in on-board hardware memory.
DSBCAPS_STICKYFOCUS	When you're switching focus to another application, you can still hear buffers with sticky focus. Normal buffers are muted when this occurs.

Creating a Secondary Buffer

Now that you've created the DSBUFFERDESC structure, you are ready to create the actual secondary buffer. The secondary buffer is created with a call to Create-SoundBuffer, defined here:

```
HRESULT CreateSoundBuffer(
  LPCDSBUFFERDESC pcDSBufferDesc,
  LPDIRECTSOUNDBUFFER * ppDSBuffer,
  LPUNKNOWN pUnkOuter
);
```

The CreateSoundBuffer function requires only three parameters:

- **pcDSBufferDesc.** Address to an already defined DSBUFFERDESC structure.

- **ppDSBuffer.** Address to the variable that will hold the newly created buffer.

- **pUnkOuter.** Address to the controlling object's IUnKnown interface. This value should be NULL.

A sample call to CreateSoundBuffer is shown here:

```
// Define a WAVEFORMATEX structure
WAVEFORMATEX wfx;
// Clear the structure to all zeros
ZeroMemory( &wfx, sizeof(WAVEFORMATEX) );

// Set the format to WAVE_FORMAT_PCM
wfx.wFormatTag    = (WORD) WAVE_FORMAT_PCM;
// Set the number of channels to 2
wfx.nChannels       = 2;
// Set the samples per second to 22050
wfx.nSamplesPerSec  = 22050;
// Compute the nBlockAlign value
wfx.wBitsPerSample  = 16;
wfx.nBlockAlign     = (WORD) (wfx.wBitsPerSample / 8 * wfx.nChannels);
// Compute the nAvgBytesPerSec value
wfx.nAvgBytesPerSec = (DWORD) (wfx.nSamplesPerSec * wfx.nBlockAlign);

// Define a DSBUFFERDESC structure
DSBUFFERDESC dsbd;
// Clear the structure to all zeros
```

```
ZeroMemory( &dsbd, sizeof(DSBUFFERDESC) );
// Set the size of the structure
dsbd.dwSize          = sizeof(DSBUFFERDESC);
// Set the flags
dsbd.dwFlags         = 0;
// the size of the buffer
 dsbd.dwBufferBytes   = 64000;
// the GUID of the algorithm
 dsbd.guid3DAlgorithm = GUID_NULL;
// the address of the WAVEFORMATEX structure
 dsbd.lpwfxFormat     = &wfx;

// Define the variable to hold the newly created buffer
LPDIRECTSOUNDBUFFER directSoundBuffer  = NULL;
// Create the sound buffer
HRESULT hr = directSoundDevice->CreateSoundBuffer( &dsbd, &directSoundBuffer,
NULL );
// Check the return code to make sure the call to CreateSoundBuffer succeeded
if FAILED (hr)
{
    return NULL;
}
```

If the call to CreateSoundBuffer was successful, the variable directSoundBuffer will be a valid DirectSoundBuffer. In the previous example, the format of the WAVEFORMATEX structure was hard coded, forcing any sound files that were loaded into this buffer to be of the specified format and up to 64,000 bytes long. Normally reading the data from a WAV file into the WAVEFORMATEX structure will give you the information you need.

Loading a Sound File into a Buffer

Now that you've created the sound buffer, you need to load the sound data into it. Loading sound data into a buffer requires you to first open the file containing the sound data and then decode its contents into the buffer. With a static buffer, all the sound data is copied into the buffer.

Because a sound buffer is an area of memory controlled by DirectSound, you must lock it before you can write to it. Locking the buffer prepares the memory to be written to. After a buffer is locked, your application can begin loading sound data into it. When you are finished loading the sound data, you must remember to unlock the buffer. Unlocking the buffer allows DirectSound to manipulate the buffer's contents again.

Locking the Sound Buffer

Locking the sound buffer gives your code a chance to manipulate and change the sound data within a buffer. Locking the buffer requires the Lock function defined here:

```
HRESULT Lock(
  DWORD dwOffset,
  DWORD dwBytes,
  LPVOID * ppvAudioPtr1,
  LPDWORD pdwAudioBytes1,
  LPVOID * ppvAudioPtr2,
  LPDWORD pdwAudioBytes2,
  DWORD dwFlags
);
```

The Lock function requires seven parameters.

- **dwOffset.** This variable specifies where in the buffer the lock should begin.

- **dwBytes.** This is the number of bytes within the buffer to lock.

- **ppvAudioPtr1.** This variable receives a pointer to the first part of the locked buffer.

- **pdwAudioBytes1.** This variable receives the number of bytes in the block pointer by ppvAudioPtr1.

- **ppvAudioPtr2.** This variable receives a pointer to the second part of the locked buffer. If you are filling the whole buffer with sound data, this variable should be NULL.

- **pdwAudioBytes2.** This variable receives the number of bytes in the block pointer by ppvAudioPtr2. This variable should be NULL if you are filling the whole buffer with sound data.

- **dwFlags.** These are the flags that specify how the lock should occur:

  - **DSBLOCK_FROMWRITECURSOR.** Start the lock from the write cursor.

  - **DSBLOCK_ENTIREBUFFER.** Lock the entire buffer. If this flag is set, the dwBytes variable is ignored.

Unlocking the Sound Buffer

At this point, you are free to read in the sound data and load it into the buffer. After that is complete, you can unlock the buffer using the Unlock function shown next:

```
HRESULT Unlock(
  LPVOID pvAudioPtr1,
  DWORD dwAudioBytes1,
  LPVOID pvAudioPtr2,
  DWORD dwAudioBytes2
);
```

The Unlock function requires four parameters:

- **pvAudioPtr1.** The address of the value from the ppvAudioPtr1 parameter used in Lock.

- **dwAudioBytes1.** The number of bytes written to the pvAudioPtr1.

- **pvAudioPtr2.** The address of the value from the ppvAudioPtr2 parameter used in Lock.

- **dwAudioBytes2.** The number of bytes written to the pvAudioPtr2.

Reading the Sound Data into the Buffer

Reading the sound data into the secondary buffer can be complex. To make the explanation easier to understand, I'll detail this process using the CWaveFile class found in the DirectSound framework classes. The DirectSound framework provides a simple way to load in sound data using the wave file format. WAV files are the default Windows sound format; they have a file extension ending in WAV.

Note

The DirectSound framework classes declared within the dsutil.cpp and dsutil.h files provide common functions that pertain to DirectSound. Some later versions of the DirectX SDK have this same functionality in the files DXUTsound.cpp and DXUTsound.h.

The first step in loading a WAV file in a DirectSound buffer requires creation of a CWaveFile object. The CWaveFile object provides you with methods for opening, closing, and reading WAV files. The line of code that follows shows you how to create a CWaveFile object.

```
CWaveFile *waveFile = new CWaveFile( );
```

Next, using the `Open` method provided by `CWaveFile`, you can gain access to the WAV file you want to use. The code that follows shows the use of the `Open` function and checks to see if the WAV file contains data.

```
// Open the WAV file test.wav
waveFile->Open("test.wav", NULL, WAVEFILE_READ );

// Check to make sure that the size of the data within the WAV file is valid
if( waveFile->GetSize( ) == 0 )
{
    return false;
}
```

This code opens a file called `test.wav` for reading. It then checks the size of the data within this file. If the file does not contain data, then the code halts reading it.

The next step is the creation of the secondary sound buffer to hold the WAV data. This process was shown earlier. After you create the sound buffer, you need to lock it before you can write the WAV data into it. The following code demonstrates use of the `Lock` function in preparing a buffer for reading an entire WAV file.

```
HRESULT hr;
VOID*       buffer     = NULL;     // pointer to locked buffer memory
DWORD    bufferSize    = 0;   // size of the locked DirectSound buffer

// Start the beginning of the buffer
hr = DSBuffer->Lock( 0,
                    waveFile->GetSize(),
                    &buffer,
                    &bufferSize,
                    NULL,
                    NULL,
                    DSBLOCK_ENTIREBUFFER);
// Check the return code to make sure the lock was successful
if FAILED (hr)
{
    return NULL;
}
```

This code locks a buffer using the `DSBLOCK_ENTIREBUFFER` flag. This causes the buffer to be locked from beginning to end. The `buffer` variable must be a valid `DirectSoundBuffer`.

Now that the buffer is properly locked, you can write the WAV data into it. Again, I'll be using methods provided through the CWaveFile class. Before you read the WAV data into the buffer, you need to reset the WAV data to the beginning. You accomplish this by using the ResetFile method. Next, you use the Read method to place the WAV data into the buffer. The following code sample resets the WAV file for reading and then places the data into the buffer.

```
// amount of data read from the WAV file
DWORD   bytesRead   = 0;

// Reset the WAV file to the beginning
waveFile->ResetFile( );

// Read the WAV file
HRESULT hr = waveFile->Read( ( BYTE* ) buffer,
                 bufferSize,
                 &bytesRead);

// Check to make sure that this was successful
if FAILED (hr)
{
    return NULL;
}
```

The waveFile variable must contain a valid CWaveFile object before its use. First, the ResetFile function is called and followed by a call to the Read function. The Read function requires three parameters. The first parameter is a pointer to the area of buffer memory to copy the WAV data into. The second parameter is the size of the locked buffer. The last parameter receives the amount of data read from the WAV file in bytes.

After the call to the Read function, the buffer is filled with the data from the WAV file. You can now safely unlock the buffer.

After the sound file is loaded into the buffer, the CWaveFile object can be deleted.

Playing Sound in a Buffer

Now that you have valid sound data in your DirectSoundBuffer, you can play the sound that it contains. After all it took to create the buffer and fill it with sound data, playing it is easy. A simple function called Play accomplishes this. The Play function is a method provided to you through the DirectSoundBuffer object. It's defined like this:

```
HRESULT Play(
  DWORD dwReserved1,
  DWORD dwPriority,
  DWORD dwFlags
);
```

The Play function requires three parameters:

- **dwReserved1.** A reserved value that must be set to 0.

- **dwPriority.** The priority level to play the sound. This can be any value between 0 and 0xFFFFFFFF. You must set the priority level to 0 if the DSBCAPS_LOCDEFER flag was not set when the buffer was created.

- **dwFlags.** The flags that specify how the sound should be played. The only flag that I'll explain here is DSBPLAY_LOOPING. This flag causes the sound to loop when the end of the buffer is reached. If this sound should only be played once, a value of 0 should be passed in the dwFlags parameter.

The following code causes a sound buffer to play its contents.

```
buffer->Play( 0, 0, DSBPLAY_LOOPING);
```

The buffer variable must contain a valid DirectSoundBuffer object filled with sound data. In this instance, the DSBPLAY_LOOPING flag is being passed, which causes this sound to loop after it completes playing.

Stopping a Sound

Normally, after you start playing a sound, you don't need to worry about it unless you have told the sound to loop. In this case, you would need to specifically cause the sound to stop playing. You do this through the Stop method provided by the DirectSoundBuffer object defined here:

```
HRESULT Stop( );
```

The Stop function does not require parameters. It passes back only a return code that informs you whether the call was successful.

You can find a full source example that shows how to load a sound file and play it in the Chapter11\example2 directory on the CD-ROM.

Using the Buffer Controls

As I mentioned earlier, DirectSound buffers can control certain aspects of the sound within them. For instance, through a buffer, you can change the volume and frequency and pan a sound. In this section, you're going to learn how to use these controls.

Changing the Volume

You can adjust the volume of a sound through the buffer in which it resides. You are able to adjust the volume between the values of DSBVOLUME_MIN and DSBVOLUME_MAX. The DSBVOLUME_MIN value represents silence, and the DSBVOLUME_MAX value represents the original volume of the sound.

Note

DirectSound does not support amplifying sounds, so you can never increase the volume past its original volume.

You can adjust the volume of a sound through the SetVolume function defined here:

```
HRESULT SetVolume (
   LONG lVolume
);
```

The SetVolume function requires only one parameter: lVolume. You can set the lVolume value to any value between 0 (DSBVOLUME_MAX) and −10000 (DSBVOLUME_MIN).

You can get the current volume at which a sound is playing by using the Get-Volume function. The GetVolume function is defined next:

```
HRESULT GetVolume (
   LPLONG plVolume
);
```

The GetVolume function requires only one parameter: a pointer to a variable that will receive the current volume.

Note

Before you can use the SetVolume and GetVolume functions, you must set the buffer to use these controls. You need to set the flag DSBCAPS_CTRLVOLUME in the DSBUFFERDESC structure when you create the secondary buffer.

Panning the Sound

DirectSound buffers allow a sound to be panned between the left and right speakers. *Panning* is lowering the volume of a sound in one speaker and increasing it in the opposite speaker. Using panning, sounds can seem to be made to move around by adjusting their volume between speakers.

Panning uses a similar concept to the `SetVolume` function. The left and right speakers can be made to raise and lower their volumes independently using two values: `DSBPAN_LEFT` and `DSBPAN_RIGHT`.

The `DSBPAN_LEFT` value, which is equivalent to −10000, increases the volume of sound in the left speaker to full while silencing the sound in the right speaker. The `DSBPAN_RIGHT` value, which is defined as 10000, does the opposite, increasing the volume in the right speaker while silencing the sound in the left. By using values between `DSBPAN_LEFT` and `DSBPAN_RIGHT`, sounds can be made to pan from one speaker to the other.

A third value, `DSBPAN_CENTER`, defined as 0, resets both the left and right sides to full volume.

The amount of panning that the sound in the buffer uses is set using the function `SetPan`, defined here:

```
HRESULT SetPan(
  LONG lPan
);
```

The `SetPan` function requires only one parameter, `lPan`, which takes any value between `DSBPAN_LEFT` and `DSBPAN_RIGHT`.

If you want to get the current pan value, use the function `GetPan` shown here:

```
HRESULT GetPan(
  LPLONG plPan
);
```

The `GetPan` function needs one parameter: `plPan`. The `plPan` variable is a pointer to `LONG` that will receive the current value of panning.

Note

Before you can use the `SetPan` and `GetPan` functions, you must set the buffer to use these controls. You need to set the `DSBCAPS_CTRLPAN` flag in the `DSBUFFERDESC` structure when you create the secondary buffer.

Summary

Using what you've learned in this chapter, you should be able to play background music or simple sound effects within your game. You can extend the lessons in this chapter to play multiple sounds simultaneously, allowing for dynamic music that can be changed and manipulated.

In the next chapter, you'll put together everything you've learned to create a simple game that utilizes each of the areas covered.

What You Have Learned

In this chapter, you learned the following:

- How DirectSound is used

- What different types of sound buffers are available

- How to enumerate sound devices installed on the system

- How to load and play a WAV file

- How to control the playback of a sound file

Review Questions

You can find the answers to Review Questions in Appendix A, "Answers to End-of-Chapter Exercises."

1. When must you use the `DirectSoundEnumerate` function?

2. What three important pieces of data are passed to the enumeration callback function?

3. Does the format of a buffer need to match the format of its contents?

4. What is the purpose of the primary buffer?

5. What value is passed to `DirectSoundCreate8` to specify that the default sound device be used?

On Your Own

1. Write a small sample program that allows you to adjust the volume of a sound while it's playing.

2. Write a small sample program to allow the sound to be panned using the arrow keys.

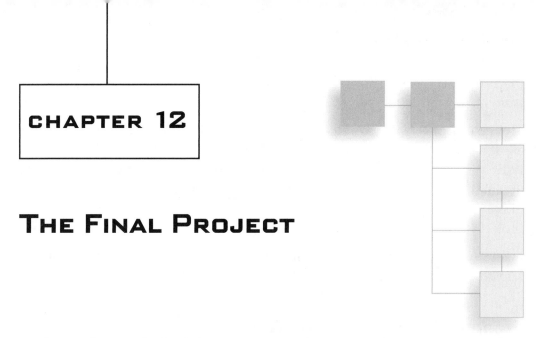

CHAPTER 12

THE FINAL PROJECT

You've made it to the final chapter, congratulations. You've seen DirectX take a simple empty window and fill it with a virtual world. Now it's your turn to create a working 3D demo using the components of DirectX.

Here's what you'll learn in this chapter:

- How to bundle common Direct3D functions

- How to design and code a simple demo framework

- How to encompass rendering of all your in-game objects

- How to allow your 3D objects to move around

Welcome to the Final Project

The final project is going to take a lot of what you've learned throughout the book and apply it to a single application. It's not going to be an overly complicated example, but it will apply a lot of what you've learned. Using this project as a basis, you can build on it creating ever more complicated applications. In addition to demonstrating how the separate pieces come together, it also provides a framework you can build on for more complicated applications.

I'm going to show you how to encapsulate the functionality of the DirectX components to keep your game code neat and easily maintained. Even though this is the final project, I'm still going to explain each step in detail, reducing the amount of time you'll spend re-reading other chapters.

The final project will take the terrain you created before and texture it while allowing you to move around it using the Xbox 360 controller. Like I said, it isn't terribly complicated or impressive, but it uses what you've learned and demonstrates how to bring it all together. In this chapter I'll be placing as much of the application code within the text as possible so you can see how the entire project is put together.

Figure 12.1 shows what the final outcome of this project will be. Now that you know where you're going, let's get started.

Creating the Application Window

The application window is the container in which your game world will live, and it's the first thing you need to create. Start out by loading up the solution file found within the Final directory on the CD-ROM. After you have the project up, open up the winMain.cpp file.

Figure 12.1
This is what the final project will look like.

I've chosen to encapsulate all the main interface and window creation code in a single place. The `WinMain` function is the entry point for any Windows application and this is where you'll start.

WinMain

The `WinMain` function serves two main purposes; first it's where you initialize your application, and second, it provides your application with a message loop. The message loop, required by every windowed application, handles the collecting and processing of any messages sent to the application by the system.

The `WinMain` function I've provided in the following code has only the absolute minimum code needed to start the application.

```
/****************************************************************
* WinMain
****************************************************************/
int APIENTRY _tWinMain(HINSTANCE hInstance, HINSTANCE hPrevInstance,
    LPTSTR lpCmdLine, int nCmdShow)
{
    // save off the instance handle
    hInst = hInstance;

    // Set up the application window
    if (!InitWindow(hInstance, windowWidth, windowHeight))
    {
        return 0;
    }

    // Initialize Direct3D
    if (!InitDirect3D(mainhWnd, windowWidth, windowHeight))
    {
        return 0;
    }

    // Init the controllers
    InitControllers();

    // Init the Game
    if (!InitGame())
```

```
    {
        return 0;
    }


    // Main message loop
    MSG msg = {0};
    while (WM_QUIT != msg.message)
    {

        // Process Windows messages first
        while (PeekMessage(&msg, NULL, 0, 0, PM_REMOVE) == TRUE)
        {
            TranslateMessage(&msg);
            DispatchMessage(&msg);
        }

        // Update user input
        GetControllercurState();

        // Update the game scene
        UpdateGame();

        ClearRenderTarget();

        // Draw the game
        DrawGame();

        SwapBuffers();
    }

    // Clean and shutdown the game
    ShutdownGame();

    // Clean up the resources we allocated
    ShutdownDirect3D();

    return (int) msg.wParam;
}
```

Since the code needed to create the application window can be cumbersome,
I've separated it into the function InitWindow.

InitWindow

The InitWindow function handles the actual window creation. As you may recall, each application window created needs to have a window class registered with the system. The window class, defined in the WNDCLASSEX structure, contains a collection of properties that the system uses to define the window. The window class, after being defined in the WNDCLASSEX structure, is then passed to the RegisterClassEx function notifying the system of its existence.

After the window class is registered, you can now create your window. The application window is created using the function CreateWindow. The CreateWindow function pulls together the properties from the window class and its own parameters to define and create the application window. The size of the window as well as its name is passed as parameters to the CreateWindow function.

```
/*****************************************************************
* InitWindow
* Inits and creates and main app window
* Inputs - application instance - HINSTANCE
          Window width - int
          Window height - int
* Outputs - true if successful, false if failed - bool
*****************************************************************/
bool InitWindow(HINSTANCE hInstance, int width, int height)
{
    // Register class
    WNDCLASSEX wcex;
    wcex.cbSize = sizeof(WNDCLASSEX);
    wcex.style = CS_HREDRAW | CS_VREDRAW;
    wcex.lpfnWndProc = WndProc;
    wcex.cbClsExtra = 0;
    wcex.cbWndExtra = 0;
    wcex.hInstance = hInstance;
    wcex.hIcon = 0;
    wcex.hCursor = LoadCursor(NULL, IDC_ARROW);
    wcex.hbrBackground  = (HBRUSH)(COLOR_WINDOW+1);
    wcex.lpszMenuName = NULL;
    wcex.lpszClassName = TEXT("DirectXExample");
    wcex.hIconSm = 0;
    if (!RegisterClassEx(&wcex))
```

```
    {
        return false;
    }

    // Create window
    RECT rect = { 0, 0, width, height };
    AdjustWindowRect(&rect, WS_OVERLAPPEDWINDOW, false);

    // create the window from the class above
    mainhWnd = CreateWindow(TEXT("DirectXExample"),
        TEXT("DirectXExample"),
        WS_OVERLAPPEDWINDOW,
        CW_USEDEFAULT,
        CW_USEDEFAULT,
        rect.right - rect.left,
        rect.bottom - rect.top,
        NULL,
        NULL,
        hInstance,
        NULL);

  if(!mainhWnd)
  {
        return false;
  }

  ShowWindow(mainhWnd, SW_SHOW);
  UpdateWindow(mainhWnd);

  return true;
}
```

At this point, the system now considers you to have a valid and usable window that you can display using the ShowWindow and UpdateWindow functions. Although you may have a window, without a window procedure, you won't be able to process any messages coming to your application. The final step needed in window creation is the addition of the window procedure.

WndProc

The window procedure is where the messages for your application from the user and the system get sent. Using a simple switch statement, you determine the messages that your application needs to handle.

For this example there are two messages that need to be handled, WM_DESTROY and WM_KEYDOWN. The WM_DESTROY message is sent to an application when the user clicks on the X button of the window. Because I also want the application to close if the user holds down the Escape key, the application is also listening for the WM_KEYDOWN message. When this message is received, the application will check to see if the key the user pressed was the Escape key. If so, then the application will exit.

```
/*****************************************************************
* WndProc
* The main window procedure for the application
* Inputs - application window handle - HWND
      message sent to the window - UINT
      wParam of the message being sent - WPARAM
      lParam of the message being sent - LPARAM
* Outputs - LRESULT
*****************************************************************/
LRESULT CALLBACK WndProc(HWND hWnd, UINT message, WPARAM wParam, LPARAM lParam)
{
    switch (message)
    {
        // Allow the user to press the Escape key to end the application
        case WM_KEYDOWN:
            switch(wParam)
            {
                // Check if the user hit the Escape key
                case VK_ESCAPE:
                    PostQuitMessage(0);
                    break;
            }
        break;

        // The user hit the close button, close the application
        case WM_DESTROY:
            PostQuitMessage(0);
        break;
    }

    return DefWindowProc(hWnd, message, wParam, lParam);
}
```

Initializing Direct3D

Getting Direct3D up and running is the next step in the project. To make setting up Direct3D easy, I've packed all the functions needed into the Direct3DFunctions .cpp and Direct3DFunctions.h files.

The Direct3D Functions

The Direct3DFunctions.cpp and Direct3DFunctions.h files bundle together common functionality that every Direct3D application needs. These files contain the following functions:

- `InitDirect3D`. Used to initialize and create the Direct3D device as well as create the swap chain.

- `ShutdownDirect3D`. Cleans up and releases the Direct3D device, swap chain, and render target.

- `ClearRenderTarget`. Prepares the screen for drawing by clearing the render target to a solid color.

- `SwapBuffers`. Calls the `Present` function on the swap chain causing the buffers to swap.

Also contained within these two files are variables used to hold the current world, view, and projection matrices. Based on the application you create, you may need to add to the functionality and variables contained within these files.

The Direct3DFunctions.cpp file is shown here:

```
/*************************************************************
* Direct3DFunctions.cpp
* Contains all the variables and functions needed to init and
* setup Direct3D
*************************************************************/

#include <windows.h>
#include <tchar.h>

#include <d3d10.h>
#include <d3dx10.h>
#include "Direct3DFunctions.h"
```

```
ID3D10Device* pD3DDevice = NULL;
static IDXGISwapChain* pSwapChain = NULL;
static ID3D10RenderTargetView* pRenderTargetView = NULL;

// World Matrix
D3DXMATRIX WorldMatrix;

// View Matrix
D3DXMATRIX ViewMatrix;

// Projection Matrix
D3DXMATRIX ProjectionMatrix;

/*******************************************************************
* InitDirect3D
* Initializes Direct3D
* Inputs - Parent window handle - HWND,
    Window width - int
    Window height - int
* Outputs - true if successful, false if failed - bool
*******************************************************************/
bool InitDirect3D(HWND hWnd, int width, int height)
{
    // Create the clear the DXGI_SWAP_CHAIN_DESC structure
    DXGI_SWAP_CHAIN_DESC swapChainDesc;
    ZeroMemory(&swapChainDesc, sizeof(swapChainDesc));

    // Fill in the needed values
    swapChainDesc.BufferCount = 1;
    swapChainDesc.BufferDesc.Width = width;
    swapChainDesc.BufferDesc.Height = height;
    swapChainDesc.BufferDesc.Format = DXGI_FORMAT_R8G8B8A8_UNORM;
    swapChainDesc.BufferDesc.RefreshRate.Numerator = 60;
    swapChainDesc.BufferDesc.RefreshRate.Denominator = 1;
    swapChainDesc.BufferUsage = DXGI_USAGE_RENDER_TARGET_OUTPUT;
    swapChainDesc.OutputWindow = hWnd;
    swapChainDesc.SampleDesc.Count = 1;
    swapChainDesc.SampleDesc.Quality = 0;
    swapChainDesc.Windowed = TRUE;

    // Create the D3D device and the swap chain
    HRESULT hr = D3D10CreateDeviceAndSwapChain(NULL,
```

```
D3D10_DRIVER_TYPE_REFERENCE,
NULL,
0,
D3D10_SDK_VERSION,
&swapChainDesc,
&pSwapChain,
&pD3DDevice);

// Error checking. Make sure the device was created
if(FAILED(hr))
{
    return false;
}

// Get the back buffer from the swapchain
ID3D10Texture2D *pBackBuffer;
hr = pSwapChain->GetBuffer(0, __uuidof(ID3D10Texture2D),
(LPVOID*)&pBackBuffer);
if(FAILED(hr))
{
    return false;
}

// create the render target view
hr = pD3DDevice->CreateRenderTargetView(pBackBuffer, NULL,
&pRenderTargetView);

// release the back buffer
pBackBuffer->Release();

// Make sure the render target view was created successfully
if(FAILED(hr))
{
    return false;
}

// set the render target
pD3DDevice->OMSetRenderTargets(1, &pRenderTargetView, NULL);

// create and set the viewport
D3D10_VIEWPORT viewPort;
viewPort.Width = width;
viewPort.Height = height;
```

```
viewPort.MinDepth = 0.0f;
viewPort.MaxDepth = 1.0f;
viewPort.TopLeftX = 0;
viewPort.TopLeftY = 0;
pD3DDevice->RSSetViewports(1, &viewPort);

// Set up the World Matrix
D3DXMatrixIdentity(&WorldMatrix);

// Set up the view matrix
D3DXMatrixLookAtLH(&ViewMatrix, new D3DXVECTOR3(0.0f, 96, -300.0f),
    new D3DXVECTOR3(0.0f, 0.0f, 1.0f),
    new D3DXVECTOR3(0.0f, 1.0f, 0.0f));

// Set up the projection matrix
D3DXMatrixPerspectiveFovLH(&ProjectionMatrix,
    (float)D3DX_PI * 0.5f,
    (float)width/(float)height,
    0.0f,
    500.0f);

// The raster description structure. This allows you
// to change the filling and culling mode.
D3D10_RASTERIZER_DESC rasterDescription;
rasterDescription.FillMode = D3D10_FILL_SOLID;
rasterDescription.CullMode = D3D10_CULL_NONE;
rasterDescription.FrontCounterClockwise = true;
rasterDescription.DepthBias = false;
rasterDescription.DepthBiasClamp = 0;
rasterDescription.SlopeScaledDepthBias = 0;
rasterDescription.DepthClipEnable = false;
rasterDescription.ScissorEnable = false;
rasterDescription.MultisampleEnable = false;
rasterDescription.AntialiasedLineEnable = false;

// Create a new raster state
ID3D10RasterizerState *g_pRasterState;
pD3DDevice->CreateRasterizerState(&rasterDescription,&g_pRasterState);

// Set the new raster state
pD3DDevice->RSSetState(g_pRasterState);
```

```
        return true;
    }


    /*****************************************************************
    * ShutdownDirect3D
    * Releases the render target, swap chain, and Direct3D object
    * Inputs - none
    * Outputs - void
    *****************************************************************/
    void ShutdownDirect3D()
    {
        // release the rendertarget
        if (pRenderTargetView)
        {
            pRenderTargetView->Release();
        }

        // release the swapchain
        if (pSwapChain)
        {
            pSwapChain->Release();
        }

        // release the D3D Device
        if (pD3DDevice)
        {
            pD3DDevice->Release();
        }
    }


    /*****************************************************************
    * ClearRenderTarget
    * Clears the render target to a solid color
    * Inputs - none
    * Outputs - void
    *****************************************************************/
    void ClearRenderTarget()
    {
```

```
    // clear the target buffer
    pD3DDevice->ClearRenderTargetView(pRenderTargetView,
    D3DXCOLOR(1.0f, 1.0f, 1.0f, 0.0f));
}

/***********************************************************
* SwapBuffers
* Swaps the buffers within the swap chain
* Inputs - none
* Outputs - void
***********************************************************/
void SwapBuffers()
{
    // display the next item in the swap chain
    pSwapChain->Present(0, 0);
}
```

The Direct3DFunctions Header File

The header file for the Direct3DFunctions.cpp file simply includes the declarations for the included functions as well as exposing the matrices and Direct3D device.

```
#ifndef DIRECT3DFUNCTIONS_H
#define DIRECT3DFUNCTIONS_H

bool InitDirect3D(HWND hWnd, int width, int height);
void ShutdownDirect3D();

void ClearRenderTarget();
void SwapBuffers();

extern ID3D10Device* pD3DDevice;
extern D3DXMATRIX ViewMatrix;
extern D3DXMATRIX ProjectionMatrix;
extern D3DXMATRIX WorldMatrix;
#endif
```

Adding Input Functionality—XInput

User input for this application is handled through the use of the XInput API. To make gathering user input easier, I've created the XInputManager. The XInputManager gathers together a few functions that allow you to get user input and store off the current input state for multiple controllers.

The XInputManager Code

The code contained within the XInputManager.cpp file enables you to get the current input state from up to four Xbox 360 controllers. The input state is stored in an array of CONTROLLER_INFO structures for you to access later. If a particular controller is not connected or becomes disconnected, the isConnected flag is set allowing the application to take the appropriate action.

A function called IsButtonDown is also included, which can be used to determine if a specific button from a controller is currently being pressed. The XInput-Manager.cpp can easily be refitted to handle the analog controls as well.

```cpp
#include <d3d10.h>
#include <XInput.h>

#include "XInputManager.h"

// Create an array of controller_info structs
CONTROLLER_INFO controllers[MAX_CONTROLLERS];

/*************************************************************
* void InitControllers()
* Function to clear out the CONTROLLER_INFO structures
*************************************************************/

void InitControllers()
{
    // Clear out the CONTROLLER_curState structs
    ZeroMemory(controllers, sizeof(CONTROLLER_INFO)*MAX_CONTROLLERS);
}


/*************************************************************
* void GetControllercurState()
* This function will query the input devices
*************************************************************/
void GetControllercurState()
{
    // Loop through the controllers
    for (DWORD i=0; i < MAX_CONTROLLERS; i++)
    {
```

```
        // Get the current state of the controller
        DWORD dwResult = XInputGetState(i, &controllers[i].curState);

        // Set whether this controller is connected
        controllers[i].isConnected = (dwResult == ERROR_SUCCESS);
    }
}


/***********************************************************
* void IsButtonDown()
* Function used to determine whether a particular button is
* pressed.
***********************************************************/
bool IsButtonDown(int controllerIndex, DWORD buttonID)
{
    return (bool)(controllers[controllerIndex].curState.Gamepad
    .wButtons & buttonID);
}
```

The XInputManager Header File

The header file for the XInputManager contains a bit more than just function declarations this time. The header defines a maximum of four input controllers as well as creates the CONTROLLER_INFO structure to store the current input state.

```
#ifndef XINPUT_MANAGER_H
#define XINPUT_MANAGER_H

#include <XInput.h>

// XInput Information
#define MAX_CONTROLLERS 4

// Define a struct to hold the controller information
typedef struct
{
    XINPUT_STATE curState;
    BOOL isConnected;
} CONTROLLER_INFO;
```

```
void InitControllers();
void GetControllercurState();
bool IsButtonDown(int controllerIndex, DWORD buttonID);

#endif
```

Texture Functions

There have been two texture functions that you have used throughout the book: GetTexture2DFromFile and GetResourceViewFromTexture. These two functions can be utilized in any game application where texture loading is necessary.

The TextureFuncs Code

```
#include <tchar.h>
#include <d3d10.h>
#include <d3dx10.h>

#include "Direct3DFunctions.h"

/********************************************************************
* GetTexture2DFromFile
* Loads a texture from a file into a ID3D10Texture2D object
* Inputs - LPCWSTR the path and filename of the texture
* Outputs - pointer to a ID3D10Texture2D object
********************************************************************/
ID3D10Texture2D* GetTexture2DFromFile(LPCWSTR filename)
{
    ID3D10Texture2D* texture = NULL;
    ID3D10Resource*  pRes    = NULL;

    // Loads the texture into a temporary ID3D10Resource object
    HRESULT hr = D3DX10CreateTextureFromFile(pD3DDevice, filename, NULL, NULL,
    &pRes);
    if (FAILED(hr))
    {
        return NULL;
    }

    // Translates the ID3D10Resource object into a ID3D10Texture2D object
    pRes->QueryInterface(__uuidof( ID3D10Texture2D ), (LPVOID*)&texture);
    pRes->Release();
```

```
    // returns the ID3D10Texture2D object
    return texture;
}


/*******************************************************************
* GetResourceViewFromTexture
* Creates a shader resource view from a texture
* Inputs - ID3D10Texture2D* texture - pointer to the texture
*     ID3D10ShaderResourceView **resourceView - the resource view being
*   created
* Outputs - void
*******************************************************************/
void GetResourceViewFromTexture(ID3D10Texture2D* texture,
    ID3D10ShaderResourceView **resourceView)
{
    if (texture != NULL)
    {
        // Get the texture details
        D3D10_TEXTURE2D_DESC desc;
        texture->GetDesc(&desc);

        // Create a shader resource view of the texture
        D3D10_SHADER_RESOURCE_VIEW_DESC SRVDesc;
        ZeroMemory(&SRVDesc, sizeof(SRVDesc));
        SRVDesc.Format = desc.Format;
        SRVDesc.ViewDimension = D3D10_SRV_DIMENSION_TEXTURE2D;
        SRVDesc.Texture2D.MipLevels = desc.MipLevels;

        pD3DDevice->CreateShaderResourceView(texture, &SRVDesc, resourceView);
    }
}
```

The TextureFuncs Header File

The contents of the TextureFuncs.h header file are shown here:

```
#ifndef TEXTURE_FUNCS_H
#define TEXTURE_FUNCS_H

ID3D10Texture2D* GetTexture2DFromFile(LPCWSTR filename);
void GetResourceViewFromTexture(ID3D10Texture2D* texture,
    ID3D10ShaderResourceView **resourceView);

#endif
```

The Game Code

Up to this point, all the code that was added was generic functionality that you'll need for most game applications. With the inclusion of the game logic, things are getting a bit more specific.

Within the game.cpp and game.h files is where all the read logic for the application takes place. Game.cpp handles initializing terrain as well as handling user input.

While you could perform the object loading and drawing within the Win-Main.cpp file, it is best to separate things in a way where the game logic is in a distinct location away from the Windows code. This allows you to remove at least some of the dependence of your game code from the underlying platform. Additionally, having a single file where your game logic is started and stopped makes things easier to follow when others need to read your code.

The game.cpp file includes the following functions:

- **InitGame**. Initializes the terrain object.

- **UpdateGame**. Called each frame to handle user input.

- **DrawGame**. This function is called once per frame and contains the calls to draw each game object being displayed.

- **ShutdownGame**. When the game is complete, this function is called to clean up any game objects being used.

Most games will need to create multiple game objects (characters, weapons, locations), but for simplicity's sake, only one object will be created here. The terrain object doesn't have any particular dependency on the game logic so it has been separated into another module. The game code only makes the calls to the terrain object to tell it to create itself, draw, and to make sure it gets removed when no longer needed.

The Game.cpp Code

The main function of the game logic is to properly place and orient the terrain in such a way so it is visible to the user. The game logic holds three variables, curX, curY, and curZ, which contain the location of a virtual camera. By manipulating these variables, the terrain can be seen to move along any of the three major axes.

These variables are then used to create the current world matrix. The world matrix is then multiplied with the view and projection matrices and passed into the shader to properly position the terrain.

```
/************************************************************
* Game.cpp
* Handles the creation, updating, and drawing of the game
************************************************************/
#include <d3d10.h>
#include <d3dx10.h>
#include <XInput.h>
#include "Game.h"
#include "XInputManager.h"
#include "Direct3DFunctions.h"
#include "Terrain.h"

// Input Variables
float curX = -256.0f;
float curY = -40.0f;
float curZ = -258.0f;

/************************************************************
* InitGame
* Initializes the game
************************************************************/
bool InitGame()
{
    // Init the terrain
    if (!CreateTerrain())
    {
        return false;
    }

    return true;
}

/************************************************************
* UpdateGame
* Handles the updating of the game scene
************************************************************/
```

```cpp
void UpdateGame()
{
    // move the terrain to the left
    if (IsButtonDown(0, XINPUT_GAMEPAD_DPAD_LEFT))
    {
        curX -= 10.0f;
    }

    // move the terrain to the right
    if (IsButtonDown(0, XINPUT_GAMEPAD_DPAD_RIGHT))
    {
        curX += 10.0f;
    }

    // move the terrain up
    if (IsButtonDown(0, XINPUT_GAMEPAD_DPAD_UP))
    {
        curY += 10.0f;
    }

    // move the terrain down
    if (IsButtonDown(0, XINPUT_GAMEPAD_DPAD_DOWN))
    {
        curY -= 10.0f;
    }

    // move the terrain closer
    if (IsButtonDown(0, XINPUT_GAMEPAD_LEFT_SHOULDER))
    {
        curZ -= 10.0f;
    }

    // move the terrain farther away
    if (IsButtonDown(0, XINPUT_GAMEPAD_RIGHT_SHOULDER))
    {
        curZ += 10.0f;
    }

    // Build the final world Matrix using the current values
    D3DXMatrixTranslation(&WorldMatrix, curX, curY, curZ);
}
```

```
/****************************************************************
* DrawGame
* Draws the game scene
****************************************************************/
void DrawGame()
{
    // Draw the terrain object
    DrawTerrain();
}


/****************************************************************
* ShutdownGame
* Shuts down the game
****************************************************************/
void ShutdownGame()
{
    // Clean up the terrain
    RemoveTerrain();
}
```

The Game Header File

The Game.h header file doesn't have anything special but just provides the function declarations for the four game functions.

```
#ifndef GAME_H
#define GAME_H

bool InitGame();
void UpdateGame();
void DrawGame();
void ShutdownGame();

#endif
```

The Terrain Object

The object, found in the terrain.cpp file, contains the most amount of code in the project. This file encompasses all the code needed to build, render, and manipulate the terrain object. While it may seem like a lot to look through, keeping all the code together that creates and operates on the terrain makes things easier to find.

The Terrain Code

The first function used within the terrain file is the CreateTerrain function. This function is called from the InitGame function within Game.cpp. The CreateTerrain function performs the following:

1. Loading of the terrain effect file.

2. Loading of the textures used by the terrain.

3. Binding of the effect variables and techniques.

4. Creating the vertex layout for the terrain.

5. Generating the vertices and indices needed to render the terrain.

6. Bundling these together into a mesh object.

The DrawTerrain function is called each frame to perform the actual rendering of the terrain object. It is the job of this function to send the projection matrix and texture to the terrain effect file as well as call the DrawSubset function on the terrain mesh.

The last function is RemoveTerrain. This function simply cleans up and releases the resources used by the terrain.

If you use the terrain object as an example, you can see how other objects can be created using a similar method.

```
/*****************************************************************
* Terrain
* This file handles the creation and management of a 3D terrain
*****************************************************************/
#include <d3d10.h>
#include <d3dx10.h>
#include "Direct3DFunctions.h"
#include "TextureFuncs.h"
#include "Terrain.h"
#include "VertexFormats.h"
```

```
// Grid Information
#define NUM_COLS 16
#define NUM_ROWS 16
#define NUM_VERTSX (NUM_COLS + 1)
#define NUM_VERTSY (NUM_ROWS + 1)

// The width and height of each cell in the grid
#define CELL_WIDTH 32
#define CELL_HEIGHT 32

static ID3D10Effect *terrainEffect;
static ID3D10EffectTechnique *terrainTechnique;
static ID3DX10Mesh *mesh;
static ID3D10InputLayout *pVertexLayout;
static ID3D10EffectMatrixVariable* pProjectionMatrixVariable = NULL;

static ID3D10Texture2D* pTerrainTexture = NULL;
static ID3D10ShaderResourceView* pTerrainTextureRV = NULL;
static ID3D10EffectShaderResourceVariable* pBaseTextureVariable = NULL;

static bool InitTerrainTextures();

/******************************************************************
* InitAndLoadEffect
* Initializes and loads the effect file needed to render
* this object.
* Inputs - ID3D10Device* pD3DDevice - pointer to a valid Direct3D
    Device.
* Outputs - ID3D10Effect* - Pointer to a Direct3D effect.
*******************************************************************/
ID3D10Effect* InitAndLoadEffect(ID3D10Device* pD3DDevice)
{
    ID3D10Blob   *errorBlob = NULL;
    LPVOID errorBuffer;
    ID3D10Effect *effect = NULL;

    // Create the effect
    HRESULT hr = D3DX10CreateEffectFromFile(L"./simple.fx",
        NULL,
        NULL,
        D3D10_SHADER_ENABLE_STRICTNESS,
        0,
```

```
            pD3DDevice,
            NULL,
            NULL,
            &effect,
            &errorBlob);

        if (errorBlob != NULL)
        {
            errorBuffer = errorBlob->GetBufferPointer();
        }

        return effect;
}


/*****************************************************************
* CreateTerrain
* Handles the creation of the vertices and indices needed to draw
* the terrain object.
* Inputs - none
* Outputs - bool, true if successful
*****************************************************************/

bool CreateTerrain()
{
    // load the effect used by the terrain
    terrainEffect = InitAndLoadEffect(pD3DDevice);
    if (terrainEffect == NULL)
    {
        return false;
    }

    if (!InitTerrainTextures())
    {
        return false;
    }

    // Bind the projection matrix to the Projection variable in the shader
    pProjectionMatrixVariable = terrainEffect->GetVariableByName("Projection")
    ->AsMatrix();

    // get the technique used by the terrain
    terrainTechnique = terrainEffect->GetTechniqueByName("Render");
    if (terrainTechnique == NULL)
```

```
    {
        return false;
    }

    // The vertex input layout
    D3D10_INPUT_ELEMENT_DESC layout[] =
    {
    { "POSITION",0,DXGI_FORMAT_R32G32B32_FLOAT, 0, 0,
    D3D10_INPUT_PER_VERTEX_DATA, 0 },
    { "COLOR", 0,DXGI_FORMAT_R32G32B32A32_FLOAT, 0, 12,
    D3D10_INPUT_PER_VERTEX_DATA, 0 },
    { "TEXCOORD", 0, DXGI_FORMAT_R32G32_FLOAT, 0, 28,
    D3D10_INPUT_PER_VERTEX_DATA, 0 },
    };

    // Calculate the number of elements in the layout array
    UINT numElements = (sizeof(layout) / sizeof(layout[0]));

    // Create the vertex input layout
    D3D10_PASS_DESC PassDesc;
    terrainTechnique->GetPassByIndex(0)->GetDesc(&PassDesc);

    HRESULT hr = pD3DDevice->CreateInputLayout(layout,
        numElements,
        PassDesc.pIAInputSignature,
        PassDesc.IAInputSignatureSize,
        &pVertexLayout);

    if(FAILED(hr))
    {
        return false;
    }

    // create the vertices array large enough to hold all those needed
    VertexPosColorTexStruct vertices[NUM_VERTSX * NUM_VERTSY];

    // Fill the vertices array with the terrain values
    for(int z=0; z < NUM_VERTSY; ++z)
    {
        for(int x=0; x < NUM_VERTSX; ++x)
        {
            vertices[x + z * NUM_VERTSX].Pos.x = (float)x * CELL_WIDTH;
            vertices[x + z * NUM_VERTSX].Pos.z = (float)z * CELL_HEIGHT;
```

```
            // Allow the height of the cell to be randomly decided
            vertices[x + z * NUM_VERTSX].Pos.y = (float)(rand() % CELL_HEIGHT);

            // Create the default color
            vertices[x + z * NUM_VERTSX].Color = D3DXVECTOR4(1.0, 1.0f,
            1.0f, 0.0f);

            // Create the texture coordinates for the terrain
            vertices[x + z * NUM_VERTSX].Tex.x = x / (float)NUM_VERTSX;
            vertices[x + z * NUM_VERTSX].Tex.y = z / (float)NUM_VERTSY;
        }
    }

    // Calculate the number of vertices in the array
    UINT numVertices = sizeof(vertices) / sizeof(VertexPosColorTexStruct);

    // Create the indices array
    DWORD indices[NUM_VERTSX * NUM_VERTSY * 6];

    // The index counter
    int curIndex = 0;

    // Fill the indices array to create the triangles needed for the terrain
    // The triangles are created in a counter-clockwise direction
    for (int z=0; z < NUM_ROWS; z++)
    {
        for (int x=0; x < NUM_COLS; x++)
        {
            // The current vertex to build off of
            int curVertex = x + (z * NUM_VERTSX);

            // Create the indices for the first triangle
            indices[curIndex]   = curVertex;
            indices[curIndex+1] = curVertex + NUM_VERTSX;
            indices[curIndex+2] = curVertex + 1;

            // Create the indices for the second triangle
            indices[curIndex+3] = curVertex + 1;
            indices[curIndex+4] = curVertex + NUM_VERTSX;
            indices[curIndex+5] = curVertex + NUM_VERTSX + 1;

            // increment curIndex by the number of vertices for the two triangles
            curIndex += 6;
        }
```

```
    }

    // determine the number of indices
    UINT numIndices = sizeof(indices) / sizeof(DWORD);

    // create the mesh object
    D3DX10CreateMesh(pD3DDevice,
        layout,
        numElements,
        "POSITION",
        numVertices,
        (numIndices/3),
        D3DX10_MESH_32_BIT,
        &mesh);

    // set the vertex buffer data
    mesh->SetVertexData(0, vertices);

    // set the index buffer data
    mesh->SetIndexData(indices, numIndices);

    // save the changes to the mesh object
    mesh->CommitToDevice();

    return true;
}

/****************************************************************
* InitTerrainTextures
* Handles the loading of the textures needed for this object
* Inputs - none
* Outputs - bool, true if successful
****************************************************************/
bool InitTerrainTextures()
{
    // Load in the base texture
    pTerrainTexture = GetTexture2DFromFile(TEXT("./basemap.bmp"));
    if (pTerrainTexture == NULL)
    {
        return false;
    }
}
```

```
    // Get the resource view for this texture
    GetResourceViewFromTexture(pTerrainTexture, &pTerrainTextureRV);

    // Bind the texture variable
    pBaseTextureVariable = terrainEffect->GetVariableByName("baseTexture")-
    >AsShaderResource();

    return true;
}


/*****************************************************************
* DrawTerrain
* Draws the terrain
* Inputs - none
* Outputs - bool, true if successful
*****************************************************************/
void DrawTerrain()
{
    // Set the input layout
    pD3DDevice->IASetInputLayout(pVertexLayout);

    // Set the texture resource view
    pBaseTextureVariable->SetResource(pTerrainTextureRV);

    D3DXMATRIX finalMatrix = (WorldMatrix * ViewMatrix * ProjectionMatrix);
    pProjectionMatrixVariable->SetMatrix((float*)&finalMatrix);

    // Render a model object
    D3D10_TECHNIQUE_DESC techniqueDescription;
    terrainTechnique->GetDesc(&techniqueDescription);

    // Loop through the technique passes
    for(UINT p=0; p < techniqueDescription.Passes; ++p)
    {
        terrainTechnique->GetPassByIndex(p)->Apply(0);

        mesh->DrawSubset(0);
    }
}
```

```
/*******************************************************************
* RemoveTerrain
* Cleans up and removes the resources for this object
* Inputs - none
* Outputs - bool, true if successful
*******************************************************************/
void RemoveTerrain()
{
    // release the texture resource view
    if (pTerrainTextureRV)
    {
        pTerrainTextureRV->Release();
    }

    if (pTerrainTexture)
    {
        pTerrainTexture->Release();
    }

    if (terrainEffect)
    {
        terrainEffect->Release();
    }

    // Release the vertex layout
    if (pVertexLayout)
    {
        pVertexLayout->Release();
    }
}
```

The Terrain Header File

The terrain header file contains the forward declarations for the terrain functions that are called from within the game logic.

```
#ifndef TERRAIN_H
#define TERRAIN_H

ID3D10Effect* InitAndLoadEffect(ID3D10Device* pD3DDevice);
```

```
bool CreateTerrain();
void DrawTerrain();
void RemoveTerrain();
#endif
```

Vertex Formats

Each time you create a vertex buffer, you have to define the format of the vertices being stored within it. Because there are only so many combinations of vertex structures, you'll find yourself commonly using the same ones over and over again. There's no point in hard coding these within your application code since that just causes code-bloat and keeps you from reusing code. By creating the vertex structures within a header file, VertexFormats.h, they can be included and used wherever they're needed, even across multiple game projects.

In the following file, a single vertex structure is created that contains a position, color, and set of texture coordinates. Additional vertex structures can be added to this file.

```
#ifndef VERTEXFORMATS_H
#define VERTEXFORMATS_H

// Triangle Vars
struct VertexPosColorTexStruct
{
    D3DXVECTOR3 Pos;
    D3DXVECTOR4 Color;
    D3DXVECTOR2 Tex;
};

// additional vertex format structures can go here

#endif
```

The Terrain Effect File

The effect file used to render the terrain uses only the vertex and pixel shaders to apply a single texture.

As input to the vertex shader, the VS function takes a vertex position, color, and pair of texture coordinates. The color and texture coordinates are passed directly to the pixel shader without change, but the vertex position is multiplied by the projection matrix first.

Because the terrain is being rendered with a texture applied, the pixel shader has to sample the texture and return the proper color using the texture coordinates. The color from the texture map is multiplied by the vertex color before being returned.

```
cbuffer Variables
{
    matrix Projection;
}

// PS_INPUT - input variables to the pixel shader
// This struct is created and filled in by the
// vertex shader
struct PS_INPUT
{
    float4 Pos : SV_POSITION;
    float4 Color : COLOR0;
    float2 Tex : TEXCOORD0;
};

////// Texture Samplers
Texture2D baseTexture;
SamplerState samLinear
{
    Filter = MIN_MAG_MIP_LINEAR;
    AddressU = Clamp;
    AddressV = Clamp;
};

/////////////////////////////////////////////////
// Vertex Shader - Main Function
/////////////////////////////////////////////////

PS_INPUT VS(float4 Pos : POSITION, float4 Color : COLOR, float2 Tex: TEXCOORD0)
{
    PS_INPUT psInput;

    // Pass through both the position and the color
    psInput.Pos = mul( Pos, Projection );
```

```
    psInput.Color = Color;
    psInput.Tex = Tex;

    return psInput;
}


/////////////////////////////////////////////
// Pixel Shader
/////////////////////////////////////////////
float4 PS(PS_INPUT psInput) : SV_Target
{
    float4 outColor = baseTexture.Sample(samLinear, psInput.Tex) *
    psInput.Color;

    return outColor;
}


// Define the technique
technique10 Render
{
    pass P0
    {
        SetVertexShader( CompileShader( vs_4_0, VS() ) );
        SetGeometryShader( NULL );
        SetPixelShader( CompileShader( ps_4_0, PS() ) );
    }
}
```

Summary

You've made it to the end of the book, congratulations. I'm hoping that you enjoyed learning about DirectX and are prepared to tackle the challenges that game programming can provide. I've only opened the door into the world of 3D graphics; there's still a whole range of topics to learn including 3D animation, object culling using binary space partitioning, and so much more.

What You Have Learned

At this point, you should know the following:

- The importance of a clean code base

- How to create a simple game framework

- How to manipulate objects in a scene

- How to encapsulate common functionality

- How to create a complete 3D demo with user input

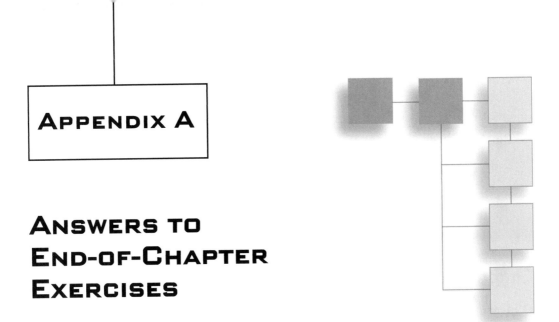

APPENDIX A

ANSWERS TO END-OF-CHAPTER EXERCISES

Chapter 2

Questions

1. What is the main difference between the GetMessage and PeekMessage functions in a message loop?

2. What's the first DirectX object that needs to be created in any application?

3. How many buffers can be created in a swap chain?

4. The DXGI_FORMAT_R32G32B32A32_TYPELESS defines how many bits for each color?

5. What DirectX function is required to blank the screen to a specific color?

Answers

1. The GetMessage function will wait for a message to be placed into the queue and then process it. The PeekMessage function will check for messages; if none are found it will continue processing.

2. The Direct3D device needs to be created first along with the swap chain using the D3D10CreateDeviceAndSwapChain function.

3. At least one buffer should be created in the swap chain to allow for double buffering. Triple buffering or techniques that use more buffers are possible but require additional memory.

4. The `DXGI_FORMAT_R32G32B32A32_TYPELESS` format allows for 32 bits of color information in the R, G, B, and A components.

5. The `ClearRenderTargetView` function is used to clear the screen before drawing.

Chapter 3

Questions

1. Which function is used to load textures?

2. Which structure is used to represent sprites?

3. Sprites are commonly used to represent what in a video game?

4. What is a sprite's translation point used for?

5. What is the process of moving a sprite called?

Answers

1. The function `D3DX10CreateTextureFromFile` is used to load a texture from a file.

2. The `D3DX10_SPRITE` structure is used to hold all the details of a sprite.

3. Sprites are used to represent characters or objects within a game.

4. A sprite's translation point is the point on the sprite where movement is calculated. Most of the time this point is at the top-left corner of the sprite.

5. The process of moving a sprite is called translation.

Chapter 4

Questions

1. What is another term for textured fonts?

2. What is a font?

3. What are some uses for text in a game?

4. Which text formatting parameter value is used to measure a string and return a properly sized rectangle?

5. What happens when text is drawn to a rectangle area too small to contain it and the value DT_NOCLIP is not specified?

Answers

1. Texture fonts are also known as bitmapped fonts.

2. A font is a series of letters and symbols written in a certain style.

3. Text is commonly used to detail instructions to the player or as a means of debugging an application.

4. Passing the DT_CALCRECT value to the DrawText function will return the properly sized rectangle big enough to hold the target text.

5. If the DT_NOCLIP value is specified and the text is larger than the containing rectangle, the text is drawn outside of the area.

Chapter 5

Questions

1. How is a point defined in a 3D coordinate system?

2. What does normalizing a vector do?

3. What is the purpose of the dot product calculation?

4. What primitive type consists of a series of connected lines?

5. What is the identity matrix?

Answers

1. Points are defined using X, Y, and Z coordinates within 3D space.

2. Reduces the vector to have a magnitude of 1.

3. The dot product calculation is used to find the angle between two vectors.

4. A line list of a series of connected lines.

5. The identity matrix is a special matrix that applies no scaling, transforms, or translations.

Chapter 6

Questions

1. What is the difference between a triangle list and a triangle strip?

2. Are index buffers required for all drawing? Why or why not?

3. Which function can be used to create a rotation matrix around the X axis?

4. Why must you be careful about the order in which matrices are combined?

5. What are the two modes the rasterizer can operate in?

Answers

1. A triangle list is a series of non-connected triangles where all the vertices that make up the primitive are defined. A triangle strip is a series of connected triangles where the first triangle is created using three vertices and each addition triangle can be created by defining one additional vertex.

2. Index buffers are not required when drawing with vertices in a vertex buffer. The index buffer exists to help reduce the number of vertices being used, allowing for vertex reuse.

3. The `D3DXMatrixRotationX` function is used to rotate an object around the X axis.

4. Matrices must be combined in the order you want the transformations to take place. Translating an object and then rotating it will not give the same effect as performing the rotation first.

5. The Rasterizer can be active in either solid (default) or wireframe mode.

Chapter 7

Questions

1. Effect files are loaded using which function?

2. What is HLSL?

3. What is the purpose of the vertex and pixel shaders?

4. What two variables are required to calculate ambient lighting?

5. What is the purpose of semantics?

Answers

1. Effect files are easily loaded using the `D3DX10CreateEffectFromFile` function.

2. HLSL is the High Level Shading Language used to write shaders.

3. Vertex shaders manipulate vertices as they are fed through the graphic pipeline. Pixel shaders allow for the manipulation of pixels before they're drawn.

4. Calculating ambient lighting is accomplished by multiplying the base object color by the ambient light color.
Ambient = baseColor * lightColor

5. Semantics are used to let the compiler know the intended use of certain variables so they can be optimized for access.

Chapter 8

Questions

1. What must be added to the vertex format to allow support for texture mapping?

2. What is multi-texturing?

3. Which shader function is used to interpolate between textures?

4. Which interface is the Direct3D mesh object based on?

5. Which function is used to create the mesh object?

Answers

1. Texture coordinates must be added to the vertex format before textures can be applied.

2. Multi-texturing is the process of applying more than one texture to a polygon. This is commonly used for effects such as light maps.

3. The function lerp is used to blend between two textures.

4. The ID3DX10Mesh interface is used to represent meshes.

5. The D3DX10CreateMesh function is used to create a valid mesh object.

Chapter 9

Questions

1. DirectInput allows for what type of input devices?

2. Which function creates the IDirectInput8 interface?

3. What is the detecting of input devices on a system called?

4. Reading from the keyboard requires what kind of buffer?

5. What is the data format type for mouse input?

Answers

1. You use DirectInput to get input from a device, such as the keyboard, mouse, joysticks, and game pads.

2. The `DirectInput8Create` function creates a DirectInput object that can access all the functionality of DirectInput.

3. Enumeration is the process of searching and detecting devices that are installed on a system.

4. The `GetDeviceState` function needs a buffer of 256 characters.

5. `c_dfDIMouse` is the format that the `SetDataFormat` function uses to access the mouse input device.

Chapter 10

Questions

1. Which function is used to get the current data from a controller?

2. How many controllers can be used at a time?

3. How is controller removal detected?

4. How is user input from a controller disabled?

5. Which structure is used to gather user input?

Answers

1. The `XInputGetState` function is used to get the current user input data from an Xbox360 controller.

2. Up to four Xbox360 controllers can be used at any one time.

3. The `XInputGetState` function returns an error code when the device is polled. If the error code is not equal to `ERROR_SUCCESS`, the controller has been removed.

4. The XInputEnable function is used to enable or disable input from the user controls.

5. The XINPUT_STATE structure is used to contain the user input data.

Chapter 11

Questions

1. When must you use the DirectSoundEnumerate function?

2. What three important pieces of data are passed to the enumeration callback function?

3. Does the format of a buffer need to match the format of its contents?

4. What is the purpose of the primary buffer?

5. What value is passed to DirectSoundCreate8 to specify that the default sound device be used?

Answers

1. You use the DirectSoundEnumerate function when you want to get a list of the sound devices that are installed on your machine. You normally use DirectSoundEnumerate when you don't want to use the default sound device.

2. The lpGuid contains the GUID of the sound device, lpcstrDescription gives you a text description of the device, and lpcstrModule gives you the text description of the sound driver being used.

3. The format of a secondary buffer does need to match the sound data that is contained within it.

4. The primary buffer is where the final mixed sound data from all the secondary buffers is stored before being played.

5. DSDEVID_DefaultPlayback is passed to DirectSoundCreate8 to specify that the default sound device is to be used.

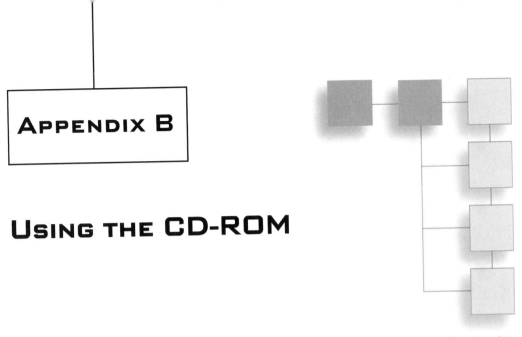

APPENDIX B

USING THE CD-ROM

The included CD-ROM contains all the source code for the examples in this book. The Microsoft DirectX SDK is also included.

What's on the CD-ROM

The code samples are located in the folder corresponding to the chapter number in which they're included. For example, you can find all code samples used in Chapter 3, "2D Game Development," in the chapter 3 directory on the CD-ROM.

The code samples within these directories are split into separate folders and are labeled example1, example2, and so on.

Within the example folders are the complete source code listings as well as the Visual Studio .NET 2005 project files.

The project files are meant to be copied from the CD-ROM to the hard drive and compiled. You might need to remove the Read-Only attribute from the files after they are copied to your hard drive.

Installing the DirectX SDK

To get started programming for DirectX, you must first install the DirectX SDK on your machine. The DirectX SDK is the software development kit from Microsoft that includes all the header files, libraries, and samples you need to write software for DirectX.

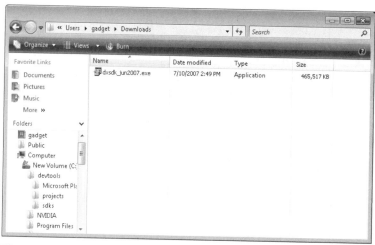

Figure B.1
The contents of the DirectX directory on the CD-ROM.

The DirectX SDK takes up approximately 1GB on your hard drive, so make sure you have enough room before running the installation.

You can find the installation program for the DirectX SDK on the included CD-ROM in the DirectX directory. Figure B.1 shows the files you should find in this directory.

You begin the SDK installation by double-clicking the dxsdk_jun2007.exe. The SDK installation will begin shortly after the setup files are placed into a temporary directory. The InstallShield Wizard dialog box shown in Figure B.2 should appear.

Select the Next button to begin the installation process. The Wizard will next present you with the DirectX SDK software license agreement shown in Figure B.3. If you agree with the terms, select the I Accept the Terms in the License Agreement option and then click the Next button to continue with the installation. In order to install the DirectX SDK, you must agree to the terms presented in the license.

The next dialog box, Custom Setup, presents you with multiple choices for the install. You want to install the entire SDK, so leave the default options as they are. If you would like to change the directory that the SDK will be installed into, select the Change button and enter the new directory path.

Click the Next button to start the installation. The Custom Setup dialog box is shown in Figure B.4.

The progress dialog box should appear. This dialog box continually updates you as to the progress of the installation. This dialog box is shown in Figure B.5.

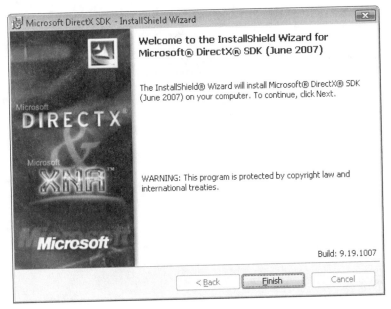

Figure B.2
The DirectX SDK InstallShield Wizard.

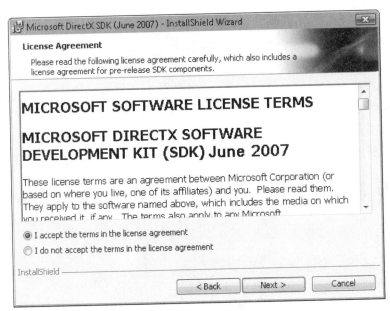

Figure B.3
The DirectX SDK license agreement dialog box.

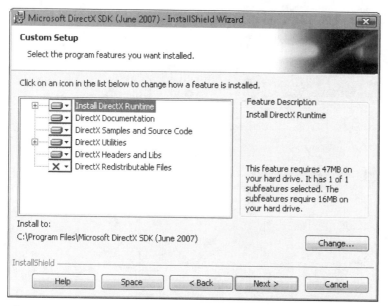

Figure B.4
The Custom Setup dialog box.

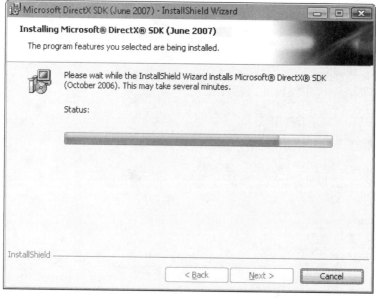

Figure B.5
The install progress dialog box.

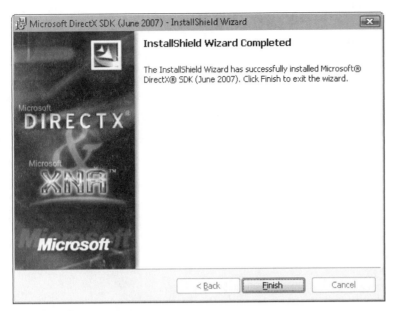

Figure B.6
The install completion dialog box.

The install continues for a few minutes, so don't be worried if it's taking some time to install. A dialog box informs you when the install is complete. Figure B.6 shows the completion dialog box.

Clicking the Finish button ends the install. At this point, the DirectX SDK should be installed successfully.

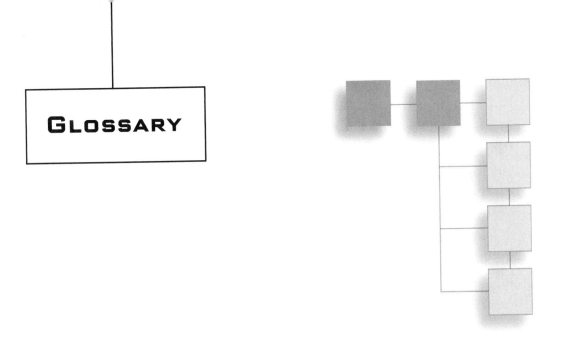

GLOSSARY

2D animation—The process of displaying still frames in quick succession to create the illusion of motion.

alpha blending—A graphical technique used to make 3D surfaces appear transparent.

ambient lighting—Lighting that is uniform and does not appear to come from any particular direction.

analog control—A control that has a range of variable input.

Application Programming Interface (API)—A set of functions that an application uses to carry out tasks.

back buffer—An area of memory to which graphics can be drawn before being displayed on the screen.

Basic Input Output System (BIOS)—The lowest level of software in a computer that handles setting up the hardware for use by the operating system.

billboard—A normally four-sided polygon often used in particle systems. A billboard always faces toward the camera.

bitmap—A series of pixels that represent a graphical image.

bump mapping—A texture mapping technique used to make smooth 3D objects appear to have an uneven surface.

Component Object Model (COM)—An architecture developed by Microsoft to create component-based software.

constant force—A force that retains a consistent direction and pressure during its duration.

cooperative level—The level of access permitted to a hardware device within DirectX.

coordinate systems—The way of defining positions within 3D space.

culling—The act of removing objects or vertices from a scene before it is rendered.

dead zone—An area of an analog control where input should be ignored.

Device Driver Kit (DDK)—A set of development code libraries used for the creation of device drivers.

digital control—A control, such as a button, which has only two states (on or off).

Direct3D—A portion of DirectX that provides functions for creating, manipulating, and viewing 3D data.

Direct3D device—An interface of DirectX that represents the graphics adapter.

DirectDraw—A DirectX component that handles 2D surfaces and images.

DirectInput—A DirectX component that gathers and receives input data from various devices.

directional lighting—Light that travels in a straight line from its source.

DirectPlay—The DirectX component that provides networking and multiplayer support.

DirectSound—The component of DirectX that handles the manipulation and playing of sounds.

DirectX—A set of APIs used in the development of game and multimedia applications on the Windows platform.

DirectX Graphics—The component of DirectX that handles graphics output.

DirectX Runtime—The DLL component that provides the functionality of DirectX.

Disk Operating System (DOS)—The low-level program that tells the system how to operate. DOS as an operating system is no longer in wide use.

display adapter—The video output hardware.

enumeration—The process of programmatically searching a system for a particular type of hardware device based on search criteria.

feedback effect—A series of vibrations sent to a force feedback device.

font system—A component whose job it is to draw and manipulate text.

force feedback—The addition of motors within input devices that provide the user with vibration.

fragment shader—See pixel shader.

frame—A single still image that is usually part of an animation.

front buffer—The area of memory that represents the viewable area of a display screen.

geometry shader—A shader capable of transforming entire pieces of an object instead of transforming the vertices individually.

Globally Unique Identifier (GUID)—A number that is used to identify a software component.

Graphical User Interface (GUI)—A user interface that represents the system through a series of icons, pictures, or menus.

Hardware Abstraction Layer (HAL)—A layer of software that provides a standard way to access different hardware without knowing the specifics of the device.

Hardware Emulation Layer (HEL)—A layer of software that provides missing functionality of a hardware device.

HLSL—High Level Shader Language.

index buffer—Memory buffers that contain index data. Index data are offsets into a list of vertices.

input assembler stage—The first stage of the Direct3D pipeline where primitives are introduced.

matrix—An ordered array of numbers.

mesh—An interconnected set of polygons that represent an object in 3D space.

message loop—The process within a Windows application of retrieving and dispatching system messages.

message queue—The area within the Windows operating system that holds events and messages created by applications.

multitexturing—Applying more than one texture to a given set of vertices.

normal—A directional vector at a right angle to a plane.

offscreen surface—An area of memory into which graphical data can be loaded and manipulated without being displayed.

output merger stage—The final stage of the Direct3D pipeline where the final image is produced.

page flipping—The swapping of the front and one or more offscreen buffers.

particle—A normally four-sided polygon used to represent small objects such as dirt, smoke, or sparks within a game.

periodic effect—A force feedback effect that occurs on a given time interval.

perspective—A type of projection that displays objects that are farther away from the camera in 3D space as smaller than objects that are closer to the camera.

pixel shader—A program running on the GPU that process pixels allowing for blending and texture manipulation.

point sprite—A way of representing particles within Direct3D.

polling—Periodically checking an input device like a joystick for input.

primary buffer—A DirectSound buffer into which sounds from secondary buffers are mixed for output.

primitive—A standard 3D object upon which meshes are created.

projection—The process of transforming 3D space into a 2D viewable form.

ramp force—A force feedback effect that gradually increases in intensity over time.

rasterizer stage—A stage of the Direct3D pipeline where the scene is transformed into pixels for display.

refresh rate—The rate at which the screen is updated.

render target—A resource considered to be an output source of a drawing operation.

resource view—Allows data to be accessed differently based on the part of the Direct3D pipeline using it.

return code—A value returned from a function that determines whether the function was successful.

sampler—Allows for the accessing of a texture during the pixel shader stage.

secondary buffer—An area of memory that loads sound data within DirectSound.

self-extracting file—An executable file that contains compressed data with the ability to uncompress this data without an external helper application.

sound buffer—An area of memory that holds sound data.

sprite—A graphic that is used to represent 2D characters or items within a game.

sprite pool—A general collection of sprite objects that can be re-purposed dynamically.

static buffer—An area of memory that holds sound data within DirectSound. The static buffer is commonly used when the entire sound can be loaded.

streaming buffer—An area of memory that holds a portion of sound data. The streaming buffer is used when all the sound data is too large to fit in memory at one time.

surface—A linear piece of memory that stores graphic data. The surface is represented as a rectangular area into which graphics can be held.

swap chain—A series of buffers on which graphics can be drawn before being displayed to the screen.

texture coordinates—A set of coordinates on a polygon that defines the portion of the texture map to apply.

texture mapping—Applying an image to a polygon to give it the illusion of a real-world object.

timer—An internal counting mechanism that keeps a constant rate of time for animations.

tranformation—Converting a 3D object from one coordinate system to another.

triangle fan—A series of triangles that share a single vertex in a fan pattern.

triangle strip—A series of connected triangles where each subsequent triangle is defined using only a single vertex.

Universal Serial Bus (USB)—A standard port on computers that enables users to connect a wide variety of devices such as mice, cameras, and game pads.

vector—A straight line segment in 3D space consisting of both direction and magnitude. The length of the vector is defined as its magnitude, whereas its orientation represents its direction.

vertex—A single point of a polygon consisting of an X, Y, and Z coordinate defining its position in 3D space.

vertex buffer—A buffer containing vertex data.

vertex shader—A program that runs on the GPU that processes and transforms the vertices coming through.

video RAM—The memory residing on the video card. This memory can be normally accessed more quickly than system RAM.

video resolution—The width, height, and bit depth of a particular video mode.

viewport—A rectangular area that defines where in a target surface a scene should be rendered.

VRAM—See video RAM.

windowed application—An application that runs within a window on the desktop.

Windows—An operating system from Microsoft that provides the user with a Graphical User Interface (GUI).

WinMain—The entry point function for Windows applications.

xfile—The native DirectX 3D object format.

XInput—A new DirectX component that interfaces with the Xbox 360 controller.

Z-Buffer—An array used to store the Z coordinate of polygons plotted in 3D space. Direct3D uses the Z value of each polygon to determine which 3D objects are in front of others.

Z Order—The depth order in which objects are drawn back to front.

INDEX